George F. Noyes

The bivouac and the battlefield, or,

Campaign sketches in Virginia and Maryland

George F. Noyes

The bivouac and the battlefield, or,
Campaign sketches in Virginia and Maryland

ISBN/EAN: 9783337810511

Printed in Europe, USA, Canada, Australia, Japan

Cover: Foto ©ninafisch / pixelio.de

More available books at **www.hansebooks.com**

THE

BIVOUAC AND THE BATTLE-FIELD;

OR,

Campaign Sketches

IN

VIRGINIA AND MARYLAND.

BY GEORGE F. NOYES,
CAPT. U. S. VOLUNTEERS.

NEW YORK:
HARPER & BROTHERS, PUBLISHERS,
FRANKLIN SQUARE.
1863.

Entered, according to Act of Congress, in the year one thousand eight hundred and sixty-three, by

HARPER & BROTHERS,

In the Clerk's Office of the District Court of the Southern District of New York.

TO

MAJOR GEN. A. DOUBLEDAY, U. S. VOLS.,

AND

𝔥is 𝔉irst 𝔖taff,

THIS RECORD OF OUR COMMON EXPERIENCES IS
AFFECTIONATELY INSCRIBED BY

THE AUTHOR.

CONTENTS.

CHAPTER I.
INTRODUCTORY.
War is a Conglomerate.—Design of these Sketches............Page 13

CHAPTER II.
OFF FOR THE WARS.
Departure from Washington. — A Word or two as to the Staff.—Mount Vernon.—Arrival at Aquia.—Sleeping in Boots and Spurs.—Sutler's Breakfast 16

CHAPTER III.
FREDERICKSBURG.
Our new Quarters.—Welcome of the Contrabands.—Want of Welcome of the Neighbors. — A Staff Breakfast.—Sudden transition from Hauteur to Decency.—The Streets.—Zion.—A Reconnoissance in Force.—Talk with a Union Lady.—The Episcopal Church.—A bitter Disappointment.. 26

CHAPTER IV.
CAMP OPPOSITE FREDERICKSBURG.
Ordered to Falmouth.—Quarters at Wallace House.—How the Army is organized.—The Titles and Duties of the Staff.—Camps and Camp Customs. — Droll Ideas as to Confiscation.—Orders to be "ready to move at a Moment's notice".................................. 34

CHAPTER V.
PHILLIPS'S HOUSE HEAD-QUARTERS.
Change of Base.—Capture of Major Lacy.—My Friend the military Governor.—The Contrabands, and their Capacity to take care of themselves.—The Quarter-master's Affirmation.—Contraband Wor-

ship.—An exciting Day.—The Black Scout of the Rappahannock.—The 14th Brooklyn and their Confederate Money.—Too much cosseting of Treason.—A crestfallen rebel Female.—General Pope assumes Command.—Quarter-master's Certificate to Rebels.—Fourth of July.—Courts-martial.—Punishments in the Army.—Burnside arrives.—Life in a Tent .... Page 41

CHAPTER VI.
FROM FREDERICKSBURG TO CEDAR MOUNTAIN.

Orders to March.—Formation of a Column.—Farewell to Fredericksburg.—First Bivouac.—Troops on a March.—Straggling.—A Soldier's Rations.—A disagreeable Race.—Fording the Rapidan.—"Poor white Trash."—Troops in Camp.—Midnight March.—Battle Speech of a fighting Colonel.—Yankee Crusaders.—Bivouac near Culpepper.. 56

CHAPTER VII.
CAMP NEAR CEDAR MOUNTAIN.

Head-quarters *al fresco*.—Visit to the Wounded.—Rebel Prisoners.—The Heroes of the late Battle.—Review by General Pope.—Visit to the Battle-field.—Riding *vs.* Walking.—A Night-scene in Camp.—Cedar Mountain.. 69

CHAPTER VIII.
FROM CEDAR MOUNTAIN TO THE RAPPAHANNOCK.

Tedious March.—Pillage by the Troops.—Sleep in the Mud.—Rappahannock Station.—Breakfast in the Saddle.—Exciting Cavalry Charge 80

CHAPTER IX.
ARTILLERY DUEL AT RAPPAHANNOCK STATION.

The Enemy open the Ball.—"Lie down."—Sleep under a Wagon.—Dead Braves on the Battle-field.—Supporting Artillery.—Courage and Cowardice.—A frightened Prisoner.—A Rebel Line cut down by Shot.—A Disappointment.—A Ride under Fire.—Exciting Charge by a Rebel Regiment.. 88

CHAPTER X.
FROM RAPPAHANNOCK TO WARRENTON.

Wagons and Wagon-trains.—Army Transportation.—Delays.—Head-quarters in a Mud-puddle.—Entry into Warrenton.—Great Demand for Supplies.—Warren Green Hotel.—The perambulating Commissary.—Quiet Sunday Afternoon......................Page 99

CHAPTER XI.
ARTILLERY DUEL AT WARRENTON SPRINGS.

Expected Battle.—Only an Artillery Duel.—Experiences among our Batteries.—Visit to the fashionable Springs.—Once more *en route*.—Company Q.. 108

CHAPTER XII.
BATTLE OF GAINESVILLE.

March toward Centreville.—Sudden Rebel Salute.—Infantry Storm the Battery.—Our Clergyman Captain.—Magnificent Battle-scene.—Yankee Presence of Mind.—Frightful Loss.—Union Cheers of Victory.—A Ride among the Wounded. — Roadside Council of War.—Rebel Prisoners.—Manassas Junction..................... 114

CHAPTER XIII.
SECOND BATTLE OF BULL RUN.

Re-enforcements.—Battle-field of Bull Run.—Double-quick against the Enemy. — A Rebel Trap. — The flanking Fire.—A terrible Death-angle.—A Retreat.—A Union Officer rallying the Second Mississippi.—A sad Night.—Second Day.—Our thinned Ranks.—Meeting of the Union Generals.—The famous Dispatch of Victory.— Every Body happy. — Ride to Centreville.—Bitter Disappointment.—Our Army in Retreat.. 123

CHAPTER XIV.
CENTREVILLE TO UPTON'S HILL.

An Army in the Blues.—March toward Fairfax Court-house.—Bivouac in Line of Battle.—A new Regiment.—An immense Wagon-train with Variations.—A March under Difficulties.—Battle of Chantilly.—A wet Bivouac.—Life in a Shanty.—March to Upton's Hill.. 141

CHAPTER XV.
INSIDE THE DEFENSES OF WASHINGTON.

Four Days of Quiet.—The Army of Virginia not guilty of Neglect of Duty.—The old Army of the Potomac.—Ordered to March.—Part of a Night in Washington.. 148

CHAPTER XVI.

WASHINGTON TO FREDERICK CITY.

A remarkable Breakfast.—Sunday Streets.—Pleasant Reception.—Camp ten Miles out.—Trip to Washington.—Cheerful Mess-table.—On the March.—Camp near Lisbon.—Rebel Wounded.—The warlike South.—Southern Endurance.—Southern Chivalry.—A better Acquaintance with the North.—Our Volunteers.—Loyalty.—A great Dinner.. Page 153

CHAPTER XVII.

BATTLE OF SOUTH MOUNTAIN.

Enthusiastic Reception.—"I don't want any Bear."—Feelings on going into Battle.—The Heights of South Mountain.—The Skirmishers.—A beautiful View.—The Rush into Battle.—"Steady, Boys, steady!"—At the Fence.—The leaden Storm.—A desperate Charge.—"Three Cheers for Victory."—One more Rebel Rally.—Ricketts's Division.—Desperate Fight on our Left.—An anxious Hour.—Asleep among the Dead.—What becomes of the Bullets?—An awful Sensation.. 165

CHAPTER XVIII.

FROM SOUTH MOUNTAIN TO ANTIETAM.

The Morning after the Battle.—A Virginia Conscript.—The Rebel Dead.—My young Lieutenant.—The Burial of our Braves.—A hospitable Staff.—Orders to Pursue.—A rejoicing Column.—"My Maryland."—The wayside Inn.—Rebel Prisoners.—Rebel Demoralization.—The Union Lady's Tale.—Nine Rebels captured by one Orderly.—The Rebel Flag of Truce.—Meeting of the Generals.—A pleasant Glen.—Tempest in a Teapot.—Chickens and Accompaniments.—A Night at Boonesborough.—Head-quarters under a Tree.—Sumner's Head-quarters...................................... 179

CHAPTER XIX.

BATTLE OF ANTIETAM.

Return to Division.—Non est Inventus.—The Roar of Battle.—M'Clellan's Head-quarters.—Glance at Battle-field.—A Hunt for the Division.—A ghastly Procession.—A hot Place of Meeting.—The Key Point of the Right Wing.—Incidents of the Battle.—A Day of Waiting.—An annihilated Company.—The Fighting on

our Left.—Rumors.—Terrific Artillery Contest.—Close Shooting.
—A thrilling Experience.—A Night on the Battle-field.—The
Absurdity of War. — What does it decide? — Forced upon the
North...Page 194

CHAPTER XX.
THE ANTIETAM BATTLE-FIELD.

An early Breakfast.—Waiting for Orders to Advance.—A Day of
Disappointment.—The Escape of the Enemy.—Army Letters.—
A quiet Hour among the Wagons.—A Ride over the Battle-field.
—Appearance of the Dead.—A pleasing Picture.—The little
Church.—Rebel Officer.—The "Slaughter Pen."—Fence-rail
Barricades.—A Law of Death.—The Burial of the Dead.—An
Army of Visitors... 211

CHAPTER XXI.
CAMP NEAR SHARPSBURG.

Our Division Staff.—The Condition of the Troops.—Need of Reading Matter.—A Suggestion.—The Evening Camp-fire.—The Quarter-master's Story.—Difference between Bribery and Corruption.—
The Army Correspondent.—A Black Sheep.—Pleasant Rides.—
Shephardstown in Excitement.—A mangled Grove.—In Memoriam.—How a Yankee Sutler outgeneraled a Quarter-master... 222

CHAPTER XXII.
THE HOSPITALS AND THE SANITARY COMMISSION.

Nature hiding away the Traces of Battle.—Sharpsburg.—Life in a
Cellar during the Bombardment.—The Army of the Wounded.—
Visits to the Rebel Hospitals.—Little Histories.—Rebel Officers.
—Our own Braves.—The Republican Legion of Honor.—Care of
the Wounded.—The Sanitary Commission.—General Rosecrans's
Testimony.. 236

CHAPTER XXIII.
ANTIETAM AND HARPER'S FERRY.

Interior Tent-life.—The unhappy Candidate for Military Examination.—A Ride to Harper's Ferry.—John Brown.—View from the
Heights.—The liberal Marylander.—Slight Change of Base.—
Charge of Hooker's Brigade.—"Spiflicating."—"Present Arms."
—An Hour among the Dunkers 248

CHAPTER XXIV.

FAREWELL TO MARYLAND.

Bakersville.—Pitching Tents by Night.—A March through the Mud.—"D—o—n—'t Shoot."—Army Songs.—A Horse Trader.—A Night at Crampton's Pass.—March through Berlin.—A Welcome to Virginia ....Page 261

CHAPTER XXV.

ONCE MORE INTO VIRGINIA.

All Hail! Virginia.—A Community of Friends.—The Flight of the Contrabands.—Berryman and Charles.—Driving out the Rebels from the Gaps in the Blue Ridge.—Our old Brigade.—A Ride back to Berlin.—A Night with Rufus Choate.—The Major's Adventures.—Sibley Stoves.—A false Alarm.—Cold Reception at Warrenton.—A few Crumbs of Sleep..... 269

CHAPTER XXVI.

WARRENTON TO FALMOUTH.

Burnside in Command.—A Roving Commission.—A Village of Fire.—Picturesque Night Scene.—A pleasant Evening.—Camp at Fayetteville.—A tedious March.—A good Supper.—Conversation with a Negro Worshiper.—A whining Do-little.—Stragglers.—Slough of Despond.—Camp near Railroad.—The Pontoon Trains.—On the Move... 278

CHAPTER XXVII.

THE PASSAGE OF THE RAPPAHANNOCK.

Laying Pontoons of Left Grand Division.—Desperate Work.—Final Success.—Not so Fortunate up River.—Bombardment of Fredericksburg.—John's Disaster.—A Look at the unfinished Bridge.—The White Handkerchief.—A Call for Volunteers.—The Passage in Boats.—The Bridge completed.—Decorations of Honor.—The Street-fighting.—A Visit to Fredericksburg.—Our Army not a pillaging Army.—Effect of Bombardment.—Approach to Rebel Sharpshooters... 291

CHAPTER XXVIII.

THE BATTLE OF FREDERICKSBURG.

The Battle Arena.—An Hour of Anxiety.—The Advance.—The Rebel Storm.—Another Advance.—That terrible Stone Wall.—

Retreat to the Ravine.—Sturgis's Division on the Left.—The Gallantry of our Volunteers.—The Battle on the Left.—A Ride to the Front.—The extreme Left.—The Whitworth Gun.—Roadside Head-quarters.—A novel Game of Cards.—The Recrossing of the River.—The Bringing off of the Pickets...................Page 304

CHAPTER XXIX.

A CAMPAIGN IN THE MUD.

Another Blast from the Whitworth Gun.—Huts of Troops.—Change in Commander.—Twice Six makes Twelve.—Corduroy.—A March through the Mud.—Head-quarters in a Puddle.—A flying Bedchamber.—An aquatic Excursion.—A doleful Ride.—Serenade.—Return of the Wanderers 321

CHAPTER XXX.

WINTER-QUARTERS.

Days of Waiting.—Future Glory of the Army of the Potomac.—Volunteers.—Defective Discipline.—Field Officers.—Waste of Ammunition.—Ratio of Casualties in Battle.—Demoralization.—Concluding Words 329

THE BIVOUAC
AND
THE BATTLE-FIELD.

CHAPTER I.
INTRODUCTORY.

"WAR is fight," declares the pithy though imperfect English translation of a well-known German work on the art of war. "War is a series of blunders, wherein he who makes the fewest is sure to conquer," said a staff-comrade to me after one of our reverses. "War is waiting," has sometimes seemed a military maxim followed and cherished by those high in command. It is, indeed, a conglomerate, made up, we may say, somewhat as follows:

    Waiting . . . . . . four parts;
    Blundering . . . . . three parts;
    Marching and fighting . . three parts.

Our campaign sketches must therefore partake of all these ingredients. Attempting no profound discussion of strategy or military policy, they seek only to portray interior views of tent life, common homely experiences, the every-day personal incidents of camp and battle-field, with such explanations and details as may instruct the uninitiated as to the ordinary camp life of the American volunteer.

A few battle-pictures must, of course, find place in our sketch-book, but they will aim at no general delineation, being necessarily limited and partial, seeking to be accurate, however, as far as they go. Indeed, no absolutely veritable description of the varied movements over an extensive battle-field can ever be expected; ten artistic word-painters will surely give us ten very different pictures, agreeing in generals, but dissimilar in details. Let a man consult the field officers of even a single regiment as to its operations in a single fight, and from the incongruities in their several statements he will be able to judge of the difficulty in painting on canvas or with the pen a true battle-picture. Of course, every narrator makes himself the central pivotal point around which the whole battle-scenery revolves, and this not egotistically, but naturally and necessarily. And just in proportion to the fidelity with which he gives us the facts as seen from his personal stand-point, drawing neither from his imagination nor the official reports, shall we have a small but veritable bit of actual history.

Leaving, then, all general descriptions of battle-scenes to the able and well-trained corps of army correspondents, and to the historian who shall be able hereafter to collate and compare the testimony, subjecting it to the dry light of an impartial criticism, I seek to record simply my own personal experiences and observations. A genre picture, not a grand historic tableau, is thus attempted, something after the style of Hogarth's every-day sketches, with no pretensions to the bolder, more comprehensive delineations of the historic school; and, though it is probably true that, during the heat of a campaign, the reader of a daily newspaper is informed as to the general design and operations before most of those actually engaged, still a staff officer has some advantages in this regard, while, as to matters of detail, he alone can speak familiarly who is an actual participant. Moreover, the every-day experiences of one brigade or one division run so nearly parallel with those of every other brigade or division in the whole army, that our sketch must contain many features common to all—will, at all events, serve as one of the scraps of narrative from which history shall gradually be evolved.

Such a sketch will, of course, have its dark shades of sadness mingled with the bright colorings of joy, its defeats as well as its victories, its dispiriting retreats as well as its jubilant advances, its awful visions of the battle-field strewn with the unburied dead as well as its cheerful evenings around the camp-fire. A campaign is, in fact, an epitome of ordinary life minus the refining, elevating, and Christianizing influence of our women and little children; of ordinary life unnaturally excited and exaggerated, with its usual experiences so overstrained, and following upon each other in such rapid succession as to carry us sometimes in a single day through the whole gamut of sensations, and give to a week the significance of months. So it happens that, in looking over my little diary, I have not yet been able to realize that the scenes herein described were all compressed within so brief a period. Years, long years they seem to me to have occupied; and, if time be measured not so much by the mere pulsations of the bodily machine as by our inner sensations and experiences, years they certainly were.

CHAPTER II.

OFF FOR THE WARS.

M'DOWELL is marshaling his cohorts at Fredericksburg, being ordered to aid the peninsular approaches of M'Clellan by moving upon Richmond, and to-day, May 22d, 1862, our brigade, having been detached from the army defending Washington, is off to join him. Never was summons more welcome. Tired of serving the country under the shadow of the Capitol, with all the glow of untried enthusiasm and all the ignorance of novices in war, our staff had really begun to fear lest the fighting would all be over before we could draw our maiden swords. Hope paints few brighter visions than those which on this day of embarkation made us happy; and now, as we gallop down to the wharf, every cheek burns with pleasant anticipation. As I gaze through the vista of our actual experiences at that hour of hope and anticipated victory, this day seems to me like a dream.

To get our horses safely on board the steamer is no easy task, for wharf and deck are lumbered up with all the paraphernalia of a campaign, and squads of heavily-knapsacked men are still hurrying on board, all jubilant and some quite intoxicated with patriotism and poor whisky. Among our troops all ages are represented; here a beardless boy, his brow yet warm with the parental blessing, and next him, perhaps, a gray-haired man, for whom a comfortable home and a warm chimney-corner seem far more fitting than the long march and bivouac of the campaign. But these are the days when the popular enthusiasm is still at high tide, submerging town and country, city and hamlet, and inciting young and old, sick and poor, to rally around the old flag. If there is any homesickness beneath these blue uniforms, it can not long resist the influx of the general enthusiasm: it is soon fused and lost in the general hopefulness and joy. "On to Richmond!" is the watchword. You may read it in every eye about you.

As we stand a while on the upper deck, cast your eye at the stalwart private near us, that you may know how a soldier looks in full war rig. The square knapsack on his back is crowned with a great roll of blankets, and contains his entire wardrobe—a change of clothes, a few toilet articles, probably a little Bible, and certainly a keepsake or two from the loved ones at home; his cartridge-box, strapped beneath, holds only a few rounds of ball cartridge: as no battle is impending, his shoulders are festooned with his shelter-tent, an oblong piece of thick cotton cloth compressed into a roll; his haversack is stuffed with three days' marching rations; his water canteen dangles at the other side, while his musket is stacked with the rest in the centre of the deck. Thus he carries his food, and drink, and clothing, and canvas house, and weapon with him; may be said, indeed, to be quite independent of society. Musket and all, his equipment weighs sixty pounds, and with it he can safely march from fifteen to twenty miles per day.

But the sergeants have picked up the last straggler and marched him on board, the last horse is disposed of, and we are finally off. Taking in tow several transports crowded with men, horses, and government stores, gradually we gather way, cheer after cheer rings out from the crowded wharf, responded to lustily by our upper deck, the band strikes up "Dixie," and so we say farewell to Washington, and glide slowly down the river. In less than thirty days we expect to be in Richmond, and fighting is as yet a myth we can not fully realize; we are simply embarked on a military pleasure excursion. The day is very charming, and the beautiful Potomac seems disposed to tender us a most hearty and pleasant welcome.

Within the cabin, sacred to the general and his staff, a quieter yet not less hopeful mood prevails. Our general, a man of many battles, who fired the first Union gun from Fort Sumter, and whose name and fame have already become historic, smiled a little at our untried enthusiasm. Near him sits our staff "major," the vade mecum of the party, a thorough martinet, and able to instruct us on any point, from the minutest question of drill to the latest decision on the "Army Regulations;" and our adjutant general, who considers the putting down this rebellion a part of his religion; and our two aids, one of whom has since finished his last earthly campaign. We shall know and love them all better by-and-by, when we have walked with them through the dark lanes of death, brave, manly fellows as they are, every one of whom has left a home well worth fighting for, and anxious hearts which shall hereafter throb at every telegraphic whisper of battle. Ah! it is the mothers and wives, the sisters and lovers who are the worst sufferers in this war. To man, the glow and excitement of action, the fascinations of campaign adventure, the reserve force of hope and courage which comes to inspire and elevate him in the hour of actual peril, the stern joy which thrills him when he remembers the holy cause to which he devotes himself. To woman, the hope deferred—the waiting, *waiting* for news after every battle—the fearful pictures of her own excited imagination—the doubt, suspense, and agony of anticipation when the air is full of rumor, and every newspaper has its long black list of death.

Our little village of vessels is now passing Alexandria, every foot of whose streets was so familiar to my boyhood, and not long after we glide past Mount Vernon, and the men crowd the rigging to catch their first look at the tomb of Washington. For one, I feel no touch of self-reproach as I gaze upon this Mecca of American patriotism. Only in defense of his principles—only to keep Mount Vernon under the old flag—only to save the Union he so much loved, are we come to tread with arms in our hands the soil of his native Virginia. The bones of the patriot soldier would rest all too uneasily upon the bloody borderland of two rival peoples—the spirit of the whole-souled philanthropist could not repose in peace under the star-bereft banner of a confederacy having for its corner-stone that system of slavery he so much deprecated and regretted. Crusaders are we, rather, crusaders of the 19th century, come not to invade, but to rescue his sepulchre, and pledged to retain it forever under the ægis of that nationality for whose establishment he fought, sacrificed, and prayed.

And now the night comes quietly down upon us; our tired boys spread their blankets in every part of the crowded vessels, and, with their knapsacks for pillows, are soon asleep. Already they have learned the first rule for a campaign—never to lose an opportunity to eat or to sleep, so as to be ever ready for any emergency. The regimental field officers join us in an impromptu supper in the cabin; the general wraps himself in his cloak upon a settee. Some of us, however, too full of busy thought and anticipation, mount to the upper deck to keep pleasant watch with the stars.

It was nearly midnight when we reached Aquia Creek and prepared to disembark. Here was confusion worse confounded. The unfinished pier swarmed with soldiers and contrabands working by the light of lanterns, discharging government transports of all sorts of stores, from a horseshoe to a locomotive, and it took at least an hour to get our men and wagons ashore. We then followed a lantern up the half-built wharf, where our orderlies found ample stable-room for the horses out in the open air. The troops marched off to a hill-side near by, stacked arms, posted sentinels, spread their India-rubber blankets, and bivouacked comfortably under the stars.

The hospitable colonel commanding the post relinquished to the general his camp-bed, while three or four of us, stretched on the floor, or curled up in boxes all too short for even the shortest of us, attempted sleep in the little bedroom. It was on this occasion that I first contracted a prejudice against having a bedfellow in boots and spurs—a prejudice which, even to this day, I have been unable wholly to conquer.

Our captain adjutant rolled himself in his blankets on a pile of bricks outside, a couch hard, but lofty;

our junior aid crept under a tent-fly; soon all were asleep, though my own rest was broken and unsatisfactory. After-experience taught us that, on a pleasant night, you can have no better sleeping-place than six feet by two of green turf. As it was, I fancy few were sorry to quit their downy couch when the sun first greeted us next morning. An "intelligent contraband" brought us a good supply of water; other toilet necessaries were in our saddle-bags; and, while the general enjoyed a private cup of coffee with the colonel, we sallied forth in search of breakfast.

Aquia may be called the Phœnix-town of America, springing up every now and then, to be burned down again whenever our army changes its base, so that it is hardly to be wondered at that Delmonico had not yet established himself. Indeed, the little collection of rough-board shanties and tents, thrown up in a day, crowded with soldiers, and clamorous with the usual bustle of the quarter-master's department, offered so few gastronomic advantages that we were just about to despair, when a current of blue uniforms, every man with a handful of pie and cheese, indicated a sutler's tent. Entering by the rear, we were soon sitting round a barrel-head table, feasting on coffee, cakes, and cheese with infinite gusto and merriment.

Our sumptuous repast ended, we walked down the pier, where we met the President and Secretary of War, who had just arrived, and soon after entered a state railway carriage, consisting of a rough freight car with a bench and two stools, beautifully decorated for this occasion with a small American flag. I had seen the President rising in a private box to acknowledge his enthusiastic reception at the Academy of

Music, but was glad to get a nearer view of our highly-respected chief magistrate. How it would have made the nerves of some German duke, with sixteen quarterings, and a domain of a few miles square, tingle with disdain, this state car, which bore on to Falmouth the ruler of twenty millions! *Vive la Democratie!*

Aquia Creek is the Potomac terminus of the railroad running to Richmond *via* Fredericksburg, and this morning we were to take the latter city on our way to the rebel capital. A staff officer was sent with orders to the troops to march at once, while the general and staff rode on without awaiting the tardy movement of the column. A pleasant ride it was on that lovely morning, through a picturesque, well-wooded, scantily-settled country—a silent, sleepy region, but little vexed with Yankee enterprise or modern agricultural improvements, its roads—romantic forest-paths instead of wide, well-worn prosaic turnpikes—arched with foliage and vocal with the music of birds. Every one was in his happiest mood, glad that our projected trip to Richmond commenced under such pleasant auspices.

A gallop of a dozen miles or more, passing very few habitations or cultivated fields, fording two considerable creeks and several "runs," brought us among the canvas cities, long avenues of wagons, and parks of artillery of our army. White-walled villages crowned the hill-sides, with their streets thronged with soldiers; here were acres of horses, cannon, army-wagons; regiments were drawn up on every hand for drill; the road was crowded with mounted officers, orderlies hurrying with their dispatches, and squadrons of cavalry going to or returning from the outer pickets. On our right we passed Shields's Division, and gazed with special interest at these veterans of six months' service, who had actually smelt powder and been in battle. Standing around their camp-fires making coffee, cleansing their weapons and accoutrements, or fitting up their shelter-tents with walls of cedar boughs, they seemed to us unfledged tyros warriors worthy of our special homage.

Stopping occasionally at the head-quarter tents of some general officer, we reached at last the Lacy mansion, a lovely residence on the banks of the Rappahannock, opposite Fredericksburg, then occupied by General M'Dowell as his head-quarters. Its green lawn was sprinkled all over with the tents of his staff; its out-buildings were appropriated as offices; sentries paced up and down its once quiet walks; its main approaches were full of horses gay with staff-trappings, and held by mounted orderlies; while the front entrance and hall were crowded with generals and the officers of their respective staffs.

The President and Secretary of War were also here, and the commanding general had assembled all his brigadiers to meet them. It was to me very interesting to see these leaders, some of whom were already famous, as they gathered in groups in the hall and grounds. Every face was full of hopeful anticipation; the President dispensed every where his dry hits of good logical common sense, wrapped up in the humorous coating of anecdote or illustration, and not a suspicion of the impending disappointment intruded itself; nor had I then a conception how much of envy and professional jealousy found lodgment beneath some of these uniforms. Artists, authors, and clergymen have perhaps been considered most liable to this weakness of jealousy, but, in this regard, professional soldiers may, as a class, be deemed their rivals; and I have sometimes really felt that this jealousy has had more to do with our past reverses than is generally imagined.

But, on this occasion, no shadow of this sort darkened the horizon of our expectations; every thing was tinged with the roseate hue of patriotic hope. We were certainly going to Richmond, and these soldierly-looking men about me were just the men to lead us on. I liked M'Dowell's looks; he seemed to me strong, self-contained, ready for responsibility, and able to sustain it. I had yet to learn how much his too frequent forgetfulness of the courtesy due even to a common soldier was to impair his usefulness and injure his popularity.

Here also was Bayard, looking really worthy of his name, young, enthusiastic, full of fire and energy. Near this spot he won his general's star, and yonder, over the river, only a mile or two away, he is hereafter to rise with it into immortality.

Imagine our chagrin when our general, having finished his interview, came out into the hall to inform us that our brigade, being the last arrival, was to be left behind to guard Fredericksburg. This was disappointment number one; we soon stopped numbering such experiences, for they are the every-day occurrences of a campaign. Whenever you get your tent fixed with unusual comfort, be sure you will march on the morrow; if you are halted for a day, make up your mind for a week's stay, and the probabilities are that you will not be disappointed.

So we mounted and followed the general down the steep road leading to the river and across the pontoon bridge into Fredericksburg, a quiet, pretty town, well entitled to the epithet said to have been given to it by the Prince of Wales — "the only finished town in America." Not commerce or manufactures, but good wholesome comfort had evidently reigned here supreme. Of course it was very different now. The constant rumble of heavy army wagons disturbed the sleepy streets; patrols of cavalry and infantry went their rounds; sentries stood guard at the street corners; soldiers invaded the shops and sidewalks; army sutlers flaunted the stars and stripes from the store windows; and in the old bank we found the headquarters of the military governor.

B

CHAPTER III.

FREDERICKSBURG.

WE were to be quartered for the present in the city, and, at the recommendation of the military governor, took possession of the house of an absent rebel officer. The usual ceremonial of lease-signing and delivering of the door-key was dispensed with, a sentry soon paced to and fro in front, and we began to make ourselves quite at home. A roomy, old-fashioned mansion it was, once doubtless the abode of a genial hospitality. How it must have disturbed the now slumbering household gods, this unceremonious intrusion without even a "by your leave."

The contrabands in the kitchen gave us hearty welcome, however, making us at once free of the house, while Nannette, the housemaid, a kind, motherly creature, in whom we gradually became much interested, could not do too much for us. But our involuntary host, probably not aware of our intended visit, had forgotten to refurnish his depleted larder, so that the provision department was decidedly wanting. As our wagons had not yet come up, a general reconnoissance among the sutlers was at once ordered. Corned meats, coffee, and hard bread were the net proceeds of this reconnoissance, and I doubt whether our host's mahogany was ever surrounded with a merrier party than that which gathered at last to banquet on these luxuries.

Supper over, we sat a while on the front stoop. It was evident that the whole neighborhood was excited at this profanation of a rebel mansion by the miserable Yankees. A girls' boarding-school occupied the next house, and from its corresponding front stoop came ever and anon whole volleys of indignant looks and contemptuous gestures. Little caucuses of angry dames convened upon the sidewalk, and, as we sat enjoying the peaceful sunset, it was manifest that no very complimentary allusions to ourselves kept flowing the tide of talk. But as no masculine joined in this attack, our young aids wore their best looks, and smiled blandly upon the fair daughters of Secessia, while the rest of us, who had wives at home, enjoyed heartily this little dash of rebel pepper, as giving pungency to our experiences. By-and-by the little squads dispersed without our reading the riot act, our headquarter wagons came up, and the different chambers were soon occupied. Wrapped in our blankets, we slept the sleep of tired men, thankful that our absent host had not borne off all his beds also on his shoulders.

The next morning, Saturday, I had occasion to ride out very early over the river, and returned with appetite keen-edged to find our party seated around the breakfast table. With hungry eyes I looked eagerly to see on what dainties I was about to break my fast. A solitary dish of hard crackers in the centre, tin plates, knives and forks, and mugs for each person, and verily nothing more. What a laugh rolled upward at the look of blank dismay which overspread my countenance. But Patrick, our cook, with Nannette as his first lieutenant, was not wanting even in this emergency. He could not be called an artist—his specialty was perhaps fried salt pork and the like—but very welcome was his appearance as he brought in something temptingly labeled "boned turkey," sardines, and similar luxuries, served in their native tin, the which, with a good cup of commissariat coffee, helped out a quite tolerable meal. The major, our present caterer, was indeed quite exercised during these days, so thoroughly denuded of articles of food was the surrounding country; but what with "good *old* eggs," introduced occasionally by way of luxury, and the help of the commissariat, managed to rub along with no more than the usual amount of grumbling, which falls as a matter of right upon the devoted head of every caterer of a staff mess.

After breakfast, in company with a friend, I had a new experience of life in rebeldom. Desiring a storehouse for government use, I called on the mayor of the city, stating my want, and asking him to name a warehouse which could be taken with the least inconvenience to its owner. He was bland, courteous, but declined to interfere. Thus left to my own resources, I called at a store on the principal street, whose half-closed shutters indicated the rebel sympathies of its occupant. The scene that occurred was quite amusing and suggestive.

Entering, I accosted the proprietor very politely thus: "Can you tell me, sir, where I can procure a store for government use?"

Responded the storekeeper, very curtly, and with a most disdainful glance at my uniform, "No; I don't believe any man in this city would lease a store to *your* government."

To which I, still politely, "Oh! you misunderstand me; I haven't the slightest idea of *hiring* a store, but only of *taking* one. By-the-by" (addressing my companion, and taking a survey of the premises), "I think *this* store will answer our purpose very well, don't you?"

Storekeeper, at once becoming gentlemanly: "Oh, you want a warehouse, sir! Well, there are some empty ones on Commerce Street, which I am sure will suit you. Shall I show you the way?"

And so the conference ended. I have never seen a more rapid transition from disdain to decency in my life.

As we walked through the streets of Fredericksburg it was evident that we were among foes. The negroes were full of welcome, greeting us with a smiling courtesy which needed no interpreter, but the ladies turned away their faces as we passed, or manifested their hostility in ways even more demonstrative. I confess that this sort of treatment, while it did not hurt my feelings, always astonished me. Somehow I had never been able to get up a feeling of hatred against the Southerner, even after the attack on Sumter—pitying him rather as the worst victim of an accursed system which surrounds his cradle, and is the companion of his childhood, whose divine origin and sanctions are impressed upon him from the pulpit, and taught him at the school, entering unquestioned into all the ramifications of his social life. His present suicidal madness had seemed to me only a part of the disease. It was not, then, with any desire for revenge, but solely to restrain him from blindly involving North and South in one common ruin, we had come hither; and it was thus impossible for me to look upon these citizens of Fredericksburg as my enemies, but rather as my countrymen, to come back by-and-by, when their insanity was over, to the old fraternal relationship, perhaps forever disenthralled from that system which was the cause of their present madness.

But our Southern friends did not seem to look at it exactly in this light, and so we had to make the best of it. If a flag floated over the sidewalk, the fair dame would sweep out into the middle of the muddy street; if a pleasant face at an open window attracted us as we walked by, what a slamming to of window-blinds was there, my countrymen! The men were, however, more prudent, and treated us usually with sufficient courtesy.

A little imp carved out of ebony had somehow joined our staff within the last day or two. He rejoiced in the name of "Zion," and acted as boot-black-in-chief with the rank of contraband. Grotesque in appearance, wonderfully endowed with dirt and rags, his bright, cheerful face and funny ways interested us. The major resolved to extricate him from his coating of mud, clothe him, and educate him as waiter; so they proceeded together to the "famous mart of Moses" in Fredericksburg for the necessary wearing apparel. Entering the shop, the major said, "Now, Zion, take off your coat."

"Whaf—whaf—for, Massa Major?" said the boy, imploringly, at the same time backing toward the door and making evident preparations for flight.

It took some time to persuade him that he was to have a new jacket and not the usual whipping; but finally he consented to disrobe. Buttons there were none; the various rags were tied on somehow, and had to be cut off with a knife. In the evening, what with copious lavations and his new suit, Zion seemed a different creature. We began to think of him as a permanent fixture; but that night he left us new clothes and all, forever. Such is life!

Sunday, May 25th. This morning a reconnoissance in force was ordered, and our general and staff rode out to the front, though our own men, now comfortably quartered in houses near the railway station, were not to participate. The object of a reconnoissance is to discover the enemy's whereabouts, drive in his pickets, feel his strength, and determine his exact position, without bringing on a general engagement. To this end, cavalry are usually sent out, followed by infantry, and frequently artillery, as supports. It is like fox-hunting, with an additional zest in the fact that the foxes in this case are two-legged, and carry rifles.

On this beautiful Sunday morning, then, several regiments moved out of Fredericksburg by two roads to meet at their point of intersection. The cavalry came first, filling the road, and also stretching out over the fields on either side, every man carrying his carbine at full cock, ready on the instant to meet a concealed foe or beat up an ambuscade. We rode out to our outer pickets, and there halted a while to see the troops go by, and soon a squadron of the Harris Light Cavalry came up at a swinging trot. Officers and men seemed highly exhilarated at the rebel hunt before them, and two of our staff obtained permission to accompany the party. The infantry were not far behind, and as the enemy had made some demonstrations in this neighborhood very lately, a lively time was anticipated. But the reconnoissance proved successful, chiefly in ascertaining that the enemy had within a day or two retreated from the immediate vicinity.

Wishing the officers of the expedition good speed, we paused on our way home to call upon some Union ladies occupying farms near by. Their story was indeed a sad one. Their husbands had been dragged off to Richmond prison, not for any act or word of opposition to the rebel government, but simply for declining to take the Southern oath of allegiance. The poor women cried bitterly as they spoke of their dreadful anxiety for the prisoners, their lonely condition, living as they had been right between the picket lines of the two armies. Behind their hedges had crouched day and night the rebel marksmen, ready to pick off any exposed Union soldier, and they went to bed every night in fear and trembling. Now, in truth, as we heard of their sufferings, did we begin to appreciate the horrors of this rebellion.

A rapid ride home gave me time to attend the Episcopal church, which I found well filled with a congregation of whom one half, perhaps, were soldiers. The rector was bitterly Secesh, but his prayer for "our brothers and sons exposed to the dangers of battle" had no allusion forbidding the sympathy of the most loyal soul. I saw nothing in the manners of the congregation or in the preacher to disturb the morning worship, and was glad to find one place at least where friend and foe might meet in seeming harmony.

For the last twenty-four hours the air has been full of rumors of the raid of Stonewall Jackson, threatening Washington, and necessitating the withdrawal of our forces from their proposed expedition toward Richmond in order to defend the national capital. Some of the brigades which had commenced their southern march had been halted; Shields's division had already started back toward Catlett's Station, and before night it was evident that the whole movement was for the present abandoned. This was disappointment number two, even to us who were not to accompany it, while the officers of the expedition regretted it exceedingly. Late at night I rode over to headquarters, and had an interview with General M'Dowell. It was evident that the giving up of this movement caused him great pain. I remember being particularly struck with his accurate knowledge of the exact position of the different regiments of his command, no easy matter in an army of 40,000 or 50,000 men.

B 2

CHAPTER IV.

CAMP OPPOSITE FREDERICKSBURG.

MONDAY, *May 26th*. This morning we were ordered to go into camp on the Falmouth side of the river. Before leaving Fredericksburg we rode through the city, and found the people in a state of intense excitement. The various and contradictory rumors, the marching and countermarching of our troops through the streets this past forty-eight hours, seemed inexplicable, and we were asked by several panic-stricken women, who came to their doors as we rode slowly along, if we were really going to shell the town. It was with a good deal of regret I bade farewell to this pretty city, for it was pleasant to walk through its streets, despite the rebel sympathy every where apparent, and it was more agreeable to see even the back of a woman's bonnet than no woman at all.

Our brigade was now assigned to guard the railroad from Aquia Creek to Falmouth. The regiments went into camp by companies at regular intervals in the woods flanking the road, sending out daily details of guards to walk post along the track, with little guardhouses, part tent, part log house, for their protection. Block-houses were at once commenced at either end of the two principal railroad bridges; the men built comfortable tents, and in less than a week were quite at home, some of the officers sending for their wives and children.

Our own head-quarters were fixed at the Wallace

House, the residence of a lawyer who had two sons in the rebel army, and sympathized fully with the rebel cause. A native-born Virginian, he was, strange to say, about the best living illustration I ever met with of the ideal Yankee, in appearance, manner, dress, stick and jack-knife, though his conversational tone of course partook of the usual *lingua Africana* of the South. We remained at his house two or three weeks, and I learned to respect him not only for the philosophy with which he bore the intrusion of his enemies, and his evident sincerity in a bad cause, but for his general intelligence and kindly courtesy. During our frequent conversations we discussed the war, its causes and prospects, with no loss of temper, and withal so frankly, that he said to me one day, after our return from a dress parade, "Your soldiers are the finest-looking as a body I ever saw—much larger and heavier than ours, and far better clothed. Our poor boys only had ragged uniforms on when they were here." He was not a man to carry water on both shoulders, for he distinctly stated that if the government should insist upon his taking the federal oath, on peril of having all his property confiscated, he should certainly let his property go. For months he had not heard from his sons; his slaves had all fled toward the north star; his fields had been taken for camping-grounds; his fences and hedges cut down; his best rooms occupied by Union officers, while the flag against which he had sent his children to fight floated in front of his house. I could not help feeling a good deal of sympathy with him as I saw him wandering round his fields and out-houses with the inevitable stick in his hand, the picture of semi-despair.

With our army cots and blankets (sheets are not fashionable in the army), we made pleasant quarters in the various chambers. Nannette, the old housemaid at our Fredericksburg mansion, had insisted upon coming over with us, and now officiated in the kitchen, supplying, with the help of Patrick, comfortable meals, served up on a table-service of tin. There was always abundance of ham or bacon as a *pièce de résistance*, with entrées of fried pork, hard bread, and other delicacies of the commissariat; and when the rare luxuries of fresh beef, milk, butter, chickens, or "store bread" did surprise us, they were all the more welcome.

Perhaps this will be the best opportunity to give some idea of the organization of the army. As at present constituted, a brigade is made up of four or five regiments; three or four brigades compose a division; three or four divisions constitute a corps. There are some twenty or more of these corps in the Union army, seven of them, for example, constituting, at the date of this writing, the Army of the Potomac. Much of the routine work of the army goes no farther than corps head-quarters, but all matters of general importance pass under the revision of the head-quarters of the army. The old incubus of right, left, and centre grand divisions has been happily abolished.

During this stay at Falmouth, ours was an independent brigade, unattached to a division, and specially assigned to the defense of Aquia Creek and the railroad. A brigadier general is entitled to the following staff:

1. An assistant adjutant general, who transacts the usual office business, and superintends the purely mil-

itary department. He issues orders in the name of the general; to him are addressed all communications from officers inferior in rank to the general; he is, in fact, prime minister, and has a very agreeable position.

2. An assistant quarter-master, who has charge of the transportation, tents and tent-equipage, clothing, tools, and fixtures generally. His is, perhaps, the most arduous and difficult position in the army.

3. A commissary of subsistence, who draws from the various dépôts of supply the necessary food for the troops, and distributes it to the regimental quarter-masters, who in turn distribute it among the companies. This department is so admirably organized and conducted that the position is considered a very pleasant one.

Each of these three staff officers ranks as captain, has a clerk and other subordinates, his own duties being chiefly supervisory. The assistant adjutant general always attends the general; the assistant quarter-master and commissary of subsistence are also permitted, when their official duties do not forbid it, to act as aids on the battle-field.

4. Two aids, who assist the adjutant general in the various duties of his office, carry orders on the field of battle, and are the only officers, under the new regulations, who are *personally* attached to the general, following him when he quits his brigadier division for another. Their rank is that of first lieutenant.

Our "major" was an artillery officer, attached temporarily to the staff as ordnance officer and acting aid. We had also a brigade surgeon, but the latter rank has since been abolished.

At brigade head-quarters is also a brigade guard,

under command of a subaltern: four mounted orderlies, the bearers of dispatches and part of the retinue of the general, and two or more foot orderlies for the convenience of the general and staff. Of course, as the command rises in dignity from brigade to division, from division to corps, the staff, with its adjutants, increases greatly in number and importance, until the head-quarters of the army becomes in itself a little city of tents; the head-quarter guard is composed of a regiment or two; the four mounted orderlies swell into two regiments of cavalry.

We were learning that to wait is one of the chief duties of the soldier, and really it is the most irksome, as a calm at sea is much more wearisome than a storm. Pleasant rides all about us; a quiet trot through the streets of Fredericksburg; a visit to the camps about the time of the evening dress-parade, lent variety to our usual duties; still this was not the campaign life we had anticipated. During this period various bodies of troops were constantly coming and going; wo to the grove or plantation near which their new camps were located. Hardly did a regiment stack arms before the trees began to come in bodily, the fences disappeared, and in an hour or two what had been a bare common was covered with huts wattled with evergreens and roofed with shelter-tents. These rustic dens were about seven feet by six, accommodating two soldiers; they were arranged in regular streets, with the officers' tents in the rear, sometimes shaded with rootless trees. It quite astonished me at first to see how quickly the old campaigners made themselves comfortable. Grotesque ideas of discipline, too, and of the law of confiscation, they had, these independent volunteers. I have seen commissioned, non-commissioned officers, and privates playing cards together, or hobnobbing around the same camp-fire. One colonel, who drilled his men near our house, though not of our brigade, was in the habit of arguing with his men as to their drill and duties, and evidently leaned a good deal upon their opinion—his parade being thus rather a town-meeting in uniform. Such a man is of course unfit to lead troops into battle, for they will probably obey him if they feel like it, but not otherwise.

As to the popularity of the confiscation law, and the readiness of the men to execute it, there could be no doubt. Two men, for example, were cooking a fat fowl at their camp-fire, when a corporal sniffed the unaccustomed odor, and thus accosted them:

"Hallo, boys! where did you get that chicken?"

"Oh, we confiscated him for talking treason."

"Talking treason! what do you mean? Chickens can't talk."

"No, but they can *crow;* and, as sure as you live, we caught this rooster, this very afternoon, crowing with all his might for Jeff. Davis."

Of course, the corporal had to be satisfied, and passed on.

During these waiting days, however, we had frequent rumors, just sufficient to keep us on the *qui vive.* By the way, there is no community on earth so frequently the sport of rumor wild and strange as a camp in the enemy's country. Woman has sometimes been ungallantly considered swift-flying Fame's chosen messenger. She can claim that position no longer. For stories the wildest, strangest, most unbelievable, of the approach of the enemy, a coming move, etc., commend me to an encampment of soldiers with little to do. Stonewall was certainly about to pay his respects to us at least half a dozen times during the past ten days. At length, on Friday, May 30th, orders came to have twenty-four hours' cooked rations, and be ready to march at a moment's notice. Of course, the novice saw a fight impending immediately, and that night I packed every thing packable, put a lunch into my saddle-bags, and had sword and pistols at my bedside, ready to be buckled on in an instant. All this we soon got bravely over, learning by experience to receive an order to "be ready to march at a moment's notice" with entire equanimity. The morning came, and we had not moved, and so we once more fell back into our old monotony.

CHAPTER V.

PHILLIPS'S HOUSE HEAD-QUARTERS.

TUESDAY, *June* 10*th*. This day M'Call's division departed to join M'Clellan on the Peninsula, and our general, being left temporarily in command of Fredericksburg and the adjacent district, made his head-quarters at the Phillips House. A fine residence it was, overlooking the valley of the Rappahannock and the pretty city, with the Blue Ridge bounding the western horizon, and treating us occasionally to a sunset of wonderful beauty. The plantation once formed a part of the estate of Mary, the mother of Washington, whose half-finished monument, just back of Fredericksburg, was visible from its balcony. It must have been a charming spot ere War, with its desolating footfall, had invaded this lovely valley; but now fences, trees, and waving grain had departed; the owner had deserted, leaving only an overseer with an immense wife and two babies, whose capacity for crying was equally extensive, with a superannuated negro or two in the outbuildings, too old to accompany their fellows on the Northern tour. If we were condemned to temporary inactivity, we could not have had a more delightful spot for our involuntary sojourn.

The 76th New York was sent over to occupy the city, and its major was made military governor. His first day was signalized by the important capture of

Major Lacy, of General Smith's staff, the wealthy owner of the "Lacy mansion," who had ventured a little too near our pickets. This capture created a profound sensation in Fredericksburg, as he was perhaps the most influential man in the county, and had labored night and day to bring about the secession of Virginia. While incarcerated in the guard-house, I made him a visit, and found him courteous and gentlemanly. On my noticing a book he held in his hand, "Yes," he replied, "I am trying to read in order to drown reflection." It struck me at the time that, as one of the instigators of a rebellion which had already brought such wo and ruin upon his native state, he would have to try some stronger spell than this; the ghost of sad reflection would hardly down at so feeble a bidding. But I know of no article of war forbidding courtesy to foes, especially when in prison; and I could not help expressing the hope, as I left the major, that we might meet again under more pleasant circumstances. He was sent North in a day or two, and has been, I presume, duly exchanged.

My friend the military governor had a busy time of it, and, being a gallant man, rather an unpleasant one. Innocent-looking females were arrested with large packages of rebel letters about their persons; bright-eyed demoiselles, with family trunks reminding one of Noah's ark by their size and antiquity, were found to be bearing southward medicines enough to stock a village apothecary instead of laces and other feminine gear. If a good lady awoke some fine morning to find that some of her two-legged property had started during the night for Washington, or that a horse had vanished from her stable, straightway she called upon the major, ordering him at once to return the missing article with an air which half implied that he himself had stolen it. Never, however, was the city better governed—no trespasses by the soldiers were permitted; law and order reigned supreme. Squads of contrabands wandered in from the country daily, besieging his office for passes northward; and it was touching to see how the poor creatures, blind to the blessings of the patriarchal institution, rejoiced at the receipt of the magic bit of paper which insured their escape from bondage. Their joy seemed to overflow their whole being, and bubbled up in wild exclamation and grotesque grimace.

We had quite a number of these newly-freed men about our head-quarters, in the employ of government as teamsters, blacksmith, etc. A patient, docile race, eminently trustworthy, with mental faculties quite undeveloped, it always seemed wonderful to me that they succeeded so well in their new experiment of freedom. It may take a generation to develop their best qualities of self-support; but even now they very readily fell into the performance of their respective duties. I have witnessed their exultation when, for the first time in their lives, they received honest pay for their honest labor, and am satisfied that this is impulse sufficient with them, as with us, to induce their best efforts. I have seen them painfully spelling out their letters—great six-foot men even, struggling over the difficulties of a child's primer, and am convinced of their capacity and desire for education. I have employed them personally and for the government, and feel that they are honest and faithful, anxious to be instructed what to do, quick in learning, and energetic in doing it.

To those who are troubling themselves so much with the question "What shall we do with them?" my answer is, Let them very much alone, and they will do for themselves. As society is at present constituted, we need a class who shall be "hewers of wood and drawers of water;" we require, North as well as South, all this labor; to expatriate it would be a substantial loss to the whole country. With proper guarantees that they shall enjoy what they honestly earn, they will soon be able to take abundant care of themselves. If exiled from free territory, or forbidden the opportunity to work, they must, of course, become a public burden; but if free market be allowed for their labor, the demand will fully equal the supply, and the question in ten years will be, "How can we do without them?" As to their fighting value, I, of course, know nothing; but this interesting question seems to be rapidly approaching a practical solution.

Our quarter-master, a wag in his way, had discovered somewhere a bright-eyed boy whom he made his servant, initiating him by the following affirmation: "You, Pompey, solemnly declare that you will support the Constitution of the United States, look out for my horses, and black boots to the best of your knowledge and belief; so help you, General M'Dowell." The boy was naturally much impressed with the ceremony, kissed a copy of the "Army Regulations," and faithfully kept his pledge.

We should expect such a people to be especially susceptible to an overwrought religious enthusiasm. Almost every night the little colony of families assembled in a building in the rear of head-quarters, making the night vocal with their prayers and hymns.

Old Uncle Berryman, the general's servant, was the patriarch of the flock, and led their somewhat peculiar worship. Standing in the centre, the vociferous and perspiring worshipers moved swiftly around him, singing, as they revolved, hymns like the following:

> "The very best thing that ever I done—
> Glory hallelujah, bress de Lord!
> Was to serve the Lord when I was young.
> Glory hallelujah, bress de Lord!"

Long and loud they repeated this verse, until, having at length exhausted it, they sang the second and only remaining stanza:

> "Then I sot down and felt very blue—
> Glory hallelujah, bress de Lord!
> Says I, O Lord, what shall I do?
> Glory hallelujah, bress de Lord!"
> *Da capo ad lib.*

Great comfort they took in these meetings, and at last it became necessary to limit their duration. Upon being spoken to in this connection, Berryman thus expostulated: "Gineral, I never speaks a word after de taps; it's some of dem other darkies. Dat other preacher is a Methodist, and you can't keep him still nohow. I is a Baptist."

"Taps," to which Berryman referred, are the three taps on the drum which are the camp-signal for the men to put out their lights, and cease all loud talking in their tents. "Tattoo," the go-to-bed signal, is beaten about 9 o'clock, and taps come a quarter of an hour afterward. The getting-up signal, beaten not long after sunrise, is called *reveillé*.

Friday, June 13th. Quite an exciting day, the vedettes coming in with reports that the enemy had attacked and driven in our pickets outside the city. A regiment of cavalry, two of infantry, and two batteries were speedily put in motion, and we were soon riding to the front. It proved to be only a cavalry attack, and, before our troops reached the spot, the enemy had retired. The men enjoyed the expedition exceedingly, and we owe the rebel attacking party our thanks for a new sensation.

Quite a large body of troops were now assembled, and occasional expeditions of cavalry were sent out to disturb the quiet of the enemy, burn the railroad bridges, and thus interrupt his communications, sometimes having a brush with the enemy's cavalry and bringing in some prisoners. Their usual guide was a native-born Virginian, in whom we all became much interested. He seemed to me a sort of Daniel Webster in ebony — a strong, clear-headed man, who had reached a true conception of the real issue in this war, and devoted himself, body and soul, on the right side. Knowing all the roads and by-ways in this section, and brave as a lion, he led our boys with all the cool courage needed in a scout, established a comprehensive system of espionage among the people of his own color, and thus brought in much valuable information. The rebels did him the honor to offer fifteen hundred dollars reward for his head, and well they might, for he was worth to the Union cause any two of the best of us. As he sallied forth with military cap, blue coat adorned with the button of old Massachusetts — its *ense petit placidam sub libertate quietem* singularly appropriate to his situation — with his revolver in his breast, and a good horse under him, he was naturally looked up to with admiring eyes by his brother contrabands.

"He sets great store on *hisself*. He's a jet black nigger; got no white blood in *his* veins." This latter physiological peculiarity, as it grows more and more infrequent at the South, is gradually becoming quite a badge of colored aristocracy; and no one could see Dabney without being convinced of the pure blood of the black scout of the Rappahannock.

About this time we were joined by King's division. With it came the red-breeched 14th Brooklyn, a regiment reminding one of the *gamins de Paris* in the freedom of their manners, and the genius they displayed in appropriating to themselves whatever they needed for their personal comfort. They brought with them some bundles of counterfeit confederate notes, and soon became excellent customers at the Fredericksburg shops. On entering, they usually accosted the proprietor as follows:

"Do you take this confederate stuff here? We don't think it good for any thing, but, if you choose to receive it, we'll make some purchases."

Shopkeeper (indignantly). "Those notes will buy any thing in my store, sir."

And so more than three thousand dollars changed hands, another illustration of the elevating influence of war.

The city was never more quiet, but the bitter, burning hate of the wealthier classes still smouldered on, unquenched and unquenchable. A change had taken place in the military government, and to some of us it seemed as if treason was treated with altogether too much leniency. In Fredericksburg, as elsewhere I presume, very many of those in moderate circumstances, the mechanics and farmers, were really Union men. Personally brought into acquaintance with several of these—men who longed to see the triumph of the old flag—men who had been driven in from their farms outside our lines, and were constantly subjected to threats of vengeance from the wealthier city rebels, I saw that what was needed was the strong hand of governmental protection to bring out a latent Union feeling which would have astonished a casual observer. With grief and shame, I saw also that this strong hand was never uplifted. Treason, being usually aristocratic, was cajoled, fed with sweetmeats, toyed with; loyalty, being usually confined to the less wealthy, was too much neglected, nay, almost frowned upon and despised by some of those in authority. Practically, as every Union man felt in his bones, a premium was held up by our officials to treason in Fredericksburg, and most bitterly did those who had suffered every thing rather than prove false to their country complain of it. Said one of them to me, "A man is a fool who comes out for the Union in Fredericksburg." I could not gainsay his bitter reasoning.

The rebel men were of course compelled to common decency, the women still indulged in little demonstrations of contempt and dislike. In passing a soldier, they sometimes swept by as if afraid of contamination. Our boys bore all this with a good deal of indifference, but once in a while flung out a retaliatory sarcasm. Thus, as a woman, in passing a soldier, lifted her skirts and moved by with a haughty gesture, he drawled out with exaggerated Yankee twang,

"Why, marm, how dirty your stockings are! Just look at 'em!" Down, down went female skirts and female pride at the same instant, while a hearty laugh from his comrades winged the sarcastic shaft and sent it well home.

June 26*th*. General Pope assumed command to-day of the Army of Virginia, including the corps of Generals Banks and Sigel, with our own under the immediate command of General M'Dowell. This concentration, with other evidences, indicated a movement, and promised us speedy relief from our present monotony. The new general took hold with a good deal of energy; a few of the good people of Fredericksburg were presently seized as hostages for their neighbors now in the Richmond prisons, the passage of supplies southward was stopped, and our rebel friends began to discover the actual signification of the word *War*. The Union citizens were of course jubilant—held up their heads again; and as they expressed their congratulations, it was evident that their feelings of relief, hope, and courage swelled up hard by the fountain of tears. Said one of them to me, a native of South Carolina, but for fifteen years resident of Fredericksburg, "Now at last I see a gleam of sunlight. I had begun to despair, but now I feel that we can put down this rebellion."

The army also partook of the new inspiration. Tired of guarding the property of men actually in arms against us, there was not a drummer-boy who did not discover that a new policy had been inaugurated. Among the general orders of the new commander was one requiring the seizure of rebel horses and forage when needed for the public service; and our quarter-master availed himself of the opportunity to exchange some of our worn-out animals for the more serviceable stock of the wealthy planters in the vicinity, giving them a voucher of the following tenor:

"The undersigned freely acknowledges to have received, on this 1st day of July, 1862, from John Smith, of Fredericksburg, for the use and service of the United States of America, four mules, which I have valued at three hundred dollars. This voucher will be payable at the conclusion of the war, upon sufficient testimony being presented that said John Smith has been a loyal citizen of said United States from the date hereof. By order of Brig. Gen. RUFUS KING.

"WILLIAM BROWN, A. Q. M. U. S. A."

This precious document may be called a "slow note," in most cases not worth the ink required to write it, as none but known rebels were invited to make this involuntary patriotic offering.

July 4th, Independence day, was celebrated with considerable *éclat* at our head-quarters. At noon a salute from our brigade battery awoke the slumbering echoes, and shortly after the troops marched in upon the green in front of the house, and the piazza was soon filled with field and staff officers, when the Declaration of Independence was read, and the usual oration delivered, the whole pleasantly varied by music from the band of the 56th Pennsylvania Volunteers. Truly the penates of the Phillips mansion, and the spirits of earth and air who, as the poets tell us, flit on invisible wings about these groves and hill-sides, must have heard sentiments uttered on this occasion by the parlous Yankee orator which had for them at least the charm of novelty. As for Virginians of mortal mould, we had but few of them, and these mainly contraband of war, who made up, however, for their lack of numbers by their open-mouthed enthusiasm. To them it was Independence day indeed.

In the afternoon two or three of us rode down to see the races on the green in front of division head-quarters. The troops lined the sides of a large hollow square, a crowd of general and other officers occupied the centre, and great was the rivalry of the different regiments, not one of which but had a horse able to beat the entire Army of Virginia. The donkey races were very amusing, defying all calculation, the fantasies of this embodiment of self-willed obstinacy never yet being reducible to any racing equation.

An hour or two of such fun is, however, quite sufficient, so I took a solitary ride through the streets of Fredericksburg. Not a fire-cracker was flung at my horse's heels, not a flag waved except in a sutler's window; it was evident that Young Virginia was in the dumps; so I hurried across the river, lest I also should be infected with the painful gloom.

I was now for a week or two busily engaged as judge-advocate of a court-martial. The weather was so pleasant that we occupied the back piazza, which, walled in with canvas, made an excellent court-room. As its sessions are open to all except while the court is considering some doubtful point or consulting as to the verdict and sentence, look in for a moment and see how we try offenders in the army. At the head of the table sits the president, opposite him is the judge-advocate, the half dozen or more officers composing the court being ranged in order of rank on either side. On the right of the judge-advocate is the accused, sitting if an officer, standing if a private; on the left stands the witness now under examination. A sentry walks to and fro in front of the court-room, an orderly or two and several spectators are in the rear. The accused is allowed counsel, but rarely exercises this right, as the judge-advocate acts for him as well as the government. The whole proceeding is eminently fair and equitable: few legal technicalities embarrass the examination; demurrers, rejoinders, and sur-rejoinders are unknown; the accused is permitted, when the evidence is closed, to tell his own story; the court-room is cleared, and the jury of officers decide as to his guilt, and affix his punishment. On the whole, I was very favorably impressed with this tribunal, and have wished that some of our civil courts could approach more nearly to its simplicity of procedure, and its common-sense method of attaining substantial justice.

The punishments in the army are sometimes novel and peculiar. I have seen a soldier standing erect for hours upon a barrel-head; another with a huge board strapped upon his shoulders, with the inscription, "I am a coward," or "I ran away from the last battle;" one man wears a wooden breastplate with the word "Thief" upon it; another walks to and fro shouldering a billet of wood instead of a musket; some drag after them a heavy ball and chain; others laboriously undergo the "knapsack drill," or carry large stones on either shoulder. The great difficulty in properly punishing our volunteers is, that the misconduct of the men is too often attributable to the want of proper discipline on the part of their officers. It is but just to remark, however, that, every thing considered, our volunteers are a well-behaved set of men, rarely needing the services of a court-martial.

Thus with little of incident passed the pleasant summer weeks, our regular routine duties, an occasional review, a gallop through the forests of oak, chestnut, and cedar, and the ever-recurring rumors of an immediate movement affording scarcely variety enough to keep off ennui. Of the lovely view from the piazza of our head-quarters I never tired. At night, after all was still, it was my custom to sit here a while, smoking with one of our aids the pipe of quiet contemplation. The sentry pacing his solitary round, the four little howitzers glistening in the moonlight, the fringe of white tents immediately about us, and the white cloud of tents resting upon the valleys beyond, all spoke of war, but the general influence of the hour led usually to subjects of a far different character. It was on such an occasion he told me that he did not expect to live to see the end of the war, a prophetic foreboding only too surely realized.

At length, on the 4th of August, the arrival of Burnside's army, which was to hold possession of Fredericksburg, indicated that the long-expected movement was at hand. Our brigade was now assigned to the division commanded by General Rufus King: his other brigades being the 1st, under General Hatch, consisting of the 2d regiment of U. S. Sharpshooters and four regiments of New York troops; the 3d, under General Patrick, composed of four New York regiments; and the 4th, under General Gibbon, made up of one Indiana and three Wisconsin regiments. Our own, the 2d brigade, was composed of one Pennsylvania and two New York regiments, to which was afterward added the 7th Indiana.

Our expected move made it necessary to part with Nannette, who went back to her children at Warrenton; and several of our colored attaches now left us, being unwilling to leave their families. Our general resigned the Phillips House to one of the new generals, as our brigade was now relieved from guarding the railroad, and it was time for us to encamp near it and learn how to live in tents. Our new head-quarters were fixed in a pretty grove adjoining the house of some ladies, who, though strongly sympathizing with the South, never forgot their sex, and did all in their power to make our brief stay agreeable.

Come into my tent, beneath the welcome shade of a stately pine, and you may see how a staff officer lives. The little house of canvas is nine feet square; a portable army cot makes on one side a good lounge by day and a right comfortable bed by night, with a writing-desk against the rear pole, a camp stool or two, a cracker-box toilet-stand in one corner with tin cup and basin, a rope stretched overhead for coats, etc., the floor strewed with evergreens, and a square yard of carpet as a reminder of civilization. Very simple furniture all this, but quite sufficient, and we shall see occasions during the coming campaign when it will appear almost palatial.

Our mess-table is spread in the latticed porch of the dwelling, and the major has lately introduced a whistle as the call to meals. If you can eat from tin, you will be welcomed to a very respectable dinner. The government now supplies us with abundance of fresh beef —even potatoes are not wanting—while the appetizing sauce of pleasant conversation seasons all. The usual order to keep the men supplied with three days' cooked rations has reached us; every meal may be the last taken in our present locality, and all are rejoicing that we are having our last experiences in "Camp opposite Fredericksburg."

CHAPTER VI.

FROM FREDERICKSBURG TO CEDAR MOUNTAIN.

AT length, on the afternoon of August 9th, as I was reclining upon my lounge after a hearty dinner, with my tent-flaps flung wide open to invite the cooling breeze, I heard the general's voice in the next tent directing an orderly to summon the staff. In a brief period all were assembled, when we were notified that orders to march had just been received. Our adjutant general at once dispatched the orderlies to the regiments encamped in the fields close by headquarters, and all were soon engaged in packing up preparatory to striking tents. After I had seen every thing ready for our baggage-wagons, I mounted my horse and rode off to make some final arrangements, noticing every where the bustle of prospective departure except among Burnside's men, who were to remain behind.

Our destination was Cedar Mountain, at which point the Army of Virginia was now concentrating, and two of the brigades of our division moved thither by another road. At 4 P.M. all was ready; the men fell in, each heavily laden with knapsack, extra ammunition, and three days' marching rations; the regiments wheeled into column, the band struck up an exhilarating air, and the brigade was soon crossing the pontoon bridge into Fredericksburg. Following the troops came the head-quarter and regimental wagons, the latter carrying the camp-kettles and other cooking utensils of the men and a limited amount of officers' baggage; and, lastly, the supply train laden with subsistence and forage, the rear closed up by the rear-guard.

The afternoon was so very warm that one poor fellow, whose zeal had outrun his discretion, quietly laid down on the sidewalk and died before his regiment had fairly quitted the city. But even the heat of the weather and their heavy burdens could not wholly repress the enthusiasm of our troops, inexperienced in the trials of campaign life and eager for a change. I had joined the general and a portion of the staff in the city, and, while the troops were marching through, we practically obeyed the campaign maxim—"whenever you can secure a decent meal, do so"—by taking a farewell repast at a quiet inn. The general then rode on to the front, leaving two of us behind to hurry up the wagon-train, which had been delayed at the river-crossing. The twilight had descended before we were ready to go forward, and as our horses walked slowly through the silent streets, one of our party, a good singer, sang one or two songs as a parting serenade. I fear that the fair rebels, who sat at their front doors enjoying the evening hour, failed to appreciate his courtesy, or to sympathize with the joyful feelings with which we went "marching along" out of their pretty but sleepy city.

A quick gallop soon brought us up with the advancing column, and, pushing past the troops, we joined the general riding at the head of the brigade. It was a lovely night for marching, the troops moved on well, their arms glistening in the moonlight, and yet, so slow is the movement of an army, that it was nearly midnight before we reached our halting-place, nine miles distant from Fredericksburg. The different regiments were at once marched into the fields on either side of the road, where they bivouacked in their blankets, a few pickets were thrown out, our horses were tied to a fence and furnished with fodder from a neighboring rick, and then the general and staff were at liberty to seek repose. The general took possession of a lower room in a neighboring farm-house, while two of us very unwisely sought repose upon a feather bed in an upper chamber. The result was highly unsatisfactory, as may well be imagined from the state of the thermometer, and little was accomplished in the way of sleep.

At daybreak next morning the men were cooking their coffee, and shortly after we quitted our couch of torment, and were ready for our own breakfast. In the course of an hour the column was again in motion; the road was in fine order, but the day was warm and enervating. If one who had formed his ideas of the marching of troops from the volunteer parades of our citizen soldiers on Broadway or Boston Common could have accompanied us to-day, he would have been wofully disappointed. "Route step" and "arms at will" were the orders. Every man was allowed to keep his own gait so long as he maintained his position in his company. The indispensable tin cup dangled from many a bayonet, while the musket described every possible angle but the right one. No martial music lent new vigor to tired limbs; not even a drum and fife marked time for the movement. Occasionally a rank or two joined in a lively chorus, but, as the heat became more oppressive, even this ceased; the most waggish volunteer lost his power to charm; wearily through the dust the column plodded on. This marching beneath an August sun in Virginia has nothing of military romance about it; it is, on the contrary, downright hard work, especially for troops like our own, unaccustomed to such service. Frequent halts afforded some relief; but our march had not continued three hours before some of the men began to straggle from the column, upon all sorts of excuses, slyly watching a favorable opportunity; some really unwell, but the majority only pretending to be unwell; they stole into the woods skirting the road, or sank down by the wayside really exhausted. The rear-guard of course compelled many of these stragglers to rejoin their commands, and helped the really sick into the ambulances, but numbers escaped their notice, some to rejoin their regiment later in the day, some never to rejoin it at all.

This straggling is the great evil of our army, lessening by a serious percentage the effective force upon which a commander can rely in going into battle. It is astonishing what sudden and severe fits of illness are apt to attack a soldier when he gets sight of an attractive farm-house, and how sad a story he always has to tell when he once gains entrance. A pretty close observation enables me to state positively that no soldier under such circumstances was ever known to have had "any thing to eat for two whole days," though his haversack might be even then plethoric with rations.

And the pleas these stragglers put in when caught with plunder are sometimes sublime in their audacity.

"Hallo, my man! where did you get that pork?" called out our major to a soldier staggering along with something wrapped up in his shelter-tent, and crimsoning the ground as he passed.

"It isn't pork, sir, it's tomatoes; you don't know, sir, how hard it is to tell pork from tomatoes in this country." The major, a pleasant hand at a joke himself, was conquered at once, and did not press his inquiries.

In this regard we are, however, no greater sufferers than the rebels. From conversations with rebel officers, prisoners of war, I learn that they lose as much in this way, and perhaps more. Straggling can only be put down by a severity of discipline, which has never yet been known in our volunteer system, but which seems absolutely indispensable.

It was my duty, as acting aid, to pass occasionally from front to rear, to see that the regiments kept well closed up, and I was pained to see, as the day wore on, so many of our poor fellows overcome by the heat, and resting by the wayside. At midday a longer halt than usual enabled the men to cook their coffee. The usual daily allowance of a soldier, called the ration, is so ample, that I give it as the best illustration in my power of the care which Uncle Samuel takes of his soldiers. It consists of three fourths of a pound of pork, or a pound and a quarter of fresh or salt beef, a pound of hard bread, or twenty-two ounces of flour, with an ample supply of coffee or tea, sugar, rice, beans, salt, soap, vinegar, molasses, and candles; and, when practicable, potatoes, onions, dried apples, and desiccated vegetables. The only trouble with the full ration is that no soldier can eat the whole of it, and some reduction might be made with benefit to the service. On a march, however, he is allowed only "marching rations," consisting of five articles—meat, hard bread, coffee, sugar, and salt; and I have thought it would be well to allow commissaries to increase the issue of the three latter articles, as nothing seems to refresh the troops so much as a cup of coffee, and at every halt during the day the tin cup was in requisition at each little impromptu camp-fire.

Once, while returning to the front, I had an adventure more exciting than agreeable. I had halted a while at the forks of the road, and dismounted to breathe my mare, a courtesy of which she took advantage to dash off at full speed. To mount another horse and pursue her was the work of a moment, and a three-mile race then and there came off, made still more delightful by the fact that we had left the road taken by our brigade, and by my consequent apprehension that I might be making my way straight into the enemy's lines. I tried coaxing, strategy, hard running, but all in vain. Several times I could almost grasp her mane, when up would fly her heels, and away she would dart unpityingly. At last I tamed my horse down to a walk, and her ladyship turned off into a field, where a couple of soldiers who had straggled from another brigade aided me in securing her; one good thing, at least, to be put to the credit of straggling.

Our destination for the day was Ely's Ford of the Rapidan, and we had taken a guide at a farm-house near Fredericksburg, who accompanied us part of the way, and then left us with full directions; but either he was ignorant, or we had misunderstood him; certain it is that about 3 P.M. we became convinced that we were on the wrong road. My mare had really taken the right course at first. Small thanks to her.

We had gone out of our way only a mile or two, but this addition to the march of our tired column was discouraging. The road on which we were now moving was also very narrow, so that it was difficult to turn the long army wagon. The army teamster is not a stoic, nor usually subdued in the expression of his emotions, and I fear that, had our guide presented himself just then, his feelings would have been slightly wounded, if nothing more. A drenching rain had just set in, which did not add to the general equanimity.

In an hour we were again in the right road, and so, over a rolling, heavily-wooded country, with scarcely a single evidence of cultivation, we approached the Rapidan. The air all day had been full of the rumors of battle—rumors coming no one knew how or whither; perhaps the birds brought them, or the leaves whispered them; certainly every one felt their influence. We had yet to learn that at this hour, as we were quietly riding through the forests, the battle was raging in which we had expected to participate, and which has made Cedar Mountain famous in American history. At about 6 P.M. we reached Ely's Ford, and forded the Rapidan, here some two hundred feet wide. The heavy shower had already raised the river so that it washed our horses' bellies, and I confess that my heart misgave me as I thought that our men must cross at this point before reaching their bivouac for the night.

Very near the ford, on the north side of the river, we found the residence of a small farmer, a long, gaunt man, put together well enough, perhaps, originally, but now quite shaken to pieces by the fever and ague. The house was small, dirty, and dilapidated, and the whole establishment worthy of its proprietor. Of thrift, comfort, good farming, there was none; it was evident that the occupants barely existed — did not live. One meets many just such dwellings and just such residents in the South; men who lie around loose rather than stand erect on God's footstool; men who seem to have no heritage of ideas or manly aspiration, but manage in a very desultory way to keep body and soul together. They are about the poorest specimens of humanity I have met with during a somewhat varied experience of travel, having more of the vices of civilization, and less of that native manliness we find even among the wild Bedouins. Labor is degrading, so of course the sons are idle; a slave or two become the scapegoats of their masters' idleness; their dialect is almost unmitigated African; when they wish to ascend to an upper chamber they always go up "stars;" when they feel chilly they hasten to shut the "dough;" as for their fondness for reading and writing, the curious may consult the census tables. I confess that I had hard work to struggle with a feeling of contempt for these, the worst victims of slavery, stigmatized by the haughty slaveholders as "poor white trash." Beautiful Virginia lies sterile, semi-barbarous, miserable, at the feet of her evil genius, only to grow young, and strong, and powerful, only to regain her once proud title of the Old Dominion, when all this race of do-nothings is gone, when free labor comes to touch with new magic the springs of intelligence, enterprise, and industry.

The whole family were gathered in the porch as we rode up, and at once began to implore for kindly treatment. Our host was quite overcome with fear, and his wife sought in vain to keep him from almost groveling entreaty. To convince them that we were friends, not enemies; that not an article would be taken without their consent, and that ample reward should repay every accommodation, was our first duty; but even after the *entente cordiale* was established, I noticed with pain a young girl, the only interesting person on the premises, still trembling with apprehension. Taught by the leaders of the rebellion that the Northmen were wild beasts in ferocity, that all chivalry and gentlemanliness were monopolized by the Southern slave-trader, it was no wonder that this, her first experience, should thus have startled her.

While quieting the fears of our host, our boys, drenched to the skin, but jolly as they always are in a rain-storm, began to move by, having forded the Rapidan probably at double-quick. Fortunately for them, the sun gave us a good-night glance at parting, and thus, under more cheerful auspices, they stacked arms, and prepared to bivouac. The ground had been selected by one of the staff before the regiments arrived, keeping in view, 1st, a good military position with reference to the presumed locality of the enemy, and, 2d, nearness to wood and water. The brigade was thus fronted toward the west in the fields on either side of the main road, and soon the camp-fires were in full glow, the evening meal in progress, boughs of trees brought in for beds, guards posted, and every body comfortable.

Meantime our hostess, aided by the kitchen cabinet,

was busily engaged in preparing supper for the general and staff, most of whom had eaten nothing since our early breakfast. Even the daughter, who had been so much frightened, was now cordial and friendly to us as we sat drying our garments at the kitchen fire. The front room was furbished up, a good fire filled it with sparkling comfort, and we were pleasantly anticipating a good long night's sleep, when an orderly dashed up with orders to bring on the brigade as speedily as possible. Our men and animals were, however, too entirely used up by the long march to be able to move a step farther without some rest, and it was nearly morning before the last wagons had fairly crossed the river. Regimental commanders were sent for, maps consulted, and the order issued to march at one o'clock. From all we could learn, to-morrow was to bring us face to face with the enemy.

But supper was now the primary object of attack, and great was the havoc in the bacon and corn-bread department. Soon we were ready for bed; the floor of our banqueting-hall and of the room adjoining was crowded with army cots, and before 8 o'clock the lights were out and all was still. My clothes were still wet, but this enabled me to try the virtues of hydropathy. Sleep was the order of the night, and, as our time was limited, we made a business of it. At 1 P.M. that luxury was over; every body turned out, a cup of coffee was swallowed, horses were saddled, and in a few minutes we had left the house.

Monday, August 11*th*. The early morning air was deliciously balmy; all that was commonplace and mean about us lay transfigured by the witchery of the moonlight, and as I moved among the camp-fires I was quite fascinated with the novel midnight scene. Hurriedly the staff dashed to and fro, hastening the preparations to depart, and at length the leading regiment moved out into the road, and the general rode to the front. As we sat on our horses at the head of the column, clear and full through the silent air came the voice of one of our colonels addressing his men: "Officers and soldiers of the 56th! At length the day for which we have so long waited has arrived. This day we are to meet the enemy." Only an occasional sentence or two of the brief address reached us, but at its close cheer after cheer attested its exhilarating influence, the band struck up a lively air, and the column moved quickly out into the road.

Not long after an aid galloped up, saluted the general, and reported, "The column is formed, sir, and the wagons all ready to draw out into the road." At once we were in motion, the advance guard under command of a captain clergyman, who to great intelligence added a bravery founded upon principle, to be hereafter nobly illustrated on the field of battle. Riding near his command, I noticed with admiration the military carriage and evident discipline of his men. Three weeks later he fell, pierced with five bullets, to lie for months upon the bed of weariness, and at length recover, to be promoted to a vacant majority in his regiment.

Next the advance guard rode the general and staff; orders to march or to halt were passed from front to rear by one or two taps of the drum; and so over a heavily-wooded rolling country, through roads arched with foliage, the moonlight filling them with fantastic shapes and shadows, we pursued our romantic way.

The peculiar quiet of the hour, and the weird influence of the forest scenery, with patches of moonlight flung in here and there among the prevailing shadow, every turn of the road seemingly a narrow pass over which giant and grotesque trees stood guard to oppose our progress, added mystic significance to those reflections which our anticipated battle naturally awakened. No longer Yankee soldiers of the nineteenth century, we were for the nonce knights of the ancient chivalry, pledged to a holier cause and sworn to a nobler issue than Cœur de Lion himself ever dreamed of. To me this was perhaps the most inspiring season of the whole campaign.

Our men marched swiftly, and shortly after daybreak we reached Richards's Cross Roads, to be halted for three hours, while, crowding the roads with cavalry, artillery, and infantry, the three other brigades of our division moved past, for here their route and our own met. The men now cooked their breakfasts, and we were glad to accept the hospitality of General Patrick's mess-table. At nine o'clock the road was clear at last, and now our march became tedious, dusty, prosaic, all the glamour of last night's romance having departed with the moonlight. With eight thousand troops and their long caravans of wagons in front of us, wearisome halts were constantly occurring; and as the heat became more oppressive, the men straggled correspondingly. During the middle of the day we did not average a mile an hour. At every bad place in the road, and Virginia highways are full of them, the wagon trains were delayed; an accident to a wheel halted the whole column, and so very slowly we crept along.

So slow a march offers great temptation to the soldiers to quit the ranks for marauding purposes. Leaving other articles untouched, they seemed to consider poultry and other eatables their legitimate spoil, and I was compelled several times to-day to drive off squads from our own and the other brigades prowling about the farm-houses after gastronomic plunder. Toward the close of the day orders came to make a forced march, as General Pope intended to attack the enemy next day, and needed our help. So the men unslung their knapsacks, leaving them with the wagons in the rear under charge of a guard, and pushed on rapidly without these encumbrances. Day grew into twilight, twilight deepened into night, and still we pushed forward. It was fully eleven o'clock before we reached our camping-ground, having been some twenty-two hours on the road, and marched twenty-six miles. Only in an hour of extremity ought such a march to be attempted in August weather. Two of our poor boys died in the ambulances from sunstroke and exhaustion, and even those of us on horseback suffered considerably from the intense heat.

The regiments were then turned into the nearest fields, and sank at once to rest, and glad enough were we to follow their example. Our wagons being now several miles in the rear, there was nothing to be done except to lie down wherever the darkness directed, roll ourselves in our blankets, and with saddle for pillow and the starry heavens for canopy, seek a supperless sleep; and a most refreshing sleep it was, untroubled by indigestion and unvexed by dreams.

CHAPTER VII.

CAMP NEAR CEDAR MOUNTAIN.

TUESDAY, *August* 12*th*. Much refreshed by our *al fresco* slumbers, we rose early to make a light breakfast of coffee and hard bread, procured at a neighboring commissariat. But the expected summons to battle did not come. The bloody battle of Cedar Mountain had been fought on Saturday, and during the last night Jackson withdrew his army, retreating toward Gordonsville. Thus our forced march of yesterday had been made in vain.

Our last night's bivouac left us in a field bare of shade-trees, close to the dusty road, about half way between Culpepper Court-house and Cedar Mountain. The Army of Virginia was all about us—every where troops and artillery; one continuous string of army wagons, moving to and from Culpepper Station, filled the road; we were in the midst of the liveliest military scene I had ever witnessed. Shortly after breakfast one of our head-quarter ambulances came up, and constituted for a while our only head-quarters, while the troops, who were not so dependent on the wagon-train, put up their shelter-tents, and thus took their needed rest, well protected from the fierce rays of the summer sun. After a while a paulin was procured from a battery and stretched over an upright, and here our adjutant transacted his business, and the general received his callers, while the rest of the staff were occupied in their various duties. For one, I was very thankful when, late in the afternoon, our head-quarter wagons reached us, and a decided feeling of exhilaration came over me as my canvas palace went up and received its simple furniture. In fifteen minutes the dusty field became for me a home, and I was enjoying a welcome bath, and the luxury of being alone.

In an hour or two I walked out toward the camp-fire to find Patrick in all his glory, having received *carte blanche* from our judicious caterer. Our entire store of canned meats and similar delusions was placed at his disposal; beef-steak, hard bread, and coffee supplied *ad libitum*. The mess-table was spread in the office-tent; and here, about dusk, around what was literally a festive board, we forgot our past discomfort. As we had still some arrears of sleep to make up, nine o'clock found our lights all out, and soon the solitary sentinel was probably the only waking person in our little camp.

Next morning, Wednesday, I rode over to the village of Culpepper Court-house—a pleasant ride through an agreeably diversified country. The little town was now a hospital; hotels, churches, and private residences were put into requisition for our wounded in Saturday's battle. Having transacted my business at the Station, I visited some of these hospitals, and found our boys comfortably clothed and bedded, and carefully tended by nurses, some of them of that sex specially adapted to this tender service. Of the wounded who are brought off from a battle-field, four out of five recover, and a majority of those whose wounds terminate fatally die within a day or two after they enter the hospital. Hence, as I moved among the beds, I found the general tone of feeling cheerful and hopeful; the men were evidently proud of their wounds, and more attached than ever before to the good cause. One handsome-faced lad, who had been shot through the body, weak and suffering, yet all aglow with enthusiasm, said to me as I paused to speak with him, "Well, I didn't flinch, anyhow; the colonel will tell you that." But there were some too weak to converse, lingering, as it were, midway between life and death; while others, pallid and still, bore upon their already wasted features the sign and seal of the death-angel, soon to liberate them and bear them back to God. Yet even to these a word of cheerful sympathy seemed welcome, for nowhere is a mournful visage so out of place as in a hospital. One should always try his best in such a place to throw in his little word of comfort, hope, and encouragement, unless he feel called upon to join with the sufferer in the nearer and more sacred service of our religion. I am free to confess that this, my first visit to the hospitals, lacked that earnest personal sympathy and almost affectionate feeling which is perhaps impossible except between those who have shared the dangers of battle together. Sympathy in its deepest sense must spring from common experiences, and it seemed to me that I, who had never put my life in peril for my country, had hardly a right to stand, full of health and vigor, among these brave men lying pale and wounded about me.

After visiting the hospitals I went up into the hall over the court-house, where a number of rebel prisoners were confined. On my entrance they crowded around me to inquire as to the news, and we were soon engaged in conversation. Of course I could not feel much sympathy here, though I felt that after all they were only the misguided tools of others who had poisoned the ear of the whole Southern people with their falsehoods. As a whole, they did not impress me favorably; with some exceptions, they seemed an ignorant, semi-barbarous set of men, dirty, ragged, and with not half so manly a look as our own soldiers. Still, on leaving, I could not help remarking, "Well, boys, I wish we were fighting side by side together instead of against each other!" "Yes, yes," was the strong and hearty response in all directions.

On leaving this prison I heard the sound of martial music, and stopped my horse at the street corner to see the troops go by. As they came on I saw that they were the men of New York, and Massachusetts, and other states, who had suffered so terribly in the late battle, their ranks fearfully reduced, regiments commanded by captains, and brigades by majors. How proudly they moved forward, these braves who had deserved well of their country. The sight thrilled me through and through, and I silently tendered to them, one and all, the homage of my personal respect and gratitude. At a residence near by lay the dead body of one of the colonels of this division, who died this morning of his wounds, and each regimental band, as the column passed the house, filled the street with the touching music of Pleyel's hymn, or the dead march in Saul, or some other familiar dirge. They seemed to me to be pouring forth a requiem for their own gallant comrades now released from life's battle and gone home. There was every thing to make the sight impressive; and when the flags, riddled and torn with shot and bullets, fluttered by, unbidden tears sprang to my eyes, and I lifted my cap almost involuntarily, compelled, even in defiance of military etiquette, to manifest in some way my pent-up emotion. God bless our brave volunteers!

Thursday, August 14th. At breakfast this morning we were notified that at 10 A.M. our division would be reviewed by General Pope, and there was a general donning of the newest uniforms. Before ten o'clock the line was formed in an adjacent field, the brigades being drawn up *en masse* in two lines, owing to the limited extent of the review-ground, the artillery taking the right flank and the cavalry the left. The division numbered about ten thousand men. Shortly after, General Pope, followed by his staff, rode into the field, halting a moment in front to receive the customary salute, and then proceeded along the lines, accompanied by General M'Dowell, each regimental band receiving him in turn as he passed by. Again he took his position in front, and the division marched past, officers saluting and colors dipping; and so ended the brief ceremony, and we were now, for the first time, fairly introduced to our new commander. As I had determined to visit the battle-field of Cedar Mountain, I was glad when the review was over, and at once started with some friends on our excursion.

The day was overcast, just suited for our ride, and for the first two miles the scenery was decidedly military, field, grove, and hill-side being tenanted by our troops. As we approached the scene of Saturday's hot struggle, I experienced that feeling of intense expectation, of curiosity mingled with awe, which inspires even the least thoughtful in visiting, for the first time, a recent battle-field. I suppose no one walks through a quiet grave-yard—God's acre, as the Germans significantly name it—without some such sense of awe, even though it be made beautiful with trees, and flowers, and running brooks, the home of happy birds; and to-day we were to visit no ordinary cemetery, but rather the high place of sacrifice whereon the loyal North offered up its best and bravest on the altar of patriotism, justice, liberty—nay, rather on the altar of God himself.

I confess that my first survey of the battle-field of Cedar Mountain disappointed me. I had formed in imagination a picture far more replete with dark and fearful shadings; I had certainly expected that the accumulated horrors of a tragedy like this, when thousands of valiant men stood face to face in the dread shock of battle, straining every nerve to kill, and calling into service all the enginery of modern warfare, would have stamped upon the landscape a far deeper impress. Within these two miles square, through these woods and cornfields, and over these plains, Banks advanced, eight thousand strong, on Saturday morning, to be driven back later in the day by the overpowering numbers of Jackson's army, the latter to be repulsed in the evening with great slaughter. Here Generals Augur, Geary, and Carroll were wounded; here more than fifteen hundred of our men were killed or wounded, and, from the most reliable estimates, a far greater number of the enemy. And yet Nature, ever active, had already done very much to wipe out forever the traces of this sad story. Already mother earth had absorbed into her own veins the crimson tide but lately staining field and dell; already she had received back again the worn-out and mangled bodies of her brave children. Over the spots where, during the brief contest, was the fiercest carnage, now waved the summer canopy of leaves, while all through the woods the birds sang sweetly, as if their pleasant homes had never known the rude blasts of war.

But as we rode over the ground, and visited more in detail the different scenes of struggle, of attack and repulse, of charge and retreat, the battle-tokens were more manifest. Little groups of slaughtered horses indicated the position of the various batteries; here were forests torn with shot and shell, cornfields crushed and trampled, and, scattered all over the field, the graves of those killed in action. On the extreme left, where Prince's Brigade met so bravely the fierce onslaught of the enemy, and faced the rebel batteries on Cedar Mountain; through this ravaged cornfield, held so persistently by Geary; in these woods and wheatfields at the right of the road, over and through which Crawford and Gordon charged, holding an overwhelming rebel force so long at bay, in trenches and single graves slept our braves. Let no one speak of their lives as prematurely cut off, of their deaths as untimely, for such a glorious ending rounds out the briefest career into a perfect whole, while it adds inappreciable significance and holy consecration to its patriotic close. Now, as ever, *Dulce et decorum est pro patria mori*.

The ground about us was strewn with the usual relics of a battle-field—fragments of shot and shell, caps perforated with bullets, garments dyed crimson, cartridge-boxes, canteens, and knapsacks. A few of these I collected and put into my saddle-bags, carefully keeping them until I had had personal experience of battle, when I threw them all away, needing no such reminders of its scenes of horror and excitement.

As we rode into a belt of woods through which the rebels had charged late in the evening, to be driven back by the batteries of Ricketts's Division, the mangled trees and rude mounds covering the rebel dead attested the horrors of that iron storm. Our enemy had not found time for decent burial, for only partially covered lay the victims of Southern treason—one stretching forth his swollen hand toward the heavens, another with naked feet or shoulder protruding, as if crowded from his grave—a scene too awful for description. Can you find, in any picture drawn by poet's pen or painter's pencil, a scene more sadly typical of the unmitigated horrors of war? Dante himself could hardly do it justice.

Friday, August 15*th.* Our men were now thoroughly rested, the stragglers had come up, and at head-quarters we had fallen into our usual quiet routine. Among the bits of camp scandal floating about as usual, we heard to-day that the Brooklyn 14th, feeling thoroughly satisfied with our late march, had laid hands on all the horses in the neighborhood, impressed a sufficient number of carts to carry their knapsacks, and proposed, when we next moved, to appear as cavalry. One of them found a condemned government horse at large in the fields, and immediately claimed him as lawful prize. As he was riding down the road on his new charger at the rate of about a mile an hour, one of our staff met and thus accosted him: "My man, I should think you could walk a good deal faster than you can ride on that horse." "Yes, sir," was the reply, "that's true; but the fact is, that even the greatest pleasures in life sometimes pall, and really I have had quite enough even of the luxury of walking."

A business trip to Culpepper, during which I once more visited the hospitals, consumed a goodly portion of the day. General Reno had come in upon us yesterday with 8000 men, a portion of Burnside's old army, and to-night, as I sat at the opening of my tent, I had the best night view of a large encampment I had ever enjoyed. Far away, in every direction over the rolling country, flashed a thousand camp-fires; every tent was illuminated, and a little aid from the imagination revealed a stately city, with its regular avenues of light. But I was feeling a little touch of homesickness, and could not help reflecting that these were not the peaceful homes and happy firesides of quiet citizenship, but the temporary shelter of those who, far away from their loved ones, had taken their lives in their hands in defense of fatherland. There was not one in all this great camp who had not left some one to mourn his absence, not one so poor and mean as to be without some tie binding him to others, and liable to be broken by the rude touch of war. At the nearest camp-fires little groups sat cosily together; others, stretched at full length in their shelter-tents, were writing, reading, or playing at cards. I heard no boisterous mirth, nor is that a characteristic of troops when engaged in the serious business of a campaign. Just then a distant tattoo broke in upon the stillness of the night; the drums of the different regiments took up the refrain, and the signal for bed resounded through the entire army. Eagerly I listened for the bugle-calls from the artillery and cavalry camps—a simple strain which always charmed me. The different bugles now sounded the call in tune, each striving to excel the others in the sweetness and clearness of his notes. Fifteen minutes afterward, three taps upon the drum sounded from regiment to regiment, all lights were extinguished except in the guard-tents and at head-quarters, and the illumination was over. No one could now enter within the limits of the camp without the countersign; a chain of sentinels surrounded each regiment, while miles away infantry pickets and cavalry vedettes, perhaps within hailing distance of the foe, insured our safety from any nocturnal visit of the enemy. And now in my own tent I enjoyed the pleasantest hour or two in the twenty-four, and then for grateful sleep.

Saturday, August 16th. General Jackson having retreated southward to unite his forces with the main rebel army, a forward movement was this day ordered, and our corps moved down to Cedar Mountain, and encamped on both flanks of it. We thus held the centre position, with Sigel on our right and Reno on our left, Banks's corps, so badly cut up in the last battle, remaining in reserve. Our own brigade moved about 8 A.M., marched five miles, and encamped a little to the west of Cedar Mountain, and very near the battle-field. Our tents were pitched in a pleasant grove upon a little knoll, the general's tent in the centre, flanked by those of his staff, with the tents of the brigade guard, orderlies, and servants, and the open-air stables of the staff horses, in the rear.

Here we remained two days; and I took the opportunity to ride over the green and gradually-sloping sides of Cedar Mountain, and visit the spots where the enemy had encamped, and where his artillery had been so advantageously posted in the late battle. Our men found in the woods about us the unburied bodies of several rebels, who, mortally wounded, had sought in vain to drag themselves away from the fatal field, and had then fallen down to die, to be laid at last in a soldier's grave by those whom they had considered their deadly foes.

Our brief sojourn at this spot was only a period of waiting expectancy; the troops were kept constantly supplied with three days' marching rations; rumors of the approach of the enemy in great force were prevalent, and every one felt that the order to march might come at any moment. One quiet Sunday was, however, vouchsafed us; on the morrow we were to bid good-by to Cedar Mountain.

CHAPTER VIII.

FROM CEDAR MOUNTAIN TO THE RAPPAHANNOCK.

MONDAY, *August* 18*th*. Definite information that the whole rebel army was advancing in overwhelming numbers had at length come in, and to-day we were ordered to fall back. A weary, weary experience was before us. At 4 P.M. we struck tents; the men were drawn up preparatory to marching, our horses saddled, and every thing got in readiness, and then we waited eight long tedious hours before leaving the ground, the road being wholly occupied by the troops and wagons of other commands. As night came on, we gathered around our camp-fire, and the troops were allowed to cook their coffee. It seemed as if the order to march would never come. Leaden-winged and slow glided on the hours, and about nine o'clock I sat down in an ambulance and tried in vain to get a wink or two of sleep. At last, about midnight, the summons to march was given, and we moved out into the road, marched a quarter of a mile, halted an hour, started again, and again halted; so that at daybreak, so crowded was the highway with men and horses, we had only accomplished about two miles. The supply trains of the entire army had preceded us, as is usual on a retreat, and General Pope, with his staff, busied themselves during the night in urging them forward. The delay was inevitable, but slightly discouraging. Our general, with his usual cheerful nonchalance, thought only of the weary troops; some of his staff, however, could not help feeling very tired and considerably disgusted. The morning was damp and chilly; the ground wet with yesterday's rain; there was no immediate prospect of our having a clear road, so the active major set some men to work in making a large fire, around which daylight found us wrapped in our rubber blankets, cold, cross, and hungry. The head-quarter wagons were in the rear, but Patrick brought up a quantity of coffee and a supply of hard bread; there was patience, vigor, and refreshment in the draught, and the whole party brightened up under its influence.

Again we started, moved a mile or two, to be again halted, and so on all day. We were moving in a northeasterly direction, toward the crossing of the Rappahannock River, at Rappahannock Station, and about noon marched through the village of Culpepper. Not far beyond we met Sigel's men, whose route crossed our own, drawn up at the roadside, and our general turned aside to pay his respects to their commander. We found him sitting under a tree, a not very military-looking man, with a face full of character; having little indicating his rank upon his person, but surrounded by a brilliant staff. Some of our own staff had growled a little during this tedious day at Sigel, probably without cause, the trouble being the reported length of his wagon-train, which, as some asserted, stretched over eleven miles. For one, I was not disposed to criticise, in this regard, one who seemed to be a fighting general.

Hotter and hotter poured down the rays of the Southern sun, heavier and heavier weighed the knapsacks and accoutrements of the soldiers, more and more tedious became our slow marching and frequent halts. These halts were not good bona fide rests, wherein a soldier could really take his ease, unsling his knapsack, and make himself comfortable for a given period, but deceptive stoppages, which might last three minutes or half an hour, and which thus kept every one in a state of expectant preparation. Every spring, pool, and rivulet within half a mile of our route was eagerly sought for, though it was not so pleasant, after all, to quench one's thirst with water muddied by the men and horses who had gone before us.

What made this long, weary marching and halting more tedious was the consciousness that we were on a retreat, and were seeking to put the Rappahannock between us and the pursuing enemy. The weary watch of the previous night, the heat, and dust, and fatigue, were not half so depressing as the feeling that we were falling back. As I rode up and down the column, or rested my tired horse under a shade-tree at the roadside, near the men who had flung themselves down for a moment's rest during a temporary halt, this feeling of depression made itself manifest in quip and sarcasm, which awoke occasionally a little forced mirth, but oftener a growl of discomfort. It did me good to meet here and there a laughing philosopher in uniform, a Yankee Mark Tapley, who prided himself in being jolly under the most adverse circumstances. Where such a man marched, there was quite a different tone through the entire company.

On a march like this, the men usually fare better, and have better sleeping arrangements than their officers, as the latter are very apt to trust every thing to the wagons, while the former always have their sleeping tents and marching rations with them. We have already seen how, by other methods, they manage to supply their commissariat. At every wayside hovel to-day its occupants were busy in baking hoe-cakes, which they sold at twenty-five cents. Chickens found their way mysteriously into the haversacks of our men. Wo to the inconsiderate sheep, or calf, or porker who disported himself within their range of vision. Quietly leaving the ranks on some pretense or other, they stole off to the farm-houses within a mile of the road, stopping long enough sometimes to have a meal cooked for them, and then rejoining with ease their slow-moving commands. Only the strictest watch on the part of the company officers can prevent this straggling, and several times to-day I felt it necessary to arrest it. Our volunteers are usually perfectly willing to pay for what they eat, but seem determined to have it any how, and the people generally acquiesced in the proposed exchange of edibles for greenbacks.

Of course, when discovered marauding, they are never at a loss for excuses, and sometimes the excuse is so droll that one is compelled to laugh in spite of himself. A private, for example, is seen coming through a field, with his gun on one shoulder and half a sheep on the other. Halted and compelled to account for this novel military accoutrement, he salutes very respectfully, and, with demure countenance, asseverates that he had to kill this sheep in self-defense; that he was walking through a field, having had permission to leave the ranks to fill his canteen, when this hostile animal, on seeing his Northern uniform, at once charged upon him with great fury, and one or the other had to die. The absurdity of the plea compels a smile, and the wag too often gets off under cover of his joke, to divide his plunder with his comrades, and feast upon it at the evening camp-fire.

The longest day and the weariest march must have an end, and by-and-by the welcome sunset came to temper the heated atmosphere and revive the spirits of the men. With a few hard crackers and spring water I had appeased my hunger during the day, and when at length we halted, about 10 P.M., the first and only craving was for a little sleep. Our horses were tied to the fence by the roadside, the known proximity of the enemy forbidding their being unsaddled. We spread our rubber blankets closely, and, with overcoats for covering, were soon asleep. One of our staff had accustomed himself to sleep with his horse's halter attached to his own leg. I confess that to this highly prudent measure I had insuperable objections. The night was damp and cool, and our sleep restless and chilly, from want of sufficient clothing. This dumping-down by a muddy roadside is not suggestive of special comfort, but we were thoroughly tired out, and had reached a point when sleep, no matter how uncomfortable, was a necessity. Once or twice during the night, as I tried to adjust my somewhat abbreviated bed-covering, a vision of my comfortable bed at home would intrude; but, before I could fill out the picture, I was again sound asleep on a mud-bank in Virginia.

Very early next morning, before it was fully day, we made our toilets with a shake and a homœopathic ablution at a neighboring pool, and were ready for breakfast. But, alas! this was to resemble the classic draught of Tantalus; only the Grecian had this advantage, that he could behold what he longed for, while, as to our breakfast, we could not even see it. Our wagons were in the rear; our saddle-bag lunches had been devoured. No officer likes to ask a soldier for a cup of coffee or a portion of his slender rations, so we growled a little together and fasted.

It was understood that our Virginia friend, General Lee, was hastening after us, anxious to cultivate a nearer acquaintance, and our column was soon in motion. Being ordered to make some arrangements for the brigade, I rode on ahead, passing the rest of our division, reached the Rappahannock in about an hour, and joined the long procession crossing the railroad bridge, the wagons crossing at the ford below.

Rappahannock Station was so crammed with troops that it was difficult to move along through the mile square of men, horses, and artillery, rather a chaotic mass at present — the different divisions having hurriedly pushed in during the night and morning — but sure to crystallize after a while into military order. How to find any body in such a crowd was a serious problem. Regiments knew not their next-field neighbors. The road was full of staff officers and men, every one with his questioning cap on, and seeking the whereabouts of this or that command. Amid this great crowd I was a stranger, and only after a plentiful use of interrogations was I able to discover the proposed location of our brigade.

This accomplished, I started to push my way back through the masses of troops, when I bethought me that a cup of coffee would be in order. Every wagon that bore any resemblance to a sutler's shop was eagerly examined, the faces of the little parties of officers who were eating their breakfasts all about me were eagerly scanned, but among them I recognized no former acquaintance. Finally, becoming desperate, I accosted some teamsters who seemed to be abundantly supplied with coffee, which they were cooking at a little fire, and offered them a generous sum for one draught of the refreshing beverage. Their response was as courteous as it was hospitable; all pecuniary reward was rejected; and so I took my horseback breakfast of coffee and hard bread with thorough zest and enjoyment. Perhaps no act of kindly hospitality I ever enjoyed has left upon me so pleasant an impression.

Of course, I felt now like a new man, and pushed my way through the crowded street with entire equanimity. Reaching the railroad bridge, I saw our brigade crossing, reported to the general, and then paused a while to witness the passage of the bridge and ford by the crowd of troops and wagons. Our brigade was one of the last to cross, and it was soon evident that they were not an hour too soon; for, while I sat on a little elevation which overlooked the bridge, I saw a long line of dust rising above the trees which skirted the plain on the other side of the river, and indicating the approach of the enemy. Shortly after a squadron of horsemen, a portion of the cavalry which had protected the rear of our column, emerged from the woods and followed on slowly toward the bridge. Suddenly I saw them turn, and with loud yells charge back into the woods upon a foe invisible to me, but which

I learned afterward was the advance cavalry of the enemy. The charging squadron belonged to the Harris Light Cavalry, with whose field officers I had become acquainted, and this little game of charging and falling back had been their pleasant occupation for the past forty-eight hours. During this service, one of them, an occasional visitor at our staff mess, was taken prisoner, but escaped by disabling his captors during the next *melée*. For adventure, excitement, and variety, the life of a cavalry officer may certainly claim pre-eminence.

Not long after our pickets were driven in by the rebel advance, our cavalry crossed the river, and the Rappahannock flowed between us and the enemy.

CHAPTER IX.

ARTILLERY DUEL AT RAPPAHANNOCK STATION.

WEDNESDAY, *August* 20*th*. The Rappahannock now interposed as a formidable barrier against the advancing rebel army; its fords were at once commanded by our artillery, and there was an opportunity for our weary cohorts to enjoy a little rest. It was believed that the enemy, whose design was either to cut us off from Washington or to attack us with greatly disproportionate force before we could effect a junction with M'Clellan's army, now *en route* from the Peninsula, would at once make a desperate effort to cross the river, and to-day was therefore one of busy preparation for his proper reception. Our general had taken for head-quarters an empty mansion just outside the village, our troops were encamped in some fields opposite, rations were distributed, and the accumulated arrears of head-quarter business attended to. A lower room was used as the office, another as mess-room, while our cots were spread in the upper chambers. A brigade staff is expected at such a time to exercise the virtue of hospitality, and several other officers partook with us of the products of Patrick's culinary skill.

Meanwhile the enemy was hurrying up his troops, and by nightfall it was probable that the whole rebel army filled the woods on the opposite side of the river. Our own, M'Dowell's corps, faced them in the centre at the Station, Sigel's corps was on our right, and Banks and Reno on our left, the whole line extending some half a dozen miles. Batteries were posted at every available position, pickets lined each river bank, and both armies, grimly facing each other, were glad to spend that night in preparatory sleep.

The next morning, August 21st, the enemy opened upon us with shot and shell, hoping probably to dislodge our artillery, demoralize our infantry, and seize a favorable moment to push across under cover of his own fire. But he reckoned without his host. Scarcely had the echo of his first gun ceased to reverberate before our batteries commenced a heavy cannonade, sweeping the opposite bank with an iron torrent more difficult for his infantry to cross than even the Rappahannock. Our own infantry were at once ordered down to support the batteries, and be ready to oppose any attempt to force the passage of the river. As we moved across the plain, the shell bursting over our heads, and the shot screaming in our very ears, I can not say that I enjoyed the situation. Now for the first time under fire, I had not become accustomed to the shrill whizzing music of the iron projectile. Had I been alone, I should probably have given my horse a chance to try his speed in the opposite direction; as it was, I had to "grin horridly a ghastly smile," and carry it bravely, as if charmed with these yelling messengers of war. I confess that I was not sorry when we reached the bluff, behind which we were comparatively safe, and could hear them shriek over us with entire equanimity.

Our brigade was now ordered to lie down, and had nothing to do but to keep still and do nothing. Another brigade of our division was posted in the woods and cornfields below this bluff; the sharpshooters on the river brink exchanged the leaden compliments of war with the rebel sharpshooters opposite; but no attempt was made to cross the river; no advance on our part was ordered; and, instead of performing wondrous feats of patriotic daring, we had only to listen to the shrieking music overhead. Even this soon lost its power to interest us. I saw no damage done in our immediate vicinity, nor in my little excursions of curiosity did I remark any thing worthy of record. A number of batteries, with infantry in blue behind them, on our side the river, were keeping up a noisy duel with a number of batteries on the other side, backed by infantry in gray, and the affair became, after a while, a little tedious. Behind us were our main body and reserves, ready for action at a moment's notice; and the iron storm howled on, plowing the fields in the rear with shot and shell, until night found us still under arms, and nothing had been done. As the enemy were trying to get at us, and not we at them, this was very satisfactory, though differing somewhat from my anticipations of battle.

With the darkness came a lull; at length the cannonading ceased, our men stacked arms and wrapped themselves in their blankets, and the general and staff prepared to follow their example. I was not sorry when the din and hurly-burly was over. Patrick had established his head-quarters in the rear, and our orderlies brought us down some supper; we then spread out our India-rubber blankets, made common stock of our woolen ones, and were soon asleep.

All this was very comfortable; but I had hardly

sunk into oblivion when I was rudely awakened by feeling on my face heavy drops of driving rain. Some of my fellow-lodgers covered up their heads and let it rain; but, being constitutionally opposed to semi-suffocation, this was to me an impossibility. Rising hastily, I groped about in the darkness, tumbling over a sleeper or two on the way, until I stumbled fortunately upon an ambulance. The interior was occupied by a general officer as his bedchamber, but I at once secured lodgings beneath him on the ground floor. The four sides of my sleeping apartment were open to the storm, and my bed unpleasantly liable to inundation, but I had at least a roof over my head, and could sleep without the patter of rain-drops on my face. Very soon I had a companion in my friend the major, who, having tried in vain to fight the storm outside, concluded to follow my example. Swathed in India-rubber cloth, we bade defiance to the rain, and a judicious arrangement of limbs enabled us to sleep quite comfortably.

Very early next morning our brigade was marched a mile or two down the river, and took position much nearer to its bank. The artillery on both sides were already busily engaged, and as we moved by I saw lying near our new position the dead bodies of two of the sharpshooters of our division, sadly mangled by shell. These sharpshooters are picked men, and the sight of their fine, manly-looking frames now stretched lifeless upon the sward shocked and impressed me. Their comrades had already taken charge of their knapsacks and other property, but near one of them I picked up part of a letter stained with his blood. How the sight carried me back to the Northern homes, ere long to be darkened by the shadow of this day's casualty! As I stood in this sad presence, and felt, as never so much before, how wicked was the devilish ambition which impelled the master spirits of the South to attack their country, it was hard to keep back the utterance of indignant curses against the whole traitor brood.

Our brigade spent this day quietly like the last, lying down in line of battle in rear of the little elevation crowned by our batteries; our horses were held by orderlies, and we passed most of the day on the crest, watching the effect of our artillery fire, and seeking to spy out the enemy's position. There was not, however, much to see; occasionally a horseman or two would emerge from the woods where lay concealed the rebel infantry, and take a look at us, but the position of their batteries was indicated chiefly by the smoke from the guns. Our own artillerymen did their work as coolly and systematically as if firing a salute, now elevating, now depressing their pieces, eagerly watching for opportunities to fire, wholly unmindful of the missiles hurled at them by the enemy. Our general had not forgotten his military art, and occasionally lent his aid in sighting the guns or advising as to the length of fuse.

Our infantry had now become so accustomed to this artillery duel that they interested themselves mainly in speculating as to the exact spot where the enemy's projectiles passing over their heads would strike in the field beyond. At one time a solid shot struck close to the top of the little crest, plowed up the ground, and still had sufficient momentum to roll directly down among our men. Neither yesterday nor to-day had I observed any indications of cowardice, except, perhaps, in a single instance. But I needed not this experience to convince me that man is not a cowardly animal, for all history teaches that, no matter what his nationality, if he be well led, he is usually only too ready to accept the wager of battle. It had been my fortune to witness some grotesque caricatures of war among the Chinese at Shanghae, when rebels and Imperialists fought for the possession of that city; but even they, when properly drilled and officered, have been found capable of stubborn resistance. Emerson declares that " a great part of courage is the courage of having done the thing before;" and it is true that we, who were novices, felt more nonchalant during to-day's cannonading. We had already begun to be quite indifferent to artillery at long range, the probability of our being hit seeming to equal that of our being struck by lightning.

Of course, there is great sustaining power in the sense of religious duty, the incitement of personal pride, the influence of military discipline, and the tie of military association. A brave man once said, "We are all cowards in the dark;" and I noticed, at Rappahannock and elsewhere, among the civil attachés of our brigade, officers' servants, grooms, and the like, who were neither led by patriotic duty nor coerced by discipline to expose themselves, who had no uniform to disgrace, no military pride to sustain, a shrinking under fire not manifested by the soldier. This shrinking did not depend upon color, as I saw it in white as well as black; but, as most of these attendants were of the latter complexion, it led some of us to leap to the rash conclusion that the race was naturally cowardly. Such is not now my opinion. Most of them remained with us through the whole of this retreat, and accompanied us into Maryland, a thing I am quite sure I should not have done had I been in their position. One poor fellow, however, a servant of one of our regimental colonels, was completely overcome by his fears, and awoke the colonel several times during last night with stories each more fearful than the last, while a few disappeared to-day, having had quite enough of war. With no country to fight for which was willing to acknowledge them, ten dollars a month paid them very indifferently for the rough work of a campaign with its present accompaniments of shot and shell. For one, I do not wonder at their leaving.

A quarter of a mile to our left, and close to the river, a Maine battery was posted; several of its gunners had been disabled by wounds, and some of the soldiers of our brigade volunteered to fill their vacant places. About noon I rode down to visit this battery, and to see how the river was held in that direction. As I passed the infantry supports, making themselves comfortable in the woods near which the battery was posted, I fortunately encountered a party of their field officers indulging in an old-fashioned chicken stew. No introduction, under the circumstances, was required. "Will you have the leg of a chicken?" said a major. "Yes, indeed, and many thanks," was my earnest reply; and I enjoyed heartily that lunch in the saddle—a bit of literal hospitality. My lunch over, I found that the Sons of Maine were getting on well, and soon returned to the brigade.

In the woods below us, on the right, Hatch's brigade had meantime been engaged in skirmishing, and we heard at intervals considerable musketry. How much of a fight was going on we could only conjecture; but not long after one of their prisoners was brought up to the spot where we were sitting, who belonged to a party of the enemy's cavalry which had crossed during the night. He seemed quite overcome by his late experiences, and stammered out, "Why, gentlemen, I never was so frightened in all my life! How much better you all are dressed than our officers! Have you got any whisky?" Becoming gradually calmer, he was quite communicative. It seems that his party had been lurking in the woods, whence they were dislodged by our skirmishers.

As I was sitting on the crest this afternoon, gazing at the opposite side of the river through a good field-glass, and waiting for something to turn up, I saw a brigade of rebels emerge from some woods, form in line of battle, and move rapidly across a vacant plain toward the belt of timber skirting the river bank. They were half way across, and just about to disappear from view, when one of our shells exploded in their ranks, cutting the line in two. I saw some fall, others ran back, but the brigade pushed on, and was soon sheltered behind the belt of timber. Afterward I saw their wounded moving slowly off to the rear. In my morbid and overstrained state of mind, this sight impressed me not half so much as many a scene on the mimic stage. The only feeling was one of anxious curiosity for the next act of the battle-drama.

We had noticed during the afternoon heavy clouds of dust across the river rising over the road leading toward our right, and at one spot, where the road wound over an exposed hill-side, we saw the continuous movement of army wagons in the same direction. Unable to force the passage of the river at this point, it seemed probable that the enemy proposed a flank movement, and during the afternoon his fire slackened, and he withdrew his batteries. So, after darkness had come to veil our position, one or two of our tents were brought down and pitched on the field, and one of our aids, in the absence of Patrick, cooked for us a very respectable supper. The men had put up their shelter-tents early in the day, and were now allowed to light a few fires, where they fried their pork and made coffee, enjoying heartily the little lull after the iron storm. Of course, we were all early to bed and soon asleep. But shortly after midnight the general received intelligence from another general officer that the enemy were making evident preparations to force the passage at daybreak. Care was taken not to awaken the troops; our little arrangements were quickly made, and then I laid down and dozed the night away.

By daybreak the men were aroused and had their breakfasts, but no summons to advance troubled us. So quiet and still, indeed, was the morning, that the general allowed our tents to remain, and we partook of a hearty meal. I then went to my tent, placidly rejoicing in the prospect of a little tranquillity, when, just as I was making up my mind to send for my writing-desk, the air was once more full of rebel thunderbolts, bursting and screaming overhead. To bring in the staff horses from the rear, strike tents, pack head-quarter wagons, and start them off out of range, was the work of five minutes; and once more we were homeless, our hopes of a day's quiet rudely dispelled.

To me it was a great disappointment, for last night's broken sleep had left me craving for a little rest; our artillery duel had lost its excitement—had, in fact, become a good deal of a bore.

It was only a third edition of the old story, and nothing came of it except a good deal of noise. Having occasion later in the morning to ride over to the railroad station, I witnessed the fierce cannonading near the bridge which ended this artillery duel. The fire at the point opposite the position of our brigade had already slackened, and the main interest had centred at this portion of the field. Perhaps half a dozen batteries on each side were on the rampage, firing as fast as the men could load; and as I had to pass in range, and at certain points the shot and shell seemed endeavoring to see how near they could come without striking, I did not pause long to admire the scenery. Arrived at the station, I found that the commissariat dépôt had been given up, while all through the adjacent fields and among the buildings lay numbers of shot and shell now robbed of their terror, some of which had left their mark in broken walls and pierced roofs.

On my return I joined a group of officers who were standing on a hill-side out of the line of fire, and had a good look at the artillery tournament, which filled the air with smoke—circlets from the bursting shells. As I stood here I witnessed a rebel regiment charge up a hill not far from the bridge, on the other side of the river, which was crowned with a redoubt. The officers waved their swords, the men cheered and pushed quickly up the ascent, while our batteries played fiercely upon them, but without any visible effect. To me the scene was truly exciting, for I supposed that the redoubt must be occupied by our men, though I was a good deal surprised that any were still on that side the river. Every instant I expected to see the rebel lines waver before the volleys of our troops. Still up, up they pushed; the top was nearly gained; surely there will be crossing of bayonets; but no! they mounted the parapet unopposed, and disappeared behind the breastworks. It was only an empty redoubt, after all, and I had wasted all my anxiety.

With this parting benison, the batteries on both sides soon ceased fire, and the three days' duel was over; three days of enormous expenditure of ammunition, with little loss of life on our side; three precious days to our army, however, and to the country, for every hour that we delayed the enemy's advance was needed by the Army of the Potomac to effect its escape from the Peninsula and hasten to our rescue. And now it is fully time to push to the right to prevent the enemy flanking us in that direction. Sigel, who has been holding the rebel wolf at bay above us, is now marching rapidly northward along the river bank, keeping his front ranks well dressed by those of the enemy opposite, while our own corps is ordered to Warrenton, a central position, to be ready for a new move on the strategic chess-board.

CHAPTER X.

FROM RAPPAHANNOCK TO WARRENTON.

THE supply trains of our corps had been sent under guard to Catlett's Station two days before, lest a temporary success of the enemy should endanger their safety; but the ammunition and ambulance trains, with the regimental and head-quarter wagons, still remained with us, and were quite enough to block up the roads, now in bad condition from the late rains. Virginia has some good turnpikes, but most of her roads become mortar-beds of mud after every rain, especially when ground up by the long wagon-trains of an army. Few are probably aware how very cumbersome these trains are. Even when the transportation is reduced to its minimum standard, a division of ten thousand men will require something like forty ammunition and fifty forage and subsistence wagons, twenty or thirty ambulances, and about sixty regimental and head-quarter wagons, drawn by four and six horses or mules. And for each of these animals forage must be drawn; so that, if we will calculate the transportation, we will find its increase to be in a sort of arithmetical progression. Thus I have seen it stated that the wagon-train of the army of the Potomac would extend at least fifty miles.

Various plans have been suggested to lessen this serious impediment to an army's rapid movement, but the naked fact always remains that so many tons avoirdupois of ammunition, subsistence, and forage must be transported. The French in Algeria carried their supplies in ox-carts, killing the oxen for rations, and cutting up the empty carts to cook them; but this method is decidedly too slow for us. Some have thought that pack-horses or mules, or light two-horse carts, would best serve the purpose; but probably our present mode of transportation is, on the whole, the most advantageous, every thing being considered. A judicious use of all these various methods would undoubtedly be advisable under certain circumstances.

One important fact touching this question of transportation differences our own country from Europe, and forbids any proper parallelisms or fair comparisons between an American and a European campaign. Europe is densely populated and highly cultivated, and a general is thus able to march hundreds of miles from any special base of supply, subsisting his men upon provisions found in the cities and agricultural districts of his enemy. In our own country, with its immense tracts of uncultivated and sparsely-settled land, one of the first questions which confronts a general, when planning a campaign, is, How shall I get supplies to my men? Poor, impoverished Virginia, for example, is hardly able, in many districts, to keep the breath of life in her own children, and there is probably not surplus food enough in the rebel portion of the state to subsist our army for a week. Let any one take his map, and see how sparsely settled are the Southern states, and what a large portion of the land susceptible of profitable cultivation is devoted to the culture of cotton and sugar, and he will be able to foresee the probable fate of an army which attempts to march through these states without cumbersome wagon-trains. I know of but one way to avoid this despair of quarter-masters, and that is by simply avoiding war altogether.

Unless while moving over well-graded roads, one hundred feet is about the space required by each long, cloth-covered wagon and its team, and thus the trains of a division will extend over some three miles of road. If a trace break in the narrow roadway, the division in rear is delayed until it is mended; if a wheel come off, the troops behind must halt until it is replaced. At one spot this afternoon we were stopped for half an hour, and, on riding forward, I found that our delay was due solely to the breaking down of an ambulance in a narrow gorge. It was finally concluded by the quarter-master to elbow the vehicular wreck off of the road, and so at last the brigade moved on.

Half past eight o'clock found us at a stand-still in the desperately muddy road about a mile south of Warrenton. Here we halted for a long half hour, until, when our patience was well-nigh exhausted, orders came to our general to encamp the brigade just where we were. On one side of the road was a hill so steep that the men could with difficulty clamber up it; on the other a low, marshy bog; it looked as if, after their weary march, they would have to sleep perpendicularly on the one side, or flounder in the water on the other. It was, however, too dark to seek a better position; the men soon tore down the fences and mounted to their bivouac, while the mud-hole on the left was taken for our head-quarters.

Supper there was none, as our wagons were in rear;

the marsh was so uninviting that at every step I sank deeply into the mire; and the only resource left us was to find a dry spot to lie in and seek oblivion in sleep. Two ambulances were speedily converted into bedchambers, and in one of them I was soon shelved, in company with my friend the adjutant general; there was just room enough—not a square inch to spare.

Sunday, August 24th. Shortly after sunrise I forced myself out of the ambulance in which I had been wedged, and at once rode into Warrenton. Our supply train being at Catlett's Station, the men had exhausted their supply of rations, and there was not a moment to be lost in replenishing their haversacks. It was during this campaign that Sigel is said to have remarked, "A biscuit is worth just now more than a bayonet," and I was now feeling very anxious in this regard. As I rode through the pleasantly shaded streets of Warrenton this quiet Sunday morning, the home look of its many handsome residences made, I must confess, the heart of one hungry campaigner ache for the moment with memories of certain pleasant homes like these nearer to the north star. But this was not the time or place for the indulgence of sentiment. The streets were already patroled by our troops, and, having visited the railway station to find it closed and cheerless, I hurried to division headquarters at the Warren Green Hotel.

Here I learned that a wagon-train was hourly expected from Warrenton Junction, and also that a large force had been at work on the railroad all night, so that supplies would arrive over this route by noon. Not twenty-four hours had elapsed since the enemy had occupied Warrenton and been driven out by our advance, and yet, so firm was my faith in the admirable management of the commissariat department, I felt quite sure that our hungry corps would not be left dinnerless even to-day. So I posted a mounted orderly on the road over which the wagon-train must enter, and another at the dépôt, with orders to notify me immediately of the approach of the looked-for food, and then felt ready to make my own toilet, have my horse cared for, and sit down to breakfast at the hotel.

Fresh bread and bona fide milk and butter made my meal luxurious, and my breakfast certainly put a new aspect upon the face of affairs. At its conclusion I inspected the hotel register, and noticed among the arrivals yesterday the names of several Confederate officers. The visits of these gentlemen must have been of the briefest, and their departures slightly hurried, for close upon their footsteps were our own cavalry, and close upon their autographs were various others with the significant initials U. S. A. Mine host was courteous but cold, and it was evident that his vision had not yet become accustomed to the sudden transition from the gray uniforms of his late guests to the Union blue which now filled his hotel.

About nine o'clock I heard the music of a band filling the street, and rode out to see my own brigade move by. The troops were marching in their best style, filling the street from curb to curb, and evidently bent on making a good impression upon the fair rebels of Warrenton. They were going into camp about two miles out of town; so I reported to the general, and returned to my waiting-post on the piazza of the hotel. These were lively days for the little Warren Green. Generals Pope, M'Dowell, and other general officers quartered here, with their respective staffs; the space in front was crowded with orderlies and staff horses, and the spacious piazza became a military exchange, where one could hear the thousand and one rumors ever prevalent during a campaign. I have seen a dozen generals conversing here together, and made the pleasant acquaintance of many officers whom I might never have met during the necessary separations of active service. Here I saw a late newspaper —a rare privilege—and heard for the first time of the resolve of the rebel Congress to deny to Pope's officers the usual rights and courtesies of prisoners of war— a pleasant little piece of intelligence just at this time.

The residents of Warrenton were, as far as we could judge, wholly sympathetic with the rebel cause, several respectable gentlemen with whom I conversed to-day frankly admitting it, with a little negative qualification by way of courtesy. One man, who expressed sentiments I have frequently heard in Virginia, spoke in somewhat this wise: "I was utterly opposed to secession, and wish Massachusetts and South Carolina could have fought this matter out together; but when the North invaded Virginia, why, of course, there was no help for us; we had to fight in self-defense." It may be that these people deceive themselves, and that this absurd plea is only the soporific with which they seek to justify to themselves their suicidal act of folly. Still it was evident that they had not caught the disease of treason wholly from South Carolina inoculation—had, indeed, a good deal of jealousy against this pestilent little pepper-pot community—but had drawn in part of the malignant virus with their mothers' milk from the old state-right heresies of their fathers. One can not but regret the belittling influence of an education which thus limits the vision of a Virginian by the natural boundaries of his own state, and makes him blind to his rights and privileges as a member of one of the most powerful and progressive nations on the globe. A man can have, it would seem, only a limited range of thought and reflection, small fellowship with great ideas, and little sympathy with those progressive principles which make up the philosophy of history, who could thus forget that he is one of a great people, to whom God has manifestly given the ownership and occupancy of a continent; who could thus sit, like Diogenes of old, in his little tub of state-rights, anxious only that the sun should warm his own homestead, and perfectly willing to abandon the grand heritage of rights, duties, and destinies which belongs to him as an American citizen. All honor to the native Southerners who, having had large experience of foreign lands, having seen their country's flag float proudly beside the haughtiest banners of earth, have felt their hearts expand to a patriotic love of the whole country, and now are among the proudest ornaments of that navy to whose splendid bravery we owe so much during this war.

As for the women, they were, as far as my very limited observation extended, nonchalant, courteous, and perfectly assured of the success of the rebel cause. One of them gave me an interesting description of the passage of Fitzhugh Lee's cavalry through the town; how she stood on the front balcony waving two Confederate flags, and how the Union soldiers, on their entrance, searched for them in vain—all this in as easy a tone as if speaking of a late ball. I fancied that these Southern ladies had not so great a dread of war, were not so alive to its horrors—in short, took it more naturally than the women of the North; but I may be mistaken.

But these experiences of Warrenton, gathered during this and another visit months later, have drawn me from the due course of my narrative. About noon the expected train did arrive, and our brigade was the first one served in the entire corps. My friend the issuing commissary had certainly a lively time of it. He had supplied us at Culpepper; he had followed us to Rappahannock, and probably stood waiting this morning, hardly willing to hold in his iron horse long enough to allow the workmen to hammer the last rivet into the last rail before he came driving headlong toward Warrenton. He had an enthusiastic reception. His office and sleeping-room were in a car, and he frequently was compelled to keep steam up ready to run at a moment's notice. A month or two afterward he wrote to me that the rebels had caught his locomotive at last, and burned up his papers; but he himself had fortunately escaped.

As I rode out to camp, having finished my Sunday's business, I found the charming hill-sides north of Warrenton full of troops, and passed Generals Pope and M'Dowell sitting on an elevation looking toward the northeast, where Sigel now watched the enemy. Our tents were already pitched in a pleasant grove; Patrick was working *con amore* at the kitchen camp-fire, and we were permitted to enjoy the latter part of Sunday as a day of rest—a privilege appreciated by both officers and men.

Our brigade rested quietly next day in this location, but at nightfall came orders to move out at daybreak to the Warrenton Springs, on the banks of the Rappahannock. The general feeling was that to-morrow we were certainly to meet the enemy.

CHAPTER XI.

ARTILLERY DUEL AT WARRENTON SPRINGS.

TUESDAY, *August* 26*th*. A lovely morning, and at daybreak our division, fully rested and in first-rate condition, leaving the regimental wagons, and accompanied only by the ambulances, with two days' rations and an extra supply of ammunition, marched down to Warrenton Springs, a distance of seven miles. Sigel had already had a passing brush with the enemy at this point, had burned the bridge over the Rappahannock, and was now facing their leading divisions farther up river. Our column had not moved a mile before the sound of the cannonading was distinctly audible, and some of the inexperienced began to congratulate themselves on the prospect of their first pitched battle. I have never known our staff more jubilant. I may remark, in passing, that this ignorant enthusiasm of the unfledged warrior, like the measles and other infantile diseases, is not apt to attack a man very violently more than once. It is not true, as a general thing, that after his first battle a man grows careless as to its perils, or is less aware of its tragic possibilities. The experience of those who have stood unflinchingly and fought bravely through a dozen battles attests the contrary. The participation in such tragic scenes usually gives a man more self-reliance, determination, coolness, and renders him less liable to sudden panic; but it is apt, at the same time, to temper his former eagerness, and cause him to regard a battle as about the most serious business in which he can engage.

Onward, through a region too picturesque to be a fitting arena for destructive war, moved our column, the music of the artillery growing louder as we approached the river, until we could see the smoke-wreaths of the bursting shells, and hear them wailing through the air. The different brigades were turned off from the road into the fields on either hand; our own, moving to the left, marched over an open space where the rebel shot flew all about us, passing just high enough, however, to injure no one. We were finally drawn up in line of battle behind a slight roll in the surface, which afforded sufficient shelter against the fire of the batteries, and the men laid down on their arms.

And this was the entertainment to which we had advanced with so much eagerness — only this, and nothing more. Lookers-on, not participants, with hardly risk enough to make the scene exciting, with no appeal to our own exertions, we were only spectators, while the gunners had all the tragedy to themselves. The general and staff now dismounted; the sun was hot, and the field destitute of shade-trees; the prospect was, on the whole, by no means enlivening. Shortly after our arrival a detail was made from each regiment of the brigade, and the detachment, one hundred and fifty strong, under command of a major, moved down into the belt of woods skirting the river, where they deployed as skirmishers. Each man selected his position, anxious not to expose too freely his own person, keeping his musket on the full cock, and eagerly scanning the opposite bank, so as to be ready for any skirmisher in gray who might show himself. At various intervals during the day the skirmishers had rather a lively time of it.

Some of the staff were permitted to advance on foot nearer to the river, where we could better scan the enemy's position. The duel was not so extended or so severely fought as that at Rappahannock Station, there being at this particular point not more than half a dozen batteries engaged on each side. What strategic advantage the enemy expected to gain by wasting so much ammunition here, unless they hoped in this way to detain our main body and thus afford opportunity for a flanking movement on our right, I could not conjecture. They had lined the opposite bank with skirmishers, but made no important infantry demonstration, contenting themselves with flinging over a shower of projectiles, very few of which produced any effect whatever. One battery, posted close to a handsome residence near the river, was especially unremitting in its hostile attentions, and I enjoyed to-day the sight of some fine artillery practice. Our major stood a little way down the road, where, with his field-glass, he could see exactly where our shots struck, and signalized by lifting or lowering his hand as to the proper elevation or depression of the pieces. Several times the enemy was compelled to change position; several times I saw our shot strike right in among his guns. He was not slow in returning the compliment, but usually aimed too high.

On the river bank, and between our batteries and those of the enemy, were the extensive buildings and grounds of the Warrenton Springs, a favorite watering place for Virginians. Having been deprived of any summer visit to springs or sea-side resort, and curious to see the place where the first families once disported themselves, I had been aching all the morning with the desire to drink of this well-known water. It is true that there were certain drawbacks in the way of a visit just at this time, especially for a quiet man, who might have no objection to be saluted as a distinguished visitor, but would certainly prefer that the saluting gunners would omit for this occasion the accompanying iron. The buildings themselves were quite below the range of the opposing batteries, so that the main trouble was to approach and return in safety.

There was no help for it; so at last I rode down the road, and through a ravine to its right, keeping as closely under cover as possible, until I reached a spot where it seemed only courteous to the rebel gunners to dismount, so as not to interfere with the free course of the artillery duel by stopping any of their balls. Tying my horse to a tree with a slight feeling of doubt whether I should find him on my return, I made a run for it over the "hot place," and was soon descending toward the establishment—a point of comparative safety, though even here the wounded trees and scattered shot indicated its proximity to trouble.

The main building was in ruins, having been burned within the past forty-eight hours, probably by our own men. It formed one side of a large quadrangle, the remaining sides consisting of halls and rows of cottages, with the various kitchens and offices of a large establishment. Once very lovely, it was now like Virginia herself, in wreck and ruin—a speaking monument of rebel madness. The spring bubbled up in a reservoir covered in by a Virginio-Grecian temple with a statue of Health. A broken tumbler lay on the tiled floor, and I drank a deep draught to the success of the good cause, my toast being honored, as at the Danish court in Hamlet's time, by the roar of artillery. As I sat a moment in the well-room, striving to repeople this lovely haunt of Southern beauty, the bough of a tree near by cracked so significantly that I at once accepted the hint that it was time to retire; so, with the same caution as before, I made my way back again to the staff, to excite their curiosity by vivid description of the glories of Warrenton Springs.

The batteries kept up their din nearly all day, except for an hour, during which a truce had been agreed to at the request of the enemy, their avowed object in sending the flag being to return a woman dressed in military costume whom they had taken prisoner. I was informed that during the pendency of this truce a body of their sharpshooters, who had been lying in rifle-pits close to the river, took the opportunity to escape from their hot position—a proceeding unfair in war.

Late in the afternoon I rode back to Warrenton on official business, returning next morning in time for a late breakfast. The brigade had passed the night very comfortably. The morning was calm and still. No note of war was heard from the opposite side of the river, and soon it was ascertained that the force lately opposed to us had followed the main body up the river. Another move in the flanking game was evidently intended; and it was time for us, if we did not wish to be cut off from Washington and the Army of the Potomac, to be pushing northward.

A long march, of which I remember little save its weariness, commencing about noon, carried us through Warrenton, and so on in a northeasterly direction, until in the evening we were pressing through the little village of New Baltimore. Near this point the Pennsylvania Reserves joined our march, the first installment of the Army of the Potomac; their colors torn with bullets, their thinned ranks and war-worn aspect, as contrasted with their appearance when they left us two months ago at Fredericksburg, attested the severity of their Peninsular experiences.

Near New Baltimore the fields and woods were lighted up with so many camp-fires that our staff imagined we were passing a brigade or division; and one of them inquired, "What brigade is this encamped here?" "Company Q, sir," responded a soldier, complacently. "Company Q" is the title given by the army to the ignoble band of stragglers who follow in the wake of an army, like sharks who swim in the wake of a ship, anxious mainly to secure something to eat.

About 11 P.M. we reached our halting-ground. The night was pleasant; the regiments were soon comfortably bivouacked. The adjutant general and myself selected our tree-canopied couch of green sward, spread our blankets, made our night toilet by simply unbuckling our swords, and were soon asleep.

CHAPTER XII.

BATTLE OF GAINESVILLE.

THURSDAY, *August* 28*th*. Early this morning our division was again in motion, marching through a pleasant country on the road toward Centreville. At twelve o'clock the men were halted for an hour or two, in order to make coffee and rest a while during the heat of the day. A pleasant bivouac it was, under the grateful shade of a chestnut grove; our horses were unsaddled and allowed to graze, and our cooks soon spread out on the grass before us a welcome though frugal meal. Several guests joined our picnic under the trees, the general was in his most humorous vein, and we rested here two or three pleasant hours. Certainly no one of us, as we reposed after our lunch, placid and content, dreamed of the tragedy which was to greet us before the sun went down.

It was late in the afternoon before we were summoned to the saddle, and the brigade ordered to advance. Hardly had we proceeded a mile before the sound of distant cannonading reached our ears, exciting, however, no very great curiosity. This music was robbed of much of its impressiveness by sheer repetition; we had, indeed, quite gotten into the habit of artillery duels, and concluded that the parties making such a din three or four miles ahead of us could attend to their own business. A subordinate in the army, no matter how deeply he may be interested in the main result, soon learns to busy himself mainly in the performance of his own immediate duties, not worrying himself much with matters outside his own range.

About sunset we were a couple of miles, perhaps, beyond Gainesville; another brigade marched just ahead of us, and we were now moving quietly and serenely over a road sufficiently wide to permit our artillery and infantry to move in parallel lines, no one having any idea that a rebel was within a mile of us, and only anxious to reach our destination. The sound of distant cannonading had now temporarily ceased, the sunset hour was very delightful, and my horse and I were just wide awake enough to keep in the beaten road and not much more. At this moment of sleepy calm, when every body was least prepared for so stern a summons to battle, bang! bang! bang! burst forth upon us an iron-shotted salute from a deep-mouthed rebel battery on a little elevation to the left, very near the road. The enemy had gotten our range with such accuracy that they seemed to be firing right down into our faces, and in a second the shells were exploding about us in fearful proximity. I saw a horse knocked over within a hundred feet of me, and it was startlingly evident that we were in a hot position. So sudden a transition from a doze on horseback to the position of target for rebel artillery exercise was by no means agreeable to me. A few of our men, half a dozen perhaps, leaped the fence and ran through the fields toward the woods beyond, about as dangerous an excursion as they could have made, for the missiles of the enemy, just escaping our heads, fell thick and fast in these fields beyond. For a single instant the ranks paused, as if uncertain what to do. The general at once thundered out, "Bring the van forward at double-quick;" and double-quick it was for some five hundred feet, until we were out of range, with a thick wood between us and the rebel batteries. Only one other brigade of the division was near us—the 4th, under the command of General Gibbon — General Hatch being already engaged with another force of the enemy two miles or more ahead of us, and General Patrick's being at least a mile behind. A hurried consultation now took place between the two brigade commanders. Our division general was in the rear, and no member of his staff was at hand to declare his wishes. To accept this rebel insult in silence was not to be thought of. It was resolved at once to move up through the woods and storm the battery. On the instant the fence was torn down by the pioneers, and Gibbon's famous fighting brigade, the men of Wisconsin and Indiana, as gallant a set as ever pulled trigger, pushed up through the woods in line of battle toward the battery. As they disappeared from view among the trees, up rode the gallant colonel of the 56th Pennsylvania, and, saluting our general, exclaimed, "Shall we push in, general? my men are eager for the fray." I could not help smiling at the familiar quotation, even under the present exciting circumstances, for now the sharp ping! ping! of the bullets began to sound in our ears, indicating that this was no mere cavalry battery, but that the rebel infantry were coming into action.

To such a question there could be no negative response. Deeply as our general felt the responsibility of going into action without orders from his division commander, he could not see our sister brigade move forward alone. "Move in the 56th and 76th at once; form in line of battle, and push up through the woods to the support of Gibbon's men." At the word the two regiments quit the road, enter the woods, and hurry up the gradual ascent. Only a few hundred feet, however, for soon the crest is gained, and, at once advancing to the front, they form beside the other brigade, and are soon hotly engaged with the enemy. All along the low ridge parallel with their position stand double lines of the rebel infantry, wave after wave of fire leaps from their serried ranks, and our boys begin to fall like the leaves in autumn. Field and company officers, and numbers of the gallant soldiers of either brigade, soon crimson that hill-side with their blood; almost at the first onset the Pennsylvania colonel is wounded, a Wisconsin colonel receives his death-wound. The combat is brief but terrible.

A portentous silence masks some woods on the left close to our position; it is necessary to uncloak the enemy if concealed therein, lest he flank us in that direction. The clergyman captain, of whom I spoke in a former chapter, springs to the head of his company, and leads them forward to draw the enemy's fire. Out of the quiet forest flashes the rebel volley; our captain, pierced by five bullets, falls faint and bleeding; but the object is gained, and the enemy is driven from his covert by good Union musketry. Some of our boys, though wounded, refuse to quit the ranks, Martin Luther among the rest, worthy of his illustrious name. And so the fight goes on. The men of the West, brave and determined as they are, find that their Eastern brothers are equally brave and determined. Not one inch is given back, though the attacking force is greatly superior, nor will there be until the fight is over.

As our two regiments entered the woods, the third was ordered up to support a battery planted on the bare crest of a field adjoining the woods on the right, and hither those of the staff not otherwise employed followed the general. The position commanded a view of the rebel lines, and, as the general sat peering anxiously forward to be ready to meet any new demonstration on the part of the enemy, the whole scene was to me awfully exciting and impressive. The shadows of night gradually descended, and it seemed to me that I saw at least a mile of lightning leaping from rebel muskets, while a perfect deluge of rebel thunderbolts went crashing into the woods, or came shrieking like fiends over and among us. The rattle of musketry was terrible and continuous—the air seemed full of lead. Ah! it is the cruel music of these bullets about his ears which most disturbs a man's equanimity. I have never been exposed to the awful discharge of grape and canister, but the whirring of a musketry volley has always seemed to me far more terrible than shot or shell.

During this fight occurred a pleasant instance of presence of mind. A lieutenant of our brigade had, with some of his men, been thrown out on the left as a picket to notify of any attempt at a flanking movement. While thus engaged, he saw in the dusk a column of men, apparently in their shirt-sleeves, hurrying up toward the rebel lines. "Who goes there?" was his instant challenge. "The 24th Virginia," was the immediate response. "All right!"

said he; "pass 24th Virginia!" fortunate that the 24th Virginia had not quietly taken off him and his little party with them.

This incident also evidences the nearness of the hostile lines, and accounts for the great slaughter in this brief contest. The battle did not last more than half an hour, and yet more than one third of the 4th brigade, and also of our own two regiments, were left dead or wounded on the field, among them five captains in one regiment, the 76th New York; and the enemy must have suffered quite as severely. Here Ewell, one of their best generals, lost his leg, and two other general officers were wounded, and their own statements admit a loss of over one thousand men. At last the dread combat was over, night having come with friendly darkness to end this bloody tragedy. Still firm and undaunted, our thinned ranks held strongly their position; the enemy's fire ceased first, and then loud and long above the woods rose three times three of good Union cheers, the claim of victory.

And now to look out for our wounded. The night was so dark, the whole affair had been so short and sudden, that no one seemed to know the position of the surgeons or their ambulances. In my search for them I had a ride of gloom whose memories can never desert me. Details were busily engaged in bringing the wounded down to the road, and here, under the trees, lay the sufferers, awaiting each his turn to receive the attention of the two or three surgeons in this part of the field. Lighted by torches or bits of candle, these surgeons were busily engaged in their melancholy labors. I heard few complaints or groans;

but, as I gazed on the poor patient fellows, my heart grew sick within me, and the whole air seemed full of anguish.

Taking the pathway through the woods where I expected to find the ambulances, I met, lying singly or in pairs, others of our poor wounded boys, who had dragged themselves thus far from the spot of their wounding, and now rested on the green turf, with no surgical aid to dress their hurts. There is always something awe-inspiring in the deep gloom of a forest at night; but you must make that forest the chamber of anguish for wounded braves, every one of whom becomes by virtue of his wound your friend and brother, calling forth your most affectionate sympathy— you must add to all this the bitter pang which tortures one unable to help them, before you can form any just idea of my melancholy ride on this sad night. Hurried words of sympathy and consolation, a heartfelt thank-offering to them of praise and gratitude, a promise of speedy help and succor, these were all I could lend of present aid; but in almost every instance came back a brave and manly response, which lent a new glow to my already excited feelings.

Hither and thither I rode through the wood, very carefully lest my horse should tread upon some prostrate form, and finding no signs of a hospital, until I became half-frantic at my want of success. At length, to my repeated shouts, came back the long-wished-for response, and, to my great relief, I found one of our surgeons, who had already, in his *al fresco* hospital, with the light of a single candle, attended to some thirty cases. I had been looking in the wrong direction. Our surgical department, called upon so suddenly to organize field-hospitals at night, was busily engaged, with a skill and tenderness no one can gainsay, the only trouble being that definite information of their position had not reached head-quarters. Very soon all the wounded were attended to; many of them accompanied our march in the ambulances, the remainder being left behind under charge of a surgeon.

On my return to the general I found him seated at a little camp-fire on the side of the road, around which also reclined the division general and the general commanding the 4th brigade. Our men had, in the mean time, been withdrawn from the front, and were bivouacked in the field close to the road, lying down on their arms; pickets were stationed, and all was still save where, around their council-fire, the generals were conversing. The officers of the respective staffs were seated a little outside the inner circle, orderlies held the horses ready for instant use in the road close by, and the firelight shone upon the anxious faces of men conscious of a grave responsibility. To all appearance, the road over which we had been marching was now completely flanked by a greatly superior force of the enemy, and whether or not they had already posted their artillery and infantry so as to prevent our changing our route was at least an open question.

Shortly after I joined the party our pickets brought in two prisoners, an officer and a private, who had, so close were the two forces and so dark the night, strayed by mistake into our lines in passing from one of their own regiments to another. The manners and appearance of the young officer pleased me. His dress was the usual gray uniform, with little decoration, and a slouch hat, with drooping feather, lent a picturesque air to his prepossessing countenance. As he stood in the glare of the camp-fire, that handsome young rebel, he answered the questions put to him by one or another of the generals courteously, frankly reserving to himself the right to say nothing which could injure his cause.

The separate examination of the other prisoner confirmed our belief that we had fallen in with Jackson's entire army, and also that the enemy was completely deceived as to our numbers, believing that they had been engaged with Pope's main body. The cheers of our men at the close of the battle, and the later cheering sent up at our general's direction after the regiments had left the front in order to make the enemy believe that we were welcoming re-enforcements, doubtless aided considerably in this mistake. In no other way can I account for the fact that we were permitted, with our broken division, to withdraw from this point unmolested.

At length it was decided to relinquish the march toward Centreville, to turn back and take the road to Manassas Junction, the march to commence at 1 A.M. The prospect was a gloomy one. The general feeling seemed to be that our march was likely to be opposed, and that the struggle with the larger opposing force would probably be a desperate one. It was now eleven o'clock; the group around the camp-fire dispersed, some to attend to special duty, others to seek a little rest. Wrapped in our cloaks, for the night air was chilly, we laid down by the roadside; but, tired as I was, my own thoughts were too full of the exciting scenes of the late battle, too busy with the expected contest, to enable me at once to sleep. It was one of those seasons when it does a man good to look at his position squarely in the face, to examine it by the clear light of duty, and seek to bring himself into true relations with the eternal verities. Not much may be said about such experiences, but out of them came strength and cheerfulness, and I was soon refreshed by a little sleep.

At 1 A.M. all were aroused; the men, alive to the necessities of the case, fell in with no noise; the wounded fit for transportation were already in the ambulances, and the column was in motion. I certainly expected that we should be attacked at any moment, and should have to cut our way through; and still think that if Jackson had known the weakness of our force, he could have eaten us up alive. But stillness still brooded over the rebel lines; we had reached and passed the point where the enemy first opened fire upon us; the expected night-attack did not come off, and we had soon turned into the road leading to Manassas Junction. The men marched swiftly, so that by 6 A.M. we had reached the Junction, where we found quite a large number of our troops already assembled. I afterward learned that the enemy moved away the same night; so that, as is not infrequent in war, both parties had had quite enough of the bloody battle-field of Gainesville.

CHAPTER XIII.

SECOND BATTLE OF BULL RUN.

FRIDAY, *August 29th*. Now, thought we, for a little rest.' After the dangers and fatigues of the past forty-eight hours, the brigade actually required repose, and we felt sure they would be allowed it. Rations were at once issued, camp-fires lighted, and the bivouac began to put on a look of comfort. This done, the staff, in the absence of our staff tents and baggage, proceeded to do their best in the same direction. A neighboring brook made an excellent washbasin. I always carried in my saddle-bags a toilet-case, towels, and a supply of paper collars. The uniform coat covers up all deficiencies, so that in half an hour I was refreshed and quite presentable. We had our head-quarters ambulance with us, and a limited cuisine, so that our cook was able to supply us with a cup of black coffee, some canned meat, and hard bread—the first thing, I believe, which had passed my lips since our noontide meal yesterday.

As we sat on the ground sipping our coffee and talking over last night's experiences, cheer upon cheer from one of the brigades of our division arrested our attention. Starting up, I saw a long column of troops moving by, and heard it was composed of some of M'Clellan's old army. I did not wonder at the cheers, for now we were assured that M'Clellan had succeeded in extricating himself from his perilous position on the Peninsula, and that our connection was fully established. For one, I had now not a particle of doubt that every man of that army, to aid in whose rescue we had been undergoing the fatigue and danger of the past three weeks, was flying to re-enforce us.

The reason, I presume, why the sight of these re-enforcements made so strong an impression was this, that the frequent excitements and want of sleep had to some extent demoralized our troops, officers and men. A man, hazy from fasting and sleeplessness, loses self-reliance, does not stand so firmly on his feet, becomes dejected and indifferent, offering a service perfunctory rather than whole-souled and enthusiastic. I know that personally I felt almost exhausted, for the bodily machine was pretty well run down. I am convinced that there was not half the fighting value in our brigade as if one day's rest and one night's sleep had been permitted us after the late fatigues.

Imagine our disappointment when, as we were finishing our coffee, orders came for the division to move forward at once to meet the enemy. The second battle of Bull Run had already commenced, and every man was needed. Our men had not had time enough to kill and cook their fresh meat, and so it had to be abandoned. I confess that I pitied the men as they reluctantly packed and slung their knapsacks. I pitied my tired mare as the orderly brought her up. I pitied my tired body as I swung myself into the saddle. All the usual excitement naturally attendant upon a march to an expected battle-field was merged and lost in mental and bodily prostration.

I shall attempt no general description of this second battle of Bull Run, seeking only to narrate my personal experiences, with such attendant circumstances as fall naturally into this connection. It was about 10 A.M. when our column was again in motion, retracing a portion of last night's journey, but turning off to the right on the road to New Market, our general direction being toward the north. The road was full of ambulances and ammunition wagons; the roar of the opposing batteries filled the air; and, as we drew nearer, the continuous rattle of musketry indicated that this was no mere artillery duel, but a general engagement. As we passed into the outer rim of the battle-field, we noticed on every hand, hiding in little valleys out of reach of the enemy's fire, parks of ammunition wagons, while over several scattered farm-houses floated the red flag of the hospital.

Having marched about six miles, we drew in about 4 P.M. to the main line of battle on the left, were halted, formed in line of battle, and advanced half up a gentle swale, whose crest was crowned with several batteries. Stretching in rear of this line of batteries, some thousands of troops were lying on their arms, sheltered by the crest from the enemy's artillery, and only needed when the enemy should attack the left, or an advance be ordered from this direction. For the present the artillery had this portion of the struggle to themselves, and terribly earnest were their demonstrations of mutual hostility. Our brigade was now resting quietly with the rest of the infantry; the general and staff dismounted, and some of us lay down and took a few minutes' sleep.

Feeling a good deal better for my rest, I was now ready to look about me. With this crest between us and the battle-field, we could, of course, see nothing, so

I obtained permission to ascend to the top, where I could overlook the valley of death, from whence rolled up to us the awful din of battle. Our major joined me, and together we passed an hour in the fruitless endeavor to comprehend the different positions, and map out the main features of the contest. Immediately below us were the Pennsylvania Reserves and some other regiments; beyond them a series of undulatory elevations, each fringed with a dense smoke, and breaking ever into fresh puffs from cannon discharges. A dense cloud rested upon the intermediate valleys; no charge of infantry, no lines of gray-uniformed rebels interested us; every thing was enveloped in a smoky veil. A pre-Raphaelite who should attempt to paint this battle would have been compelled to give us mainly a smoke-enwrapped landscape, unless he threw aside his pencil and went in with the infantry. But we could not forget that beneath the veil our brothers, loyal and patriotic, were fighting for the good cause, and peered anxiously forward, thinking every moment might lift the concealing vapor and disclose something of the struggle going on below.

With the result of all this fighting—how Sigel, and Hooker, and Kearney, and the rest drove back the enemy's left, swinging our own right forward to occupy their former position, all are familiar. But meantime while, alas! some of the long-expected divisions of the Army of the Potomac are held back at Alexandria, Longstreet and the whole force of the enemy are hurrying to the rescue of their nearly discomfited comrades. That Longstreet is indeed already taking position opposite our left wing we are to have fearful personal evidence only too soon.

For now, about 6 P.M., comes to us an aid from General M'Dowell with orders to advance. Swiftly from regiment to regiment, now lying *en masse*, a little compact square of men, passes the order; the men leap to their feet, sling knapsacks, take their muskets, and fall in. Field officers lying asleep, worn out by fatigue, rouse themselves and are soon in the saddle. The general and staff lead the way, and the brigade moves out into the road, followed by the 1st brigade, the division being now under the command of General Hatch. The other brigades are not with us, though one follows not long after. Eight regiments of us, and only some twenty-five hundred fighting men—a sad commentary upon last night's losses, and also upon the fatigues and privations of the past few weeks, more destructive to an army than any battle.

Hardly have we fairly started before the order comes to move at double-quick. M'Dowell himself is at the roadside, and as we move quickly by the news flashes through our lines that the enemy is retreating, and that we are sent forward to pursue and pick up the stragglers. Cheer after cheer swells up from the ranks; officers wave their swords; the fatigue of last night's fighting and marching is forgotten; the heavy knapsacks do not weigh a pound; tired limbs lose their stiffness; officers and men receive new and wonderful inspiration. Ah! that was an exciting ride, cheered by the breath of anticipated victory, quite wild indeed with enthusiasm.

On our right and left we note the batteries lining the ridges, with large bodies of troops behind them, marking our main line of battle; and as we rush past, cheer upon cheer greets and encourages us; for now the hot throats of our cannon were silent; the fighting at this point was over, and our tired army, having fought bravely through that bloody day, were holding quietly but sternly the new lines of advance won from the enemy. On! on! three fourths of a mile beyond our main lines, up the Warrenton turnpike still moved at double-quick our two brigades, accompanied by a single battery of artillery; on! on! far ahead of all our supports. How beautiful and still this sunset hour! how treacherously quiet the fields, and woods, and glens on either side of us!

Where, however, are the rebel stragglers we were sent forward to capture, where the evidences that the enemy is in flight? Ah! it is not to pursue a disheartened and flying foe we have come hither; but right into the rebel den are we rushing—right into the deadly embrace of Longstreet's entire force, waiting for us, three lines deep, just arrived and fresh for battle. A little ahead of our main body skirmish our sharpshooters, thrown out on either hand, creeping cautiously forward, peering into wood and glen, every man ready on the instant to bring down a skulking foe or develop a hostile force hiding in ambuscade.

And now we are moving up a gentle ascent in the road, when suddenly the sharpshooters halt, and all along their line rings out the sharp crack of their rifles, admonishing of danger. Yonder wooded slopes just beyond us, looking so still and beautiful, are full of rebels; already their advanced skirmishers have opened the bloody tournament. On gallops our single battery to the top of the ascent, the guns are unlimbered, the horses brought back a hundred paces to the rear, and in an instant roars forth our answer to the rebel welcome. The infantry hasten forward, deploy in line of battle in the fields on both sides the road, move swiftly to the top of the crest, and pour volley after volley down toward the enemy. That enemy, sheltered in natural rifle-pits, protected by stone walls and woods, have only to lie quietly in their hiding-places until they can take fatal aim upon our exposed regiments. A fatal and disastrous game this, even if our numbers were equal; as it is, the odds are overwhelming, and our ranks are swept by the besom of destruction.

Close in rear of the men the general, and staff, and field officers of the regiments cheer, encourage, and force up the troops to their work. Again and again our brave boys deliver their fire, to bend again and again beneath that murderous rush of bullets, which howls about us as the storm howls through a harvest-field in autumn. Bravely the company officers stand fast to their position; a field officer seizes his regimental colors and bears them forward in front, and the lines dress up with steady obstinacy. I saw one captain standing beside his men on the crest, exclaiming, "Fire away, boys! give it to them!" ducking his own head ever and anon as the leaden storm in fiercer blasts came wailing by. Smile not at this, for here was a worthy example of high religious principle triumphing over great bodily fear. He afterward remarked, "Nothing but my sense of religious duty kept me from running away a dozen times." Another captain in our brigade, wounded in last night's battle, is here fighting beside his men, and the consequence is that he will be lame for life.

The wounded are now creeping to the rear, while

some of our best and bravest lie dead upon this fatal field; and still, low-lying and secure, the enemy sweeps our ranks with a whirlwind of bullets. On our left, and close to our left flank, is a dense wood, still and calm as if unconscious of the bloody carnival. Early in the fight the fire of one of our regiments had been turned in that direction, so as to unmask any concealed foe—not answered, however, by a responding volley, but a voice exclaims, "Don't shoot here; you're firing on your friends." Supposing that our skirmishers were holding the woods, no farther attack was made in that direction. But now, all of a sudden, out of this treacherous grove comes a murderous enfilading fire. Nothing is so demoralizing to troops as an attack in flank and rear, and it is fearfully evident that our position is too hot for us. Already many of our men are killed and wounded; our staff major's horse is killed, another staff horse wounded in two places: how any man can live under such a fire as this seems wonderful.

This standing as targets for a sheltered and unseen foe is not good tactics. One of two things must be done: either we must charge with the cold steel into the woods, and down upon those stone walls and copses, or we must retreat. Flanked and outnumbered we can not, must not remain in this hideous death another instant. Our general straightens himself in saddle, and upon his face may easily be read the determination never to quit this field alive. But the madness of such a course is only too evident, and at last retreat is ordered.

As soon as we begin to fall back the enemy unmasks his troops, and charges in front and flank upon our ranks, now broken and retreating in disorder. The sun has set, and the darkness descends to lend new horrors to the scene; foes become undistinguishable from friends, and still at frequent intervals fresh volleys from the advancing enemy wail over our heads with a terrible emphasis. At several points the desperate exertions of some field or staff officer succeed in rallying little battalions of men, again to fall back before the outnumbering foe.

It was while making a rally like this that a friend of mine met with a singular adventure which well illustrates the confusion caused by the darkness of the hour. His horse had been killed in the battle, and his leg injured, and as he limped away he was overtaken by a body of men moving in the same direction. Supposing them to be our own troops, he resolved to attempt to make a stand, and sought to face them to the front, using even blows in his excited eagerness. At length some one exclaimed, "Who are you, sir?" "Major of the 76th!" was the reply. "76th what?" said the stranger. "76th New York," replied the major. "Well, sir, you are my prisoner, for you are trying to rally the 2d Mississippi." And so the gallant major had to make an excursion in a southerly direction, to escape once during the night, and be again captured as he groped his way through the darkness, to meet with various adventures, to be paroled, and finally exchanged. On his return to his regiment he was warmly congratulated by his friends on his success in rallying a Southern regiment.

Sadly from this field of disaster we rode with the general, two of our staff absent, each of whom I had seen greatly exposing himself in the fight, and of whose fate I was very apprehensive. The night was now so dark that it was impossible to collect the men, but we busied ourselves in getting them together in detachments. Arrived once more within our own lines, we found our main line of battle marked by a few scattered camp-fires; but most of the troops had lain down in their blankets, and all was still save where the pickets challenged an approaching party, or an officer called out the rendezvous of his scattered men. Dinnerless and supperless, the only wish was to lie down and be alone with the recollections of the drama of death through which we had just passed. "Why had we been sent out upon so forlorn a hope?" was the engrossing question. So at last, amid mingled feelings of pain and thanksgiving, of bitter sorrow at our disaster and heartfelt gratitude for my own escape, each in turn in the ascendant, I fell asleep, and one more day of danger, fatigue, and excitement was over.

Saturday, August 30th. With the morning our two staff officers, safe and sound, and the different detachments, which had camped in various portions of the field, came in, and it was enough to give a man the heartache to see the little brigade drawn up in line, not five hundred strong. More than fifteen hundred rank and file had marched with us out of Fredericksburgh; some had undoubtedly skulked behind; some were absolutely worn out by our long marches, sleepless nights, and battle fatigues; some, separated from their commands during last night, had not yet rejoined them; but probably the larger portion of the missing were prisoners to the enemy, lay wounded in the hospitals, or slept the last sleep of the patriotic brave.

The hill-side where our brigade now stood was close behind our main line of battle, and here our batteries were posted, with the infantry drawn up just in their rear, or moving toward their new positions. The morning was very beautiful, and not a warlike sound disturbed the peaceful calm. No martial music awakened the enthusiasm of the troops; not even the drum and fife marked time for their marching. I am convinced that this is a mistake, and that, indeed, in many respects the military life of our volunteers has been made too tame and matter-of-fact. The patriotic impulse has not been sufficiently appealed to and aroused by encouraging words uttered by their officers on the brink of battle; the martial spirit not sufficiently excited by music, medals, brevets, and similar encouragements. Some of the choicest patriots and best fighters I have happened to meet with have as yet received very scanty acknowledgment. When I read of the little addresses made to the men by the leaders in other wars, of the promotion upon the field of battle, the constant appeal to ambition, pride, patriotism, I think I see one reason why our army, composed as it is of the best fighting material, has not proved itself invincible. War is a business, but it is something more, and needs far other and higher incitements to make it successful.

All this in passing. Very soon an aid brought the order for our advance, and in a few minutes our caricature of a brigade moved without drum or fife to the front—only a short distance, however, as they were posted among the reserves in the centre of the army.

Close by our position was the hillock selected by General Pope as his post of observation, and thither our general proceeded after placing his brigade. In a few minutes he sent me an order to come up also, and here I saw Generals Pope, M'Dowell, and Hooker, with a dozen other general officers and their staffs— a brilliant military cortége even in our plain American uniform. Near by stood almost a regiment of orderlies holding the staff horses, aids were galloping up or hurrying off with orders, and every body seemed to be in the best of spirits, while the general-in-chief, with the inevitable cigar in his mouth, walked from group to group, evidently overflowing with good-humor. Well he might be proud and happy, for it was now believed that the enemy was in full retreat. The hill-sides, which yesterday echoed with fierce artillery, were now silent; the little valleys, then swarming with graybacks, were now quiet as if there was no such thing as war. The dense forests in front of us might indeed be full of treason, but that treason had not yet given tongue, and some imperfect reconnoissances indicated that it had fled away discomfited. Probably a happier party never joined at the meet in the palmiest days of old Virginia field-sports than now stood and talked together in little knots of three or four upon that hillock, every one speculating upon the probable line of the enemy's retreat, and eager to be in at the death.

As I stood conversing with other officers, General Pope's adjutant general was transcribing that famous dispatch which announced the glad tidings of victory to the country, and gave it twenty-four hours of real joy. But I had no time to lose, for the general had directed me to proceed at once to Centreville, where our wagon-train was now parked in charge of our brigade quarter-master, and to bring up supplies from that point, or wherever attainable. With no relish for fighting, I yet had a fancy that I should enjoy, by way of a change, the pursuit of a flying enemy and "picking up stragglers;" but there is no court of appeal in such cases, and I was off at once with a regimental quarter-master.

As we rode by our troops drawn up in line of battle around the old flag, I felt grateful as perhaps never before for this victory, which seemed to me the salvation of our afflicted country. Our last night's disaster—all the weariness, and hunger, and want of sleep were forgotten in the deep satisfaction of the hour. Even the red flag of the hospitals, where our wounded boys were lying, could only tone down this feeling, for I felt that they had suffered not in vain—that now we had reached, perhaps, the last act in this sad tragedy. Every officer I met, instead of passing rapidly by with the usual military courtesy, now had a word of hearty congratulation. Jocund was every countenance, for the good news had flown through the entire army; and the faces even of those who, being wounded only in hand or arm, were walking toward Centreville, were full of hope and joy.

So we rode pleasantly on toward Centreville, reaching that strongly fortified position about noon. Such an immense concourse of wagons I never witnessed—acres upon acres of them, parked by divisions, under charge of their respective quarter-masters. The news had preceded us; the embargo put on the mails was now removed, and I scribbled a letter in pencil full of glad tidings. Before that letter reached its destination the telegraph had told a far different story.

Amid such a city of wagon-trains, it took me half an hour to find our division train and reach the tent of our brigade quarter-master. Fortunately, the needed supplies were procurable, the necessary orders were given, and I was soon seated at a meal which put to shame any thing I had enjoyed in this line for a fortnight. For good living under all circumstances, commend me to a quarter-master's mess-table; if there be any fatness in the land, be sure that a full share falls into his larder.

While thus engaged the wagons were made ready, and my friend and myself, refreshed in body and jubilant in spirit, were soon in the saddle. As we rode through Centreville I was accosted by a foreigner on General Sigel's staff, just in from the front, and "fiery red with haste." The man was absolutely boiling over with enthusiasm, and almost embraced me, though a stranger, as he exclaimed, "I go to Washington wiz ze news." "Bon voyage," was my reply, and on he dashed rejoicing.

Thus full of measureless content, we with difficulty tamed ourselves down to the slow movement of the train, so anxious were we to get forward. We now made up our mind that a long ride was before us, and that we should have to follow our pursuing army perhaps all night. In the footsteps of victory we should have been glad to remain in the saddle until we reached Richmond. Not far from Centreville we met Franklin's division, then halting by the wayside, and I could not help wishing that they were in front, that they might aid in the wholesale capture of the rebel army. I had not a thought how desperately their presence, which might have saved the day, had been actually needed.

We had proceeded perhaps a couple of miles, when we began to meet occasional squads of two or three soldiers walking toward Centreville, many without musket or knapsack; but most of them were wounded, and I regarded the rest as only the usual débris of stragglers which drifts away from every field of battle. Even when these squads became more frequent I felt no touch of alarm, but considerable indignation rather, impelling me in several instances to protest against this movement to the rear. In one of these instances I was by no means fortunate. Halting a couple of our soldiers, I exclaimed, "Why, boys, have you lost your road? The enemy is in the opposite direction." To this they replied by simply lifting up their wounded and bandaged arms, which had been concealed under their jackets, flung loosely over their shoulders. Half lifting my cap, with a low bow of apology, I rode on without another word.

And now the rush of men, singly and in detachments, mingled with sutlers' wagons, artillery caissons, and supply wagons, began to look fearfully ominous, but even yet I would not, could not descend from the heights of hope into the valley of despond. I began to be afraid to ask any questions, and every one was pushing by in too much haste to volunteer any information. At length I could stand it no longer. Turning to my companion (we had been riding for some minutes in silence), I remarked to him, "Really this begins to look a good deal like a retreat; how does it strike you?" "I have been thinking so for the last quarter of an hour, but didn't like to speak of it," was the unsatisfactory reply.

So at last we began to question the passers-by, and

to receive but one response. Every man spoke of his own regiment as "fearfully cut up," but most agreed that our left wing only had been routed, while the centre and right stood firm. Yet stronger and stronger grew the retreating tide, darker and darker became the story of disaster; and now we began to meet ammunition trains, even batteries, and battalions of men marching back in something like order. From intelligent officers we learned that the defeat was general, and that our whole army was falling back to Centreville. Our wagon-train had with great difficulty crept forward thus far; the night was coming on, and the road was so blocked up that it would have been folly to attempt to proceed farther; so I ordered the train to turn back and return to the division park, inside the defenses at Centreville. We concluded to push on a little farther; soon became convinced that it was useless to attempt to stem the tide, and busied ourselves in aiding the passage of the sometimes entangled coil of wagons which now filled the road.

I am bound to say that I saw very little of that panic which is said to have characterized the retreat from the first battle of Bull Run; no break-neck driving of wagons, no cutting of traces, no headlong rushes of troops; the current set one way rapidly, but with little foam. This must be considered a retreat, not an absolute rout; and toward the last the troops moved off in good order. Franklin's division was drawn up in front of Centreville; so that, had the enemy pursued, he would have met with a proper reception.

It was night before we reached Centreville, to find the little place crowded with soldiers, many of its houses being also filled with the wounded of yestert day's battle. A strong guard was posted across the road to prevent the farther retreat of stragglers, and it was evident that the first flurry was over. I had been able to gain no positive intelligence as to the fate of our brigade and staff, but it was useless to seek them in the darkness, so we returned to our quarter-master's camp, and were comfortably lodged for the night.

And what a night that was! Doubtful as to the safety of my comrades, almost desperate as to the prospect before us, stung to the quick by shame and sorrow, there rose hardly a single star of hope above its black horizon. Let all this pass as a frightful and fearful dream.

CHAPTER XIV.

CENTREVILLE TO UPTON'S HILL.

SUNDAY, *August* 31*st*. With the earliest dawn I was again in the saddle, anxious to find the brigade, and to learn how my comrades had fared in yesterday's battle. The morning was cold and rainy; every thing bore a look of sad discomfort, in unison with my own feelings. The scene through which I rode was, indeed, one needing only a faithful limner to present a picture strikingly illustrative of military life in its most depressing form. Around me were the *disjecta membra* of a shattered army—here were stragglers sneaking along through the mud, inquiring for their regiments; little squads just issuing from their shelterless bivouac on the wet ground; wagons shipwrecked and forlorn; half-formed regiments, part of the men with guns and part without—wanderers driven in by the patrols; while every one you met had an unwashed, sleepy, downcast aspect, and looked as if he would like to hide his head somewhere from all the world. At one side of the picture our artist would introduce the long lines of handsome hacks, each with its sour, surly driver, enraged at having been sent out here from his pleasant stand on the avenue by an inexorable provost-marshal, who needed his carriage as an ambulance for our wounded: for these vehicles, so suggestive of home luxury, offered a speaking contrast to the rough miseries of war; while, that his sketch might not want touches of practical satire and irony, he would paint in some of these groups of kid-gloved citizens in their fine apparel, who now paused disconsolately in the mud, having come out on a pleasure excursion to visit our victorious battle-field. Perhaps the artist might find humorous touches in the scene; I confess that I could not see them through my sad eyes on that unhappy morning.

But there were also divisions and brigades bivouacked in true military style. The Centreville fortifications were well manned and occupied by batteries; a division or two still in front of them faced the enemy, and a more thorough inspection convinced me that the Army of Virginia still lived. Most of last night's runaways had found their commands, while many of the brigades, among which was my own, had marched back in good order. As I gazed around I discovered the little cohort drawn up on the right, and was soon exchanging earnest, friendly greetings with the staff. The brigade had suffered very little in the conflict of yesterday, only four men having been killed and wounded in the whole number. It was comforting to find my friends all safe; to me it was like coming home after an absence full of misfortune; but our meeting was not joyous; we met rather as men meet after shipwreck, in which, though saved themselves, they have lost their all. I think I can safely say that I saw no smiles that day.

We had no tents, but were busied in necessary outdoor duties; provisions were distributed, the men made coffee, and still poured down upon us the drenching rain; so we shivered through an hour or two, until orders came to our division to march in the direction of Fairfax Court-house. Our supply train was ordered to Alexandria with all the tents and head-quarter baggage also, and our march of five miles was brisk and unencumbered. Having reached a good position wherein to repulse the enemy should he seek to sweep round our right, avoiding the Centreville fortifications and attacking us in rear, or making a cavalry raid upon our wagon-trains, we were halted in some fields north of the road, and drawn up in line of battle; the men stacked arms, unslung knapsacks, and were allowed to rest. The other brigades of the division were drawn up near us, the remainder of the corps was not far off; batteries were posted, and quiet waiting was now in order.

Here we remained all day. Shortly after our arrival the sunshine came to cheer us; we spread our blankets beneath a shade-tree, swords were unbuckled and hung up on its limbs, a fire was built near by to drive off the dampness and cook our dinner, the horses were picketed and fed in the neighboring grove, a few pickets thrown out in front, and we threw ourselves down to rest. It was not long before a respectable camp dinner, served upon the grass, invited us, and here beneath the welcome shade we dined.

Under other circumstances this would have been a cheerful party. But now I noticed that no gayety sparkled, no pleasant anecdote gave zest to our meal. It was only a satisfying of hunger, and nothing more. Every one was wonderfully silent, moved through his duties mechanically, had no extra courtesies to spare for his fellows. Few allusions were made to our late defeat, still a sore subject with all; and each felt, I presume, like myself—quite crushed, as yet, under the shame and sorrow of our lost victory. Had the enemy attacked on that day he would have encountered men thoroughly desperate—not so much demoralized as savage—and burning to wipe out the memories of the late disaster.

With a cracker-box for an open-air writing-table, I managed to write a little in the afternoon, but most of the staff spent the time in sleep. Meantime a continuous train of wagons and ambulances filled the road, all moving toward Alexandria, and no hostile demonstration disturbed our quiet bivouac. As night came on we borrowed a paulin from a battery, and, by stretching it over a transverse pole supported by two stakes, made a comfortable canopy, beneath which, at sunset, we spread our blankets, and slept heavily until morning.

Monday, September 1st. Marvelous was the effect of a good night's sleep upon our party, and a more cheerful tone was evident in all. Still in our quiet bivouac, busied in various duties, we passed most of the day. The 7th Indiana, some seven hundred strong, was this day added to our brigade; some of our missing had returned, so that we could now muster perhaps fourteen hundred men. I was interested, in standing by the roadside this morning, to see the mile after mile of wagons as they rolled by, mingled with other vehicles of every description. Under the lee of a huge army wagon crept a diminutive jackass, drawing a diminutive cart laden with knapsacks, followed, perhaps, by an old, broken-down family carriage of the ancient style peculiar to the F. F. V., creaking complainingly along under a load of other soldier-gear, while an ox-team or two moved leisurely on with the quiet dignity of their kind. I fear that these equipages were the products of private confiscation, and that no entry of them ever reached the quarter-master's returns.

Later in the day the necessity for haste became too urgent to permit these nondescripts to lumber up the road. Staff officers were stationed at various points hurrying up the trains. The wagons moved in two parallel lines; the teams broke into a trot wherever practicable, and the luckless wight whose ox or jackass could not keep the pace was elbowed off the road. For hours to-day General M'Dowell, whose head-quarters were near the roadside, opposite to our position, sat under a tree where he could inspect and hurry up the movement. It was clearly a military necessity that our immense caravan should be sheltered as soon as possible behind the forts at Alexandria.

The day passed on with no signs of the enemy, and about 4 P.M. our brigade was ordered off as a protection to Fairfax Station, a new disposition of the troops being now required. Shortly after we had marched through Fairfax Court-house we were met by a most drenching storm. The rain laughed to scorn our rubber cloaks, filled our top-boots to the brim, trickled in rivulets between our shoulders, while the wind fairly swayed our horses before its fury. The road speedily became a lake, and our brigade made a sorry figure indeed as, with muskets reversed, they waded through the mud, staggering against the blinding storm. In the midst of this fury of the elements, heavily and continually the sound of cannonading on our right broke upon our ears, seeming almost a horrid mockery, and once more treason and loyalty fought to the death on the field of Chantilly. In this battle

G

Kearney and Stevens, two of our very best generals, met their fate; many a brave fellow was killed or wounded, but the victory was ours, and the enemy's attack was repulsed with great slaughter.

It was quite dark before we reached our position, and here upon ground which had become a marsh, and in the midst of this fierce storm, our poor boys were compelled to bivouac. Pickets were at once thrown out, and he who desires a true conception of the hardships of a soldier's life should have waded to the front with these outlying sentinels, and stood with them under the rain, watching for some indications of an approaching enemy. Nor was the main bivouac much better; no fires were lighted, lest they should attract the attention of the foe; hard bread and water constituted the evening meal; boughs were piled up for beds; India-rubber blankets warded off a portion of the deluge, and so somehow the saturated troops caught a little sleep.

We of the staff were more fortunate. Close to our line was a little hovel, with one side all fireplace, and tenanted by a couple who were glad to lease the lower room to us for the night. It took half an hour for the general and his aids to make the proper dispositions of his regiments, but when all had assembled before the fire the steam of drying garments ascended to the rafters and overhung us like a cloud. Beneath this canopy, on half-baked lumps of dough and the ever-present Virginia bacon, with coffee and sugar from our own haversacks, we feasted, and made soon after of the floor our common couch. Our orders were to be ready to jump at a moment's notice, as it was a pleasant feature of these experiences that no one knew when or where the enemy might attack, so that even the removal of boots was dispensed with; but, as I had already absorbed much of the water with which my own had been filled, that was a matter of little consequence. With many a thought of the poor soldiers outside, and sandwiched between two good fellows, I passed a very comfortable night.

Tuesday, September 2d. A lovely morning after the storm, and the men were now allowed to light fires and cook their breakfasts, so that when orders were given to fall in they seemed to have forgotten last night's discomforts. At 8 A.M. we marched back through Fairfax Court-house toward Centreville. The most exaggerated rumors as to last night's battle and as to the intentions of the enemy met us on every hand, and another battle was generally anticipated. We rejoined our division some two miles beyond the Court-house, and the brigade was again drawn up in line of battle, only to remain for a few hours, for early in the afternoon the division was ordered to march back toward Washington, through Fairfax Court-house and Falls Church village, a distance of about ten miles. We reached Upton's Hill about sunset, where our men bivouacked on the hill-side, while we spread our blankets on the floor of a house near by. And so ended Pope's retreat and our first campaign in Virginia.

CHAPTER XV.

INSIDE THE DEFENSES OF WASHINGTON.

WEDNESDAY, *September 3d.* And now the armies of Virginia and of the Potomac were united within the defenses of Washington, under the command of General M'Clellan. Here we remained four days, awaiting the movements of the victorious enemy. That he would follow up his advantage no one doubted. Many believed that another great battle was to be fought in front of Washington; a feint or two was indeed made in the direction of Chain Bridge, but all doubt was soon removed by the intelligence that he had crossed the Potomac into Maryland.

Of these four days of quiet on Upton's Hill I have little to chronicle. After our fatigue and excitement, this rest medicined and strengthened us, until gradually the depressing effect of our late defeat wore away, and once more hope rose into the ascendant. To me it was a great privilege, when our wagons came up from Alexandria, to get once more into my own tent; to lie down in my own camp-bed with the feeling that an uninterrupted night's sleep was before me; to have my own den, whither I could retire and be alone. No less pleasant was it, after having been so long cut off from communication with the North, to come into epistolary and journalistic connection; for batches of letters and files of newspapers now reached us, and we had abundant time to read and to reflect upon our late experience.

In calmly reviewing the results of the late campaign, I confess that, though there was much to regret, there seemed little of which to be ashamed. The government had proposed to the Army of Virginia one specific object, viz., by a strong demonstration, threatening Richmond from the right, to extricate the Army of the Potomac from its dangerous position on the Peninsula. This object it fully accomplished, and M'Clellan was thus enabled to withdraw his forces without losing a man. Pursued by the whole rebel army, and compelled to fall back by disparity in numbers, it contested every point, giving ample time for the Army of the Potomac to come up, join forces, and overthrow the enemy. And there seems to be no good reason why this union was not accomplished; why our campaign did not culminate in a crowning and decisive victory. Before the impartial tribunal of the future, in the days when all personal animosity has subsided; when the investigations of congressional committees, courts-martial, and courts of inquiry have crystallized into history, I feel sure that the verdict of guilty of neglect of duty will not be entered up against the Army of Virginia. Half-fed for days, often exhausted by fighting, long marching, and want of sleep, I have yet to learn that they were found wanting in courage and patience in the hour of trial.

So much in justice to the Army of Virginia, and to the gallant divisions of the old Army of the Potomac, who so bravely supported and aided it during its last experiences. And if there be any generals of that old Army of the Potomac of whom this can not with truth be asserted, this is not the time or the place for accusing them, nor am I qualified to sit as judge. But if there be in all this land men with souls so mean that in this crisis of their country's destiny they could fail to throw their whole mind, body, and spirit into our last battle, could keep back their men lest haply they might reach the field in time to change the issue of the day, or obey their orders so tardily as utterly to foil the plans of the commanding general, then may God help them in that hour when they shall see in vision the accursed treason of their act, and its fearful consequences to the country and the world. Then shall the graves of the victims of *their* treachery send forth each its bloody witness, while all the tears and all the agony of the widows and orphans, who owe their grief to them, shall testify against them. The man who stabs his friend when unarmed and trusting him, we call a murderer, and punish him accordingly; but how insignificant his guilt compared to theirs who, intrusted by their country with high commands, in an hour like this could prostitute their patriotism to personal jealousy, forfeit their official oaths, and forswear themselves before high heaven at the shrine of political intrigue or personal ambition—who could wickedly permit their countrymen and brothers to stand the odds of our last bloody field unaided and alone. For the honor of our common human nature, I pray that this charge may not be true.

In reading the history of the struggle of the Greeks for independence, I remember to have been impressed with the thought that a people whose generals and political leaders could so basely permit personal jealousies, low ambitions, or political aspirations to interfere with their official duties, and thus defraud their country of their best services, was really unworthy of freedom—could not, in the nature of things, expect to attain it. How often, in these sad, sad days, as I sought to pierce the heavy clouds and cast the horoscope of my country's destiny, did it seem to me that we were in danger of shipwrecking our freedom on the same rock. But enough on this unpleasant theme.

I seldom mounted my horse during this quiet interval between two campaigns, passing most of my time in my tent in bringing up my arrears of business, of news, and of correspondence. The wardrobes and weapons of our men were thoroughly renovated; fresh arrivals of convalescents from the hospitals and of stragglers from their wanderings swelled their ranks; abundance of food strengthened them; abundance of sleep rested them; all was made ready for the expected move. Our major was not to accompany us, returning to his regiment, to the great regret of his old companions, who admired him for his skill and courage as a soldier, and loved him for his many excellencies of head and heart as a man.

At 6 P.M. on Saturday, September 6th, our division was ordered to march through Washington into Maryland. We left Upton Hill with little regret, and with the hope that a new and brighter experience was before us. As usual, we found the road blocked up by other troops preceding us, for the whole army was now in motion, so that, after proceeding a mile or two, the men were halted at the roadside, stacked arms, and rested. It was evident that it would be hours before our brigade could have a clear road, and, having business to transact in Washington for the command,

I obtained permission to ride on at once. At 10 P.M., with a subordinate, I was on the road. The moon was near its full. We found the road crowded with troops, wagons, and artillery, all pushing toward the Chain Bridge; but by keeping well into the fields we made good time, and before midnight crossed the river into Georgetown. Soon after we met large bodies of troops—ten thousand at least—moving into Maryland, chiefly new regiments, whose bright uniforms, fine bands, and full ranks were in striking contrast with our own thinned battalions. So through the moonlit streets we rode on, until, our horses comfortably stabled, we secured two cots in the parlor of a crowded hotel, and were soon wooing the drowsy god, thankful that our retreat was ended, and that tomorrow we turned over a new leaf. Against the same army, whose strength had been at least partially broken as it dashed itself against the Army of Virginia, was now moving the new Army of the Potomac, composed of the united strength of the two Union armies, increased by large re-enforcements of fresh troops. The result could hardly be doubted.

CHAPTER XVI.

WASHINGTON TO FREDERICK CITY.

SUNDAY, *September 27th.* I relinquished my cot in the corner of the hotel parlor with a good deal of reluctance this pleasant morning. But, while we had been sleeping, our division had been marching through the silent streets, and we were anxious to accomplish our business and follow on as speedily as possible. Early as was the hour, we found Pennsylvania Avenue sprinkled with uniforms and gay with staff officers and orderlies, and learned that, two or three hours before, our division had moved out Seventh Street into Maryland. An hour or two put our matters in train, and then we hitched our horses at the Kirkwood for an early breakfast.

I wonder if my sable friend, who placed before me that morning the unaccustomed napkin, milk, and butter, with the hot coffee, boiled eggs, and other accompaniments of a judicious breakfast, was aware to what a novel banquet he gave me welcome. And yet a red-faced monster sitting next me, unctuous and plethoric with good living, his plate fronted and flanked by rows of delicacies two lines deep, actually growled and snarled over a meal before which I sat speechless, my heart and mouth too full for utterance. Never before or since have I taken a meal at the Kirkwood, nor do I dare again to attempt it, lest a second trial should rob me of a pleasing delusion. For this must ever be to me the ideal breakfast of my life. It had been my fate to banquet on Chinese indescribables in Canton; to sit cross-legged over my coffee with the Oriental in Damascus; to see myself reflected in the mirrored walls of the best restaurant in Paris; but there was a gastronomic fascination about this meal which eclipses them all, and I left the Kirkwood full of kindly feelings for my host and for all mankind.

As we rode hither and thither during the morning, the sight of the well-dressed men, women, and children in the streets seemed strange to me. I felt very much as if I had just returned from a visit to another planet; and when the church-bells rang out, an indescribable longing came over me for an hour or two of the subdued light and soothing contemplation of cathedral aisles. But the putting down of this rebellion was now my religion, and, as we have no Sundays in the army, no conscientious scruple disturbed me; so I flung off such feelings and all the home thoughts which these Sunday street-scenes awakened, hurried through with my duties, and, about one o'clock, was riding with my companion up Seventh Street toward the front.

We had proceeded only a mile or two before the turnpike became one crowded military mass; troops, artillery, and wagon-trains were moving in double lines, and our progress through was necessarily slow. The dust rose in great clouds; we breathed, tasted, smelt it; our clothes put on the hue of the butternut; but the men appeared to be in good humor, and their faces, muddy with dust and perspiration — yellow masks through which gleamed their eyes — rippled into frequent grins. For a demoralized army, as some have styled them, they certainly marched well, and with but little straggling. At the gateways of some of the elegant country-seats stood their occupants tendering cups of water to the men, and, what was far more refreshing, the tokens of patriotic sympathy. Probably these ladies, who stood waving flags, or handkerchiefs—woman's usual banner in grief or in joy—little knew how gratifying all this was to men who had for months hardly seen a woman's face beaming with pleasant welcome. Entirely unaccustomed to such a reception, if my cap was off once it was off thirty times during to-day's march; and there was not the roughest soldier in the ranks who did not march better, ay, and fight better, for these and other sympathetic demonstrations in Maryland. Many a closed residence still frowned upon us, but it was also evident that we were moving among friends. And here let me say, after good opportunities of judging, that though there was far too much of private marauding in this Maryland campaign, still it was evident that the troops recognized the distinction between friends and foes, and generally permitted the sheepfolds and poultry-yards to remain unscathed.

We were passing through a country far different in appearance from our old campaigning ground in Virginia—a smiling country, as yet scarcely conscious of the presence of destroying war. About ten miles out we reached the camps of the advance. Grove and hill-side were full of tents, and a thorough reconnoissance was necessary before we discovered our brigade, snugly bivouacked on a gentle swale, skirted by a pretty brook and near a shady grove. The big office-tent alone was pitched, and here, soon after my arrival, dinner was served, whereat I excited the envy of my companions by the vivid description of the late breakfast. We also made of this tent a common chamber; our cots were brought in, and we sank to rest with the sun.

The next morning all our tents were pitched in regular order, fronting upon a vacant quadrangle, beyond which, laid out in streets, with their officers' tents in rear, stretched the shelter-tents of the troops. I confess that my first feeling on entering my own mansion was one not of gratitude, but inquiry, the mental question being how many hours this was to last. There's a pleasant sense of uncertainty in regard to such matters as food and lodging in the army. To-day I heard for the first time that Hooker commanded our corps, and Burnside our wing of the army, two fighting generals. It was evident that we should have something to do. Our adjutant general, who had left us at Upton Hill in order to enjoy a few days' illness in Washington, came in upon us to-night, still looking thin and pale, but as glad to join us as we were to welcome him.

Tuesday, Sept. 9th. Our division was ordered to march at noon, but I was sent back to Washington with a supply train, and by eleven o'clock that night had started with it to return to the front, moved out some five miles, and parked the wagons to rest the animals. The whole country was full of soldiers, so that I was not much surprised, on knocking at the door of the wayside inn, to be informed by a person in a night-cap that not only was every bed occupied, but also the parlor and kitchen floors. The moonlight had already disclosed to me little groups of men bivouacking in the piazza, so I concluded that the hotel was full. But at a farm-house near by, in a venerable four-poster, I secured my quantum of sleep, and, after a substantial breakfast next morning, again took the road.

After a while I left the train in charge of my sergeant, and pushed on ahead, to reach, about 2 P.M., our division in camp near the town of Unity. Pleasant exceedingly looked the tented city, nestling with its ten thousand citizens in a picturesque vale hemmed in by woods. I found our general and staff engaged on very important duty at our mess-table, which was sheltered from the sun by a fly. Another hungry man soon joined the party, to receive from the surgeon a ration of roast beef which had been roasted in a frying-pan, and of other delicacies secured by our caterer in our late passage through Washington. A pleasant mess-table that always was, around which glowed a friendly feeling, deepened in fervor by our common experiences, and binding us to each other and to our honored chief by associations never to be forgotten. What though the fare was sometimes meagre, so was not the spirit of good fellowship which flashed forth in many a happy jest and pleasing anecdote.

We were still sitting at the mess-table when the clatter of hoofs attracted our attention, and a dispatch was soon brought to the general. Before Captain H. broke the envelope we knew instinctively that it was "marching orders." Having already passed most of the day in the saddle, I was rather disappointed; and as the starting of a division with its long trains requires time, I flung myself upon a truss of hay and rested more than an hour. At last all had left the field except myself and a disappointed sutler, who had set out his tempting wares just in time to see his customers march away. The natives were already coming in to seize upon the cracker-boxes, barrels, and other débris of a broken camp; the last wagon was moving out of sight; so I at length departed, and in fifteen minutes was riding with the general at the head of the brigade.

This day we marched perhaps three miles, to accomplish which the division was kept in the road four hours, and finally had to bivouac after nightfall in the midst of a cold rain. Not a very profitable day's work, and rather a comfortless prospect at its close. But by 9 P.M. we had our tents up; the men were making ready for sleep, having finished their supper. All about us were the bivouacs of a large army, reddening the misty evening air with an unusual glow. Still rumbled the long wagon-trains over the road; but in another hour all was still, and sleep settled down upon the Army of the Potomac.

Wednesday, Sept. 10th. "Wake up, captain; we're ordered to march, and breakfast will soon be ready," was the pleasant greeting flung through my tent-folds early this morning by my friend the adjutant general. So I took ten minutes to reflect about it, then rose from my six feet by two of camp-bed, shaved by a mirror at least four inches in diameter, washed in a tin basin well battered by transportation, and carried off my camp-stool just in time to join our staff at the open-air mess-table. While we were eating our tents were struck and packed, and before we had concluded the leading brigade of the division was moving up the road. As we were now drawing near to the enemy, the wagon-trains were consolidated and moved in the rear.

Our march to-day was not a long one, but very tedious on account of the frequent halts caused by the movement of so large an army in front of us over the same road. Through a pleasant farming country, undulating and picturesque, under rather a hot sun, our boys marched and halted, and reached, about 6 P.M., our camping-ground near Lisbon. Here our artillery and infantry were drawn up to cover the Lisbon cross-roads, and our camps were arranged after the usual form of a line of battle, fronting the presumed locality of the rebel army. It seemed as if our baggage trains would never come up; miles of wagons rolled by, but none turned off into our particular field. Near a pretty grove with running water we had selected a spot for head-quarters; our horses were tethered, and we were anxious to have our tents pitched before dark, and something made ready to strengthen the inner man. It was getting dark before the voice of our indefatigable acting quarter-master was heard urging on his drivers, and in an hour we were tented, fed, and comfortable.

Our next day's march commenced at 9 A.M., and offered no new experience. Part of the day I rode with our division staff, and dined at the wayside inn of a good Union woman at New Market, whose sentiments were better than her dinner; two or three general officers partook of her hospitality, and what was wanting in luxury was made up in pleasant conversation and lively humor. Speaking of humor, one hears sometimes a good deal of genuine fun as he rides slowly along with the troops. A party of herdsmen amused me to-day as they manœuvred their battalion of cattle, every order being given in true military style, as if the herd were a small army. On being asked "What division is that," the sergeant in charge at once replied, "Hook-er's division, sir;" and, chuckling at his own conceit, he followed his four-legged infantry. As our troops marched through New Market, a good deal of enthusiasm bubbled up to welcome them, and at 7 P.M. we went into camp just beyond the little town.

So, slowly feeling our way, we moved against the invading enemy. Fine marching weather; a land flowing with milk and honey; a general tone of Union sentiment among the people, who, being little cursed by slavery, had not lost their loyalty; scenery not grand, but picturesque, all contributed to make this march delightful. Of course there were frequent rumors of expected battle, but these had now lost their power to excite our interest. I bear in my memory but few incidents worthy of record during these days; the men were in fine spirits, and now we began to meet little squads of rebel prisoners taken in the cavalry skirmishing ahead of us.

One picture framed itself in my recollection during our next day's (Saturday) march. Our horses had fared very poorly of late at the hands of our quartermaster, and I was standing near a barn wherein my half-starved mare was enjoying a feed of oats. Looking behind, I could see the long column of troops winding around the summit of the mountain over which I had just passed, their bayonets glistening in the sun, and the mighty coil of armed men stretching down the mountain sides, past the spot where I was standing, until it was lost to view by the winding of the road far in front. It was the best view of an army on its march I had ever enjoyed.

In the upper part of the barn were some twenty rebels; some sick, others wounded in the late cavalry skirmishes, and left by the Southern army as it fell back before our advance. A guard or two attended to their comfort, but they all looked wan, and pale, and thin from the many privations and fatigues to which they had been exposed. The good farmer told me that most of the large body of rebels who had passed his house were half-clothed and dilapidated; but I knew how well these men fought, and his statement elicited not my contempt, but rather my respect for men who, under such difficulties, and want of food and clothing, have stood up bravely and persistently in a bad cause. These men must be sincere. As a friend once said, "though not inspired of God, they certainly are possessed with the devil," and act bravely the part which their master commands them to play.

And this warlike South is fearfully in earnest. The leaders in this rebellion know full well that the North never desired to interfere with a single constitutional right, disturb a single domestic institution—have, indeed, always been too ready to listen to every Southern appeal; but the large mass of the people are ignorant; the number of those who can not even read or write is astonishingly large, and the newspapers, the only teachers of the people, have been controlled by ambitious and unprincipled men, determined to rule or to ruin. What wonder that the Southern ear has been poisoned by the whisperings of the serpent?

what wonder that to most of these poor fellows, now suffering every thing, their sacrifice seems a pious offering upon the altar of their country and their God? We must respect such a sentiment, however much we may wonder at it, and my little word of pity was not held back from these poor wounded rebels in the wayside barn. Blinded by ignorance and prejudice, fed on falsehood until they have learned to look upon the peaceful North as ambitious to subjugate and enslave them, they are the victims of an institution which pampers a few lazy thousands, while it condemns the millions to a lean and beggared existence. Gladly would I welcome them back to the manifold blessings of that government whose ten thousand benefits they will only begin to discover should this wicked rebellion succeed.

I have learned from this war to give to the South credit for one quality I did not suppose it possessed—that of endurance. Five years of my boyhood I passed in a Southern school, and have mingled with Southerners at college and elsewhere, and had come to think of them as men of show rather than substance—of momentary bravado rather than true courage—of flash and pinchbeck assumption rather than real chivalry. But I have found out that they are patient and can endure; and, despite the many exceptional instances of gross brutality and neglect of the courtesies of honorable warfare, it seems to me that they have, in general, borne themselves in this war chivalrously as well as bravely. I do not pretend that the Southerner illustrates the highest type of the gentleman. He is rather the gentleman of the Middle Ages—ignorant, overbearing, insolent, but with a good deal of the leaven of a true chivalry; not a Bayard certainly, but more after the style of a Black Douglas or a Harry Hotspur.

And I am inclined to think that we of the North are to be better understood hereafter by the South. They had learned to appraise the Northern valor and principle by the standard of our political subserviency. They went into this rebellion with no idea that the North would dare to resist in arms—the poor, cowardly, truckling North, which they had frightened into compromises, and then frightened into breaking them, and which had so long trembled in the national Congress beneath the Southern rod. This mistake is gradually being corrected also. The hands accustomed so long to peaceful labor only are learning the trick of war; the muscles trained only at the plow or in the workshop are becoming skilled in the use of the musket and the sword; and it is evident that the North has not only the courage, but also the skill needed to put down this rebellion. The men who have stood against each other in the battles of this war can never fling upon each other the charge of cowardice—must acknowledge and respect in each other their common manhood; so much, at least, is gained.

Leaving the wounded rebels, I paused a while in the shade to see our columns move by. From St. Paul to Passamaquoddy, every state had its representatives—next, perhaps, to a regiment of farmers from Wisconsin moved a regiment of lumbermen from Maine; the New York fireman found himself in the same brigade with the shoemaker from Lynn or the fisherman from Marblehead—the whole mass fused into a common brotherhood by a common patriotism. Will not this war do much to unify these separate states, consolidate and weld into one these distant communities? Fortunately for us at the North, our education is expansive, enlarges the mind to the grasp of national ideas, and is thus free from the belittling state jealousies of the South. Still it is manifest to the most casual observer that we have far too little affectionate loyalty in America. Stand with a party of Englishmen when "God save the Queen" thrills through the air; talk with a Frenchman of his country and her destiny; pause in your pilgrimage through the Alps to inquire of your guide as to William Tell, and you will see how near and personal is to each this affectionate feeling of nationality. Are we not also to have a more enthusiastic love for the old flag, a deeper personal affection for our whole country, now that we have followed the one into the jaws of death, and have made such sacrifices for the other?

But I must hurry on, or this day's march will never be ended. It was interrupted by few tedious halts, so that by 2 P.M. our division went into camp on the Monocacy River, a lovely spot now crowded with troops. From the hill we could see the pretty city of Frederick hiding away in the foliage, all around us were tents and artillery, and soon came floating up strains of pleasant music from the camps of the new regiments. Our own head-quarters were fixed at a farm-house, and the staff tents were pitched in the yard. Our caterer gave us timely notice that something remarkable in the way of dinner might be expected, and postponed it until, all our duties being accomplished, we could really enjoy it. My post-prandial hours until midnight were devoted to writing, and before I sought repose all was still through the immense camps about me.

CHAPTER XVII.

BATTLE OF SOUTH MOUNTAIN.

SUNDAY, *September* 14*th*. A little after daybreak this morning an orderly came to my tent to announce that we were to march at once; but, while tents were packing, we had plenty of time for breakfast. Little did we think, as we sat around that cheerful mess-table, through what a scene of danger, excitement, and death we were to pass before sunset. It was a fine marching day, every one was in good spirits, while of the exact whereabouts of the enemy we might speculate or conjecture, but did not know. We had heard that Burnside had taken possession of Frederick a day or two before, the little squads of rebel prisoners occasionally passing us indicated the proximity of our foe, but how, when, and where he was to give us the meeting was quite concealed from us.

Our march through the pretty city of Frederick was a perfect ovation — one continuous waving of flags, fluttering of handkerchiefs, tossing of bouquets, and cheering by our men, who grew fairly hoarse before they had passed through its main street. Men, women, and little children were equally enthusiastic. I understood, however, that the wealthy slaveholders did not in general join in this loyal demonstration, nor could it be expected. Without dwelling long on this subject, and looking at it from the practical point of view of a "down-East Yankee," I calculate that the net value to us in the South Mountain battle of this new inspiration which came in upon us from the eyes and fingers of our fair friends in Frederick was equal to about one thousand fresh men.

Once clear from this pleasant ripple of patriotic sympathy, we made a rapid march over the wide national road, through the little village of Middletown and the lovely valley beyond, with the wagon-trains in our rear, and nothing to encumber our rapid advance. And there was sufficient reason for haste, for not long after we left Frederick the booming of distant cannon announced that our advance had found the enemy, and that a battle was impending.

One of our staff jests at such a time as this was based upon the old story of the sportsman who, gun in hand, had toiled for two days over brake and fern, through forest and mountain path, in the eager pursuit of a bear. Near the close of the day the footprints of a gentleman of the ursine species were distinctly visible, and pretty soon a growl from a rocky ledge near by attested his presence. Halting, scratching his head, our hero turned to his brother sportsman: "Look here, Bill, these tracks are getting a little too fresh. I believe I don't want any bear after all, so I'll go back home."

I know that there was one man in that column, and presume that there were very many who, as we gazed up at that steep mountain side, and thought of our wives and little ones at home, sympathized a good deal with the honest bear-hunter. The eager enthusiasm of the military novice had been toned down by experience; the exciting edge of novelty had worn off; the terrible scenes we had witnessed had left an ineffaceable impression; nothing but a sense of duty, the innate pride of man, and the hope that through this bloody lane might come peace and safety to the country, kept us to our duty. Marshal Lannes once said, "None but a coward will boast that he never was afraid," and I have met thus far with but one man, modest as he was courageous, who, in our review of two battles wherein he had displayed great bravery, said to me that he could not remember even a momentary feeling of fear. I feel sure that he spoke the truth, but his case was exceptional.

I do not doubt that many men have a constitutional fondness for fighting; that many others, with little to live for, standing, perhaps, on the narrow edge of a path of desperate despair, are wholly careless and reckless of consequences; that in some breasts an overpowering ambition quenches all thought of danger; while others — the few and chosen ones — are really able to offer up their lives, and, harder still, to say good-by to their beloved, as a free and unreserved sacrifice at the shrine of their country. I suppose we all *ought* to feel thus, and, indeed, there are hours in a man's experience when he does feel thus. But human nature seldom escapes the lower attractions of this dear old earth of ours, and probably very few of us were burning with eagerness to charge up those heights before us, upon whose well-wooded sides occasional smoke-wreaths and the roar of cannon attest the presence of the enemy.

And yet there is no sign of shrinking, nor will there be, with, of course, some exceptions, when the hour for storming that height shall come. The division pushes on with unusual rapidity; there is less straggling than usual. The column is soon marching through the excited streets of Middletown, over the rolling paradise beyond, to be halted about noon, after a march of twelve miles, on Catoctin Creek, near the foot of South Mountain. Here I left the command, and rode on ahead to get a nearer view of the situation. On either side of the wood, batteries of artillery and ammunition trains were snugly sheltered in the ravines, for the storming of these heights was work mainly for infantry alone. Some of our batteries were, however, engaging the enemy in the woods on the left of the road, high up the pass, and two or three were in position on the lower elevations, trying occasionally the effect of a shot at long range. Bodies of troops were already massed in the fields just at the base of the mountain, especially on the left of the road.

I had not been sitting long on my horse, trying to get some idea of the projected movement, before I saw General Burnside and his staff taking a look at the heights from a point near by. He was in command of General Reno's corps, already partially engaged, and of our own corps, under command of General Hooker, not yet brought into action. Shortly after General M'Clellan joined him, and I awaited with much interest the result of their deliberations.

The broad turnpike winding up and through the pass looked safe and quiet. I saw no rebel battalions threatening our passage, no cannon crouching open-mouthed to warn us off from the narrow entrance. Peaceful, and calm, and beautiful the hills on either side the pass slept in the summer sunshine. Gently over the face of their dense forests swept the shadows of flitting clouds. But what mean those quick-rushing smoke-puffs just rising above the trees, and the heavy boom which follows them? Look quickly off to the left, and you will see corresponding smoke-puffs, and hear almost instantaneous response to the rebel batteries from our own artillery, now, as they tell us, seeking, with the aid of infantry, to dislodge the foe that stops the way. Listen a while, and you will hear the rattle of musketry. Ah! those deceitful forests! they are full of an unseen foe; and now, perhaps, invisibly to us, the opposing cohorts stealthily advance or rush madly against each other. The smooth white turnpike begins to look a little dangerous to us; it was best to wait a while before attempting its passage.

Hoping to get a better view, I now rode on a little farther to a house on the roadside, near which a branch road comes down from the mountain on the left of the pass. It seemed quite untenanted, but I was told that its occupants had taken refuge in the cellar, an occasional shell having strayed this way during the day's fighting. Here I saw some of our wounded brought down on hand-litters, and resting a while under the protecting lee of this brick tenement, and from them got some vague idea of the struggle going on above. But as to the main details of this engagement on the left of the pass, the capture and recapture of one of our batteries, the gallant fighting of General Reno's corps, and the death of their honored chief, I remained in ignorance until the morrow.

But it was time to return to my brigade, for I was disappointed in my expectation that the division would advance in this direction. Our 4th brigade was drawn up behind a battery a little way down the road—a brigade which, later in the day, was to illustrate by the most determined bravery the gallantry of the men of Wisconsin and Indiana. Other movements had taken place during my brief absence; large bodies of troops were now drawn up in line of battle, and still from the heights above broke forth at intervals the booming of the opposing batteries. It was evident that the attempt to cross the mountain was to be made before nightfall.

To General Hooker had been assigned the storming of the hill on the right of the pass, and I now learned that the three remaining brigades of our division had moved off on a road skirting its base at right angles to the turnpike. At various points on this road I met bodies of our troops moving off to the right, and, looking up, I could see the long line of our skirmishers already half way up the mountain. With what almost breathless anxiety is their progress watched by thousands of anxious and eager men, as slowly, slowly, now halting as if to listen, now crouching a while on the ground, with muskets ever ready for instant service, they push up toward the woods, every tree in which may conceal a rebel sharpshooter. These men belong to our second, General Patrick's, brigade; our own brigade must be very near them. A few hundred feet in their rear moves the long dark line of the reserves, upon whom the skirmishers are to rally when they have unmasked the enemy.

But I am now becoming anxious to find the brigade, and can not pause to gaze longer on this exciting picture, and a turn in the road soon shuts it out from view, and brings me to the spot where General Hooker, with his staff, is directing the movements of the troops destined to carry the heights. I learn that my own brigade is already part way up, and I am soon passing the reserves, who have not commenced the ascent, reach the brigade, and climb with the general through the corn and wheat fields which clothe the lower half of South Mountain.

The brigade is still moving in column when I join it, but shortly after we form in line of battle, and now begin to move quickly up the steep acclivity. The rattle of musketry in front of us is now growing louder and louder; it is evident that the skirmishers have unmasked the enemy; that the other brigades of our division are engaged; that we are needed at the summit. So steep is now the ascent, that several of the staff dismount and lead up their horses, that they may be fresh for the work ahead. Passing through the last cornfield, we reach an elevated plateau very near the summit, fronted and flanked by woods, through which the rebel bullets are already flying over our heads. The twilight hour has come; the air is bland and delicious; and, while the men halt for breath, we turn and look back at the valley through which we have been marching to-day. Frederick City is not visible, as a turn in the valley interposes a hilly elbow; but Middletown lies below us, while stretching off toward the north and east is a lovely swale, buttressed by hilly ranges, smiling with orchards, fields of ripening grain, and cheerful farm-houses—truly a valley of content and beauty. There is little of the sublime about this view, but it is very soothing, and offers so strong a contrast to our present fearful business as to daguerreotype itself upon my imagination forever. Ah! how the thought of the Sunday evening calm now brooding over certain familiar streets and home-circles adds one feature more to this impressive contrast!

"What a magnificent view!" exclaims the general, as he turns in his saddle to inspect his brigade, and catches one glance of the beautiful panorama. A moment's breathing period, and he orders the brigade to march by the flank into the woods on our right, where, facing to the front, we move up at double-quick to meet the enemy. The little twigs above us, splintered and cut by the bullets, are cracking and falling about our heads; here and there a coward or two comes skulking out from the fight, a wounded brave limps past or lies half exhausted at the foot of a protecting tree. Yonder, behind a hickory, crouches one in the uniform of an officer—shame on his cowardice and evil example; on the instant his name and regiment are demanded, and he is driven back to his duty, perhaps, so singular is human nature, to fight bravely through the rest of the battle.

As we press on, our brigade line wavers a little, the flanks pressing ahead of the centre, or one flank outmarching the other a little, yet preserving, on the whole, a good, strong, steady line of attack. The air is now full of shrieking lead, and we hear just ahead of us the cheers and yells of the opposing troops, the never-ceasing rattle of musketry, and all the awful din of battle. Out of this carnival of noise and fire rushes the adjutant of the 1st brigade, a noble specimen of American chivalry, exclaiming, "Our brigade can not sustain itself much longer, as we are nearly out of ammunition. For God's sake, to the front!" At the word the brigade is moved up even more rapidly, restrained, however, by the field and staff officers still riding in front: "Steady, boys, steady!" is the word all along the line. Another minute, and the edge of the woods is gained, and there at the fence which skirts it is Hatch's brigade, standing, falling, desperately fighting at this bloodily-contested boundary. Cheer upon cheer from our men goes up to heaven, and now, in admirable order, they rush into their places, Hatch's brigade falling back to rest a while after their fierce encounter.

Beyond this fence is an open space of about a hundred feet in depth between the fence and a cornfield, and in this space a strong force of the enemy, partially protected by rocky ledges and inequalities of surface, forming natural rifle-pits, is pressing heavily upon our position, charging gallantly two or three times, to be as gallantly repulsed before they reach the fence, and sweeping it meanwhile with sheets of fire. Conscious of the weakness of our own line, with no reserves near us, unable to form any idea of the force opposed to us, the only thing to be done is to hold this fence at all hazards, lest the enemy, breaking through at this point, shall flank and put to rout the troops on both sides of us. It remains for the staff to watch closely the line, cheer and encourage the men, look out for a moment of panic, and so keep all to their duty.

And hold it they do, inflexibly. For half an hour against this barrier of Northern patriotism dashes wave after wave of Southern treason, to be again and again hurled back broken and discomfited. Individual instances of valor are not wanting: the color-bearer of the 76th New York rashly leaps out to the front, waves his flag, exclaiming, "There, boys, come up to that!" and falls in the instant, shot through the head. But why attempt to designate, where all did so well? At intervals a lull, a mere pattering of musketry, and then the rebel storm bursts forth afresh, and before it some of our men go down, or slowly fall back, wounded and bleeding, to the rear. The twilight gloom is descending, throwing the rebel den into shadow; the darkness adds new horror to the scene; and suddenly a portion of one of our regiments begins to crowd up together, the men pressing against each other, and firing into the air in a sort of frenzy. Terribly contagious is a panic like this. Unless it be instantly quelled, the men will be shooting each other, or rushing to the rear in sudden and disastrous rout. Somehow and swiftly, military authority must assert itself. The first thing to do is to order them to cease firing. To shout forth such an order at such a time would be like attempting to drown the thunder of Niagara. It must be driven in, as it were, individually, mouth to ear, and almost with the point of the sword. Somehow the effort succeeds; discipline asserts itself, the rank is re-formed, our brave boys are themselves again.

Before the fight is half over an aid dashes up with the news that the gallant General Hatch, the division commander, is severely wounded, and our general is thus in command of the division. Our only colonel has already been crippled by a wound, a lieutenant colonel takes command of our brigade, while a captain finds himself at the head of a regiment. Our 1st brigade is in the rear, having exhausted its ammunition; our 3d brigade holds the line on our right;

our 4th is on duty perhaps a mile away on our left. Our general, therefore, remains with his old brigade as the most central position.

And now there are intervals of comparative calm, and we begin to congratulate ourselves that the baffled enemy has departed. But the contest is not yet over; for suddenly out of the darkness in front of us leaps another volley, wounding hardly a man, but so near as to seem in our very faces. Along the files of perhaps a single company, gradually growing louder and louder, rises a low murmur, not like an exultant cheer, but rather a cry, excited and panic-stricken, and suddenly half a dozen or more start off for the rear. One minute more, and probably the whole regiment will be on the wing. To meet them on the instant with the threat to run the first man through who moves a foot farther to the rear seems the best thing to do, and it proves entirely successful. A staff officer exclaims, "Why, boys, what are you running for? we've beaten the enemy. Three cheers for victory." A wild, irregular cheer bursts forth upon the evening air, and every man of them once more takes his position at the fence.

It is indeed true that we have beaten the enemy; these impetuous attacks are only his last flurries; he is, though we do not know it, and can not discover it in the darkness, at his last gasp. It is now so dark that our men can only aim at the flashing of the rebel muskets, and these rebel muskets have ceased firing. The general now orders our brigade also to cease firing; an advance into the unknown localities in front would be sheer madness, and so our men stand silently and grimly at the fence, while for several min., the as it seemed, hardly a single report breaks the stillness of the night. Just as we are saying to each other, with thankful hearts, "This fight is over," the enemy, thinking perhaps that we may have fallen back or are unprepared for him, charges desperately up toward the fence, delivers a volley, too high as usual, which shrieks through the air, followed by a continuous fire for a minute or two minutes perhaps, though it seemed very much more. It is no use; they hurl themselves against this living barrier in vain, and are soon compelled to fall back before the terrific volleys of our men. To me this is the most impressive incident in the fight; the utter stillness of the night, broken in upon by the cheers and yells of the opposing troops; the rattle of the musketry discharged, and the wailing of the bullets, followed by a stillness deep and intense, as if each party held its breath to listen for the next move of its enemy.

The contest is nearly over; only a few scattering volleys after this, except on the left of our brigade, where a desperate effort is made to turn our left flank, to meet which the 7th Indiana and 76th New York swing a little to the left, and so repulse the attack successfully. Our division is now relieved by the division of General Ricketts, which moves up and takes post at the fence, the officers dressing the ranks as if preparing for a review; it is evident that the position is in safe hands; but our general orders our brigade to lie down on their arms a hundred feet from the fence, as we have still some ammunition left, and a night-attack seems probable. A few more scattering volleys, and at this particular point all is still.

General Patrick's brigade, having done its work nobly, is now resting on our right, while on our left, but near to the turnpike, the brigade of Gibbon is still fighting very desperately. Our own contest appears to be over for the present, but we listen to the unceasing rattle of this musketry on our left with great anxiety. At one moment it seems as if our troops must be falling back, at another the firing sounds farther off, as if they were gradually driving the enemy from the hill. The excitement of our own fight is over; the woods are now so dark that objects ten feet distant are undistinguishable, and the thought of a night-attack upon our exhausted troops inspires me with dread. A prisoner just brought in informs us that the troops in front are chiefly Virginians under command of General Pickett, and that Longstreet himself has been here, striving in every way to encourage the men, calling them his pets, and coaxing and imploring them to their work. Already we had some idea of the success of his efforts, but we were to see it more fearfully evidenced when daylight disclosed the battle-field on the morrow.

Gradually the musketry on our left ceases; silently, but fully prepared, Ricketts's men hold the fence, while our own little brigade rests upon its arms. Our mounted orderlies seem to have had business elsewhere, and we are compelled to stable our horses by tying them to the trees. The wounded are now cared for, our hospitals being fixed about half way down the hill; and after a while, the necessary dispositions being completed, we lie down, wrapped in our cloaks, and seek repose. Far from feeling easy in my own mind, apprehensive of the result of a night-attack should the enemy attempt it, uncertain as to the issue of the struggle on our left, I lie down as one rests by the wayside, and not as anticipating a good night's sleep. But, despite all this uneasiness, despite the excitement of the evening, despite the dead now sleeping, some within ten feet of me, exhausted Nature asserts her claims, the myriad reflections of such an hour hold only momentary sway, and I am soon asleep.

I have spoken of the storm of bullets which swept our ranks to-night; and it may be asked—a question I have asked myself a hundred times—How is it that any escaped alive? This is to me the great wonder, the crowning mystery of war. In this contest, so stubbornly fought, for the possession of Turner's Gap, the loss along our whole line was 328 killed and 1463 wounded, and yet I have sought to give a fair illustration of our own part in the conflict. It is marvelous, this waste of ammunition in battle. It takes, so it is stated, nearly a man's weight in lead to kill him. The shrieking volleys, seemingly about your ears, fly above you; the men, excited, and anxious to fire as frequently as possible, discharge their muskets with no pretense at aim, thankful only that they are permitted to do so alive. I have more to say on this subject.

If I were asked what was the most awful sensation during this battle-hour, I should speak of the quiver of my nerves when once or twice my mare stumbled in the darkness over the body of some dead brave. It is not true, as a general thing, that a wounded man groans loudly or utters any cries upon the battle-field; he either limps off or is carried to the rear, or he lies down with his hurt quiet and still. Think for a moment of thus treading upon one of these silent wounded, every hair in whose head was sacred to me! This horror, at least, thank God! was spared to me.

CHAPTER XVIII.

FROM SOUTH MOUNTAIN TO ANTIETAM.

MONDAY, *September 15th*. Our sleep last night was rather nominal than real, broken by frequent interruptions, as from time to time reports were brought in to one or the other of the generals lying near; and it was rather shivery also, our cloaks not affording sufficient protection against the chilliness of the air, especially as we had lain down to a dinnerless and supperless sleep. Our little snatches of oblivion served mainly to pass away the hours of darkness, and with the first gray of morning we were up and moving among the men. The first inquiry was, "Where are the enemy?" General Ricketts's troops still held the fence, but in front of it there were no signs of the foe; all was still, and the little interval between us and the cornfield seemed untenanted save where, through the morning mists, we could dimly discern the prostrate forms of the rebel dead.

A soldier or two now ventured out over these rocky ledges. Suddenly from behind a stump a long, lank stripling of perhaps seventeen years, without weapon, and dressed in the usual gray uniform, leaped eagerly forward, exclaiming, "Don't shoot! I'm your prisoner!" When brought before the general, he described, with a childlike simplicity very amusing, his late experiences and sensations. The boy had evidently never before broken loose from the maternal apron-string, and told us, with fearful emphasis, how he had been conscripted, drilled, and finally brought up this mountain to be shot at, winding up somewhat as follows: "I told 'em I was a coward, and couldn't fight, but they drove me up here, where I came near being killed; so I dropped, and crawled behind a stump, and waited there all night." But he didn't know whether the enemy was still in the cornfield or not, so we learned little of any value, though his quaint remarks upon his own cowardice afforded some merriment.

No one had yet explored the cornfield, and a large body of men might easily be concealed there; but half a dozen of our men were now moving among the rebel dead, and I was convinced that it was safe enough to go out also, being thereunto moved by a desire to see some of our late antagonists. So closely had their desperate charges brought them to our line, that only ten paces distant from the fence lay some of the poor fellows—one resting with head on arm, as if asleep; others lying across each other, but most of them looking with calmly-staring eyes upward toward heaven. Among them, as also among our own dead, I was surprised to notice that the features bore usually a placid expression, with little trace of battle excitement or death-agony.

Among the foremost lay an officer, afterward identified as Colonel Strange, of Virginia, evidently killed just at the moment when, every nerve at its highest tension, every courageous impulse at fever heat, he was leading his men in a most desperate charge. Upon his stern, determined face still lingers that look of battle, his right hand still grasps his sword. This man's death was evidently a great loss to the enemy.

A few feet to his left I noticed another officer, and still farther on a young lieutenant, whose very handsome face and placid expression greatly attracted me. As I stood and looked down earnestly, as if, perhaps, I might read in that countenance some fragments of his history, I felt that this was a man who probably illustrated some of the best features of the Southern character — a warm-hearted, generous fellow, whom while living I could have loved. There's a sad gap somewhere caused by this death; perhaps the plain gold ring on his finger might give us the key to his whole life-story. How all feeling of enmity disappears in presence of these white faces, these eyes gazing upward so fixedly in the gray of the morning hour!

The ground was of course strewn with muskets, swords, and military trappings of every description; but I needed no such mementoes to aid my recollections of this battle. Some of our men were, however, picking up these spoils of war, and on returning from the left I saw two or three kneeling and stooping around my lieutenant; hastening up, I was horrified by seeing one wretch trying to force off with his knife the plain gold ring. I have rarely been more indignant, and drove the harpy off from his prey. Shortly afterward a detail was sent out to bring in the body of Colonel Strange, and all other soldiers were ordered back inside the fence.

More than thirty of the rebel dead were lying within fifty feet of the fence; I did not visit the cornfield, but learned that here also the dead were very numerous. On our side the loss was much less, but here, also, our men were busily engaged in collecting the fallen, and ranging them side by side, each regiment or brigade by itself, that their own immediate comrades might lay them to rest with the scant ceremonial of a soldier's burial on the battle-field. No little firing-squad poured forth a farewell volley; no minister read over their graves the beautiful burial-service; no coffin incased their limbs; just as they were, in their uniforms crimsoned with patriotic blood, they were taken closely to the bosom of Earth the mother, and on the very summit of the mountain, in a spot consecrate by their heroic sacrifice, and glorious as the classic ground of victory, they slept well.

In looking back at these and kindred experiences, I sometimes wonder at my own apparent callousness of feeling, and have often asked myself how it was that men—our own staff, for example—whom I know to be tender-hearted and humane, could pass through these scenes so unmoved. I suppose that repetition blunts the edge of feeling, but presume that it is mainly to be attributed to the excitement of the hour, and to the general tone of feeling induced by the unnatural life we have been leading. Things which would have greatly impressed us had now become matters of course, fell in naturally with every-day duty; and I have actually been more moved by the sight of a serious street-accident at home than by all the scenes through which we have passed this morning. The whole sad picture framed itself with much of the unreality of a dream, and so did not come home for the time into our very consciousness.

It was now fairly sunrise, and it was made known that the enemy had retreated, and that we could claim an unmistakable victory. We were yet to learn how the rebel rout, flinging away their guns, had fled headlong down the mountain, or dispersed through its forests to give themselves up in scores as prisoners of war. Our little brigade was now permitted to light fires and make coffee, and, by mutual consent, a search was made in the staff saddle-bags for something to eat; it resulted only in a limited supply of hard bread, but we sat down together and made the best of it. Hardly, however, had we finished our first biscuit, when General Ricketts and staff drew near, with an orderly who had just brought up a basketful of breakfast, and made us free of its contents with a kindly hospitality.

While thus engaged, orders came up to our general to march the division toward Boonesborough, and the staff were speedily in the saddle, bearing orders to brigade commanders, and to the artillery batteries still quietly resting under the eastern slope, and to the wagon-trains parked in the rear; the temporary field-hospitals were abandoned, and our wounded were sent back to Frederick in the ambulances.

As I rode back under the bullet-scarred trees through which we had pushed last evening, and out over the plateau where the rebel bullets had first saluted us, I met little squads of stragglers finding their way back to their regiments, and caught up with a few of our slightly wounded making their way on foot toward the rear. From this outlook I could see the turnpike crowded with troops, artillery, and wagons hurrying up the pass; the fields on either hand were white with army wagons still in park, while far down the road toward Frederick pushed on a living tide of men. As I drew near and mingled with the crowd, the joy and satisfaction every where evident, the jokes at the expense of the enemy flung from file to file, the very marching of the men, indicated that this was not a retreat, but an actual pursuit of a flying enemy. Volunteer bayonets not only think, but they talk a good deal also, and this morning they were enjoying full license in this direction.

Having fulfilled my errand to the rear, I gave my half-starved horse the rein, and permitted him to jog up the road with the crowd, enjoying heartily the humor which sparkled here and there in the column; to me the sensation was novel and peculiar; how it feels to be retreating I knew all about, but this was, I believe, my first experience in pursuing a retreating enemy. "My Maryland" was now sung by our men with an alteration of the words to suit each singer. The new regiments were especially enthusiastic, and I had not ridden long near the column before I found my own spirits rising into something like the old enthusiasm. There is no army ration, after all, so good for troops as an occasional touch of victory.

On the national road, and near the summit of the pass, stands a wayside inn, kept by a good Union man. The rebels had ransacked and dismantled it a day or two before; every thing eatable and drinkable had gone; but now its yard, piazza, and rooms were crowded with Union generals and their staff. The first point to which I headed was the barn, and here I found a small quantity of hay, of which my mare was soon making her first meal for twenty-four hours. I found the general and staff near by; the division was resting in the fields close to the road, awaiting the artillery and ammunition trains, without which it could not go forward. In an hour or more the general moved off at the head of his division, and I sat down on the porch, constantly interested in gazing upon the moving mass of troops, meeting many acquaintances, and glad to have so good an opportunity of seeing the leading generals.

A counter-current of rebel prisoners was now setting quite strongly from the front toward Frederick, and I got into quite an interesting conversation with an officer of a South Carolina regiment, one of a party who were quenching their thirst at the tavern pump. Unlike most of "the chivalry," he was a quiet, earnest man, admitted with perfect frankness last night's defeat, but kindled into a fervor, which seemed to have little infusion of personal bitterness, as he assured me that the South would fight to the end. The remainder of his party were of an inferior stamp, and all of them very naturally looked jaded, travel-stained, dilapidated. Neither on this, or on many similar occasions, did I hear any taunts or insults from our men; every body seemed to have the Anglo-Saxon instinct which forbids the striking a man when he is down. Of course a procession of gentlemen in gray always excited a good deal of curiosity, but the conferences were always good-humored.

The western slopes of South Mountain were to-day full of straggling and demoralized rebels. As we learned subsequently, the fight had terminated in a rout: brigades, regiments, and companies were resolved into their individual elements. A good Union lady, whose handsome residence I visited a few days afterward, gave me an amusing practical account of this demoralization. One day, during the week preceding the battle, while the rebel hosts were moving forward, she received a call from a relative, the captain of a battery, who came in to dine with her. He brought several brother officers with him, and the whole party was full of the most pleasant anticipation. All they asked for was one more chance at the Yankees. All they feared was that our demoralized army, driven from the Peninsula and out of Virginia, could not be brought up to the contest. "We are going to wipe them out this time finally, and then for Philadelphia and New York! The cowardly Yankees will find out for the first time what war means when we get into their country. As for Maryland, we will lose the last man before we retreat."

So with high hopes rode out our rebel cavaliers to exterminate the Union army. But, before daybreak on Monday morning, our friend was awakened by a crowd of half-starved, weaponless men, dressed in costumes of ragged gray, who besieged the yards, garden, barn, and door-steps of her residence, asking for food and full of fear. Panic lent a wonderfully exaggerated tone to every statement, so that, from their own account, it appeared that their whole army had been exterminated, and the Yankees were after them, horse, foot, and dragoons. At least two hundred were on her premises at one time that morning, and, having dispensed freely all the provisions in her house, she sat a while at her window, and overheard their conversation as they lay on the lawn. The remark, "Well, I only wish I could be taken prisoner," passed unrebuked, and several told her husband that they were waiting for the Yankee cavalry to come up and take them. About nine o'clock, in rushed her relative the captain.

"Why, John, is that you? I thought you were going to Philadelphia."

"It's no use talking about it, aunt; we have been badly whipped, and I don't know where a single man or a single gun of my battery can be found."

By noon the rebel cavalry were scouring the whole neighborhood, and drove the stragglers inside their lines at the point of the sabre. But several managed to hide under the straw in the barn, and were not discovered. Rebel vedettes patroled the vicinity all day, and it was not until the next morning that our own cavalry came up, when these hiding rebels gladly surrendered to two of our men. If we could only have been a little quicker in that pursuit!

Another little incident, coming nearer home, will well illustrate their demoralization, and afford a good instance of presence of mind. As our division moved down the road this morning, one of our orderlies, spying a comfortable-looking farm-house about a mile distant, left the column to purchase some chickens for the staff mess. Entering the yard, he rode round to the front door to see, to his astonishment, seven armed rebels sitting in the porch. To use his own expression, he was "mightily scared," but he knew that if he attempted to run they would shoot him off his horse, so he pulled out his revolver, dashed valiantly up, and ordered them to lay down their arms. All complied save one, who swore he never would throw down his gun for any Yankee, whereupon our hero tried to persuade him by leveling his six-shooter at his head, and giving him half a minute to make up his mind. With a bitter oath, down fell his gun also. "Fall in!" now exclaimed the orderly. Again there were some objections; but these also he overruled, and the parade began, though not exactly in the mode prescribed by tactics, for in this case the commander rode *behind* his battalion, and, instead of a sword, flourished a revolver. As they marched along, they fell in with two others of the same stripe, sitting weaponless under a tree. Anxious for recruits, our orderly induced them also to enlist in his company, marched his nine rebel prisoners down to the road, and delivered them over to our junior aid—a very successful chicken-hunt, minus the chickens.

As I sat in the inn porch, a deputation from rebeldom came up bearing a flag of truce, and creating quite an excitement among the group of orderlies in front. At its head rode a rebel surgeon in a gray uniform profusely ornamented, bearing aloft a stick surmounted by a white handkerchief, followed by four rebel soldiers carrying a bloodstained stretcher, the little party escorted by one of our own officers. Asking to see the ranking officer, the surgeon was brought up to General Hooker, saluted, and requested permission to seek and bear off the body of Colonel Strange, who met his fate, it will be remembered, in the fight with our division. General Hooker very courteously referred him to General M'Clellan, whose head-quarters were still in the rear, and I learned afterward that his request was complied with.

The different generals seemed to enjoy heartily this meeting by the roadside, joining their respective commands as they in turn moved by. A little later in the day Sumner's corps occupied the road, and I now saw for the first time this old warrior, whose appearance and character remind one of the best days of the Roman republic. At four o'clock the road was still crowded with troops and artillery. I presume that more than half of the whole Army of the Potomac had passed in review before me since morning. With the general appearance of the troops I was more than satisfied, and, if there was any demoralization among them, I certainly failed to discover it.

But the thirty miles of subsistence and forage wagons still lingered in the rear; I was becoming weary with waiting, and my gastric apparatus began to suggest the necessity of rations. It being doubtful whether I was to be privileged to sleep to-night, I resolved, at all events, not to suffer the pangs of hunger also, and with a gentlemanly surgeon started on an armed reconnoissance. Of course it was useless to try any of the farm-houses near the road, for every vestige of edibles had long since been swept from their larders; we therefore struck off to the right through a pleasant lane, promising prosperous future. Hardly had we left the turnpike when General M'Clellan, followed by a brilliant cavalcade and body-guard, proceeded rapidly toward the front.

The quiet, sleepy country-road, shaded by over-hanging foliage and half overgrown with grass, had a most soothing influence upon men tired of excitement, and glad to escape the sight of a crowd in uniform. We had ridden half a mile, perhaps, when we saw a low-roofed cottage, with piazza overgrown with verdure, nestling in a quiet nook half way down the western slope of South Mountain. It was evident that this was our place to drive.

I am free to confess that I am not a true lover of life in the country. Pleasant indeed is it, during the heated term, to rest under the shadow of the mountains or on the shore of the sounding sea; but I can usually find more to interest and inspire me in the crowd of earnest and frivolous, grave and gay, rough and cultivated, who throng our city streets, than in all the trees, and brooks, and flowers I ever saw. Of course, no man of taste, of poetic imagination, and all that, would make such a confession; perhaps, even in my own case, the fact is not that I love nature less, but human nature more. It is very certain that on this afternoon I could hardly repress a feeling of unmistakable envy at the lot of the happy denizens of this mountain glen. Ah! it is evident that I was never made to be a warrior.

We were soon riding in at the gate of the little inclosure, and found a good Union family of Germans, with some female friends who had fled hither from their own homes higher up the mountain. For several minutes it was useless to attempt even a hint at dinner, for four or five stout and strong-lunged women at once poured forth upon us their stories of last night's horrors, and all talked at once. With resignation we listened to their vivid descriptions of the bursting of shell over their quiet homes, heard in all its details the tragic story of the shot which came so near striking Mrs. Van Snuff's barn, put in a word or two of respectful sympathy when a word or two was possible, and bided our time. Then, with gentle suggestions of abundant reward, we made our modest request, to be at once crushed under a mass of adjectives emphasizing the utter impossibility of granting it. Another lull gave opportunity for a more extended proposition; the feminine element still bubbled on;

but I noticed that the master of the house moved out toward the poultry-yard, followed him until the fate of one chicken was sealed, and felt sure that our point was gained. Having pulled some green corn for our horses, we sat down in the front room, when the doctor, who had been up all night attending to the wounded, went instantly to sleep, and I soon followed his example.

In due time the chickens, with potatoes, bread and butter, a fair cup of coffee, and various *entrées* of the Dutch style of cookery, smoked upon the board, and in due time had fulfilled their destiny. During the whole meal, our kind attendants, with voices preternaturally sharpened by excitement, entertained us with tales of wonders dire, the offspring of our late battle. Strange indeed to these secluded homes must have been the roar of artillery, the rattle of musketry, the shrieking shot and shell, and the squads of half-crazed men—the drift-wood of the receding rebel tide—who rested a while in their porches, and then fled hurriedly away through the darkness of that fearful night. In one sense it was perhaps a Godsend to our German friends, for it had afforded them interesting topics for fireside talk during the rest of their lives.

Fully fortified within for at least twenty-four hours, we bade good-by to our entertainers, and were soon back in the main road. Not long after I met an officer, who reported to me that it would be late at night before our division train could draw out into the road, and it was evidently of no use for me to remain longer on the summit. As we descended the western slope the sunset hues were filling the west with gorgeous beauty, and the eye drank in a landscape rich in all those quiet charms suggestive of comfort, peaceful habitations, and pleasant homes. Few districts in America are more lovely to look upon than this, for it is a region little cursed by slavery, and beautiful with the smiling farms of men who till their own soil with their own honest hands.

At Boonesborough, a small country town with little business and many pleasant residences, we learned that our division had moved on to Keadysville, some six miles distant. Our soldiers had monopolized the village: inns and shops overflowed with uniforms, while the halls and churches were tenanted by the rebels wounded in last night's battle. My effort to secure a chamber in the hotel was unsuccessful, but the host kindly recommended me to call upon a wealthy Union citizen, who, he thought, would be glad to receive me. The result was that in an hour my horse was comfortably stabled, and soon after I was shown to a handsome sleeping apartment. Last night shivering on the battle-field of South Mountain, to-night occupying a good bed in a peaceful home—such are some of the contrasts in campaign experience.

Tuesday, September 16th. Though up very early this morning, my kind hostess would not permit me to leave without breakfast, and sent me on my way with a glow about the heart at her sympathetic hospitality. During the last half of the night one unending train of wagons had been moving past the house, and I soon found those of our division. But our progress was still slow, especially after we reached Keadysville, where a strong counter-current set in of cavalry and artillery, moving off toward the right of the future battle-field; and here I pushed on ahead, and found, about 3 P.M., our division bivouacked a mile or two beyond the village, with head-quarters under a tree. No one could tell me much as to the position of the enemy. Some felt sure that he had already fled across the Potomac, others that a desperate battle was impending. The fields in every direction were full of troops; and when at last the wagon-trains arrived, the division proceeded to make itself very comfortable.

I was now ordered to retrace my steps toward Keadysville with a detail of four men on business connected with my department. It was slow work, our attempt to push through the densely crowded road, the wagons hurrying forward two abreast, and occasionally coming to a dead-lock, which brought out to its fullest extent the profane capacity of the army teamster. Having reached our destination, I bivouacked my squad under some trees, and found decent shelter for myself and my horse in a house near by. Not long after I was domesticated an aid of General Sumner's galloped up and took the house for his head-quarters, followed very shortly by the old hero himself, with his staff and cavalry escort. Early hours are fashionable during a campaign, and I was shown to my room—rather warm quarters, being exactly under the roof.

I

CHAPTER XIX.

BATTLE OF ANTIETAM.

WEDNESDAY, *September 17th.* Before retiring last night I had seen my horse safely stabled by my host, but, as General Sumner's cavalry escort had bivouacked all over the premises, and as I suspected that the distinction between meum and tuum in the matter of horseflesh was somewhat neglected in the code of cavalry morals, I took with me to sleep a half uneasy feeling, and was awakened by it before daybreak. Upon going to the stable I found all right; the cavalry-men were making coffee; and as soon as daylight came I mustered my squad, accomplished my errand, breakfasted in the tent of the officer whom I had come to seek, and was soon on my way back to the division.

By this time the incessant roar of artillery, apparently a couple of miles distant on the right, indicated that a battle was going forward; the dusty street of the little village was full of orderlies and staff officers, riding hither and thither on various duties; every house boiled over with excitement, and gathered upon its stoop a knot of half-frantic women, whose terror it was pitiful to behold. Of course my own thoughts were full of the impending conflict, of whose happy result to the good cause I could not doubt. We certainly had forced the enemy into a dangerous corner, and I felt sure that the music of these cannon was ushering in the salvation-day of the republic. Our victory at South Mountain had not lost its inspiration, and there was thus every reason for being hopeful and enthusiastic.

I was soon riding into the last night's camping-ground of our division, but the ashes of their camp-fires were cold. Troops were, however, massed in the fields beyond, and thither I hastened, to be again disappointed. Presuming that they must have advanced still farther to the front, I rode on to find other troops drawn up in line of battle, but these also were strangers to me, and no one could give me the desired information. I was now on the battle-field of Antietam, and near the front of our centre.

I should like to give a full description of this famous battle, but the attempt would fail for various reasons, one difficulty being that personally I know little about it. The newspaper press, with its corps of keen observers in every part of the field, has given its general features artistically, and as faithfully as is perhaps possible. I may be permitted, therefore, to give only my own limited and partial experiences and observations.

At the point where I now paused for a moment, just about the central point of our army, and on the east side of Antietam Creek, I saw no indications of a hostile force in the fields and woods opposite. Our forces were coming into position near me, but on the other side of the creek all was still. Very few missiles had yet come this way; but, as I rode away, I saw one shell burst in a group of our men, wounding two or three severely. A house upon a commanding elevation was pointed out to me as the head-quarters of

General M'Clellan, and thither I at once proceeded, as the last resort for the information I sought. Here was the immense cavalry escort waiting in the rear, staff horses picketed by dozens around the house, while the piazza was crowded with officers seeking to read with their field-glasses the history of the battle at the right. On an elevation a couple of hundred yards in front, commanding a still better view, groups of officers, newspaper correspondents, and citizens were assembled, and I at once joined them, leaving my horse for a moment in the valley below.

It was only the usual battle panorama, and I could not distinguish a single battery, nor discern the movements of a single brigade, nor see a single battalion of the men in gray. Smoke-clouds leaped in sudden fury from ridges crowned with cannon, or lay thick and dim upon the valleys, or rose lazily up over the trees; all else was concealed; only the volleyed thunder was eloquent; and no man so stolid, of all who now stood gazing down upon the field of death, but pictured in his excited imagination a scene with some at least of the features of the dread reality.

Only a short outlook was permitted me, for here I had discovered that beneath that smoky canopy my own division was engaged, having last evening been sent from the centre to the extreme left. It was necessary to return toward Keadysville, turn to the left over a road which crossed the Antietam by a stone bridge, and, after a two miles' ride, I had little need to inquire the way. It was now about nine o'clock, and already the ebb-tide which flows from every battle-field had fairly set in, bearing out some stragglers, but chiefly those of our wounded, whose injuries, being slight or in the upper portion of the body, permitted them to walk slowly back toward Keadysville, having already been bandaged in the field-hospitals. Ambulances bringing off the more desperately wounded, or returning for fresh freights of agony; pale-faced men looking up at me from the grassy wayside where they had paused to rest; a captain of our old brigade smilingly holding up both arms bandaged and bleeding, and assuring me that we were doing well on the right—such are some of the pictures left in my memory by that morning's ride.

And still, as I hastened on, the roar of the artillery and infantry grew more terrible, and I was soon passing a hospital sheltered in a low-lying valley on the verge of the battle-field. Farm-houses, barns, outhouses, all were tenanted, and still the stretcher-bearers brought in from the front a constantly fresh addition. I had no time to-day to visit this hospital, but, as I rode past the barn, a collection of amputated limbs lying outside the door attested the hurried and wholesale character of the work going on within. At any other time such a sight would have shocked me, but to-day it came in naturally as part of the scene.

For now the ghastly procession of the wounded—some tottering along unsupported, some leaning upon their comrades, some borne upon stretchers, some carried in the arms of their friends, every step an agony—passed me almost continuously; full five hundred mangled and bleeding men, some of them with hardly life enough in them to reach the hospital. There were sights that day whose sad horrors can never be forgotten, too sad and horrible for any description here. And it was through this bloody avenue I must pass forward to the battle. It was no time to grow sick and faint, for into that hell of smoke and battle-din, out of which come these bleeding braves, I must enter, come what, come may. Let me admit that it was a terrible morning's ride.

I was now on the Hagerstown turnpike, across which cavalry were drawn up with drawn sabres to prevent the egress of stragglers from the battle-field. And now in what part of that awful hurly-burly of cloud and noise just ahead is my division? The cavalry-men were ignorant; none of the wounded could tell me; I must push on, and trust to fortune. As I rode down the turnpike, I passed under a hilly crest to its left, upon which a battery was posted, now hurling shot and shell over my head at a rebel battery opposite. On my right I saw troops drawn up in line of battle; on my left I soon met other troops drawn up in a grove near the road; but still I heard nothing of my division, except that it was somewhere in front. And now I was passing between spots desperately fought over already this morning, when over the fields, or in the road just ahead, I was astonished to see some of our troops apparently falling back, and soon also I discovered the general.

We were now in rather too hot a place for the exchange of courtesies, but I saw at a glance that I had come at an inauspicious moment, and a word or two of hurried explanation told me the whole story. I had arrived just at the period when, General Hooker having been driven fainting with his wound from the field, our right wing, which had driven the enemy through these fields above us into a thick grove farther up the road, at least a mile, with great slaughter, had been compelled to fall back by the outnumbering force which the enemy, whose centre and right were left unattacked during all these morning hours, was able to concentrate against it. The bravest fighting could not withstand such fearful odds, especially as our old opponent, Stonewall Jackson, had sheltered his reserves behind rocky ledges waist-high, and wonderfully adapted for defense, had deepened natural depressions into rifle-pits, had laid up long lines of fence-rail breastworks, and so was all ready for a formidable resistance.

Our old brigade retained the position in which it was first posted in support of artillery, but the other brigades were falling back to a new position in excellent order, and the general and staff were overseeing the movement. A bitter disappointment all this to me, but how much worse to the men who had moved through such a storm of leaden rain up this turnpike, through yonder cornfield, close up to the rocky citadel—"slaughter-pen," as a friend designated it—where the rebels from behind stone bulwarks shot down our exposed ranks. But, though the anxious strain still rested on their features, there was not even a shadow of despair, and nowhere was there a single symptom of panic among our officers or men.

The division was soon halted, and drawn up in line of battle on both sides the Hagerstown turnpike; but the enemy did not follow up his temporary advantage, and the infantry fighting at this point was over. The artillery on both sides still filled the air with shot and shell, but not long after this ceased also; the general and staff dismounted, our horses were tethered on the west of the road, and there was a little rest. It was now about 10 A.M., and the right wing had been engaged since daybreak. The enemy, having overpowered our attack in this direction, was now able to give his undivided attention to his centre and right wing, which were to be attacked in turn later in the day.

After a brief interval under the trees, an orderly brought orders from General Meade, now in command of our corps since General Hooker's wound, to march the division on the east side of the turnpike, near our present locality, where we formed in line of battle behind several batteries, and the men were ordered to lie down on their arms. The woods and fields in front of this key-point of the right wing were now voiceless and still; not a grayback could be seen; not a battery saluted us; the scene of the late encounter seemed quiet and deserted. Thirty cannon of various calibre were silently looking toward the foe; grimly behind their pieces stood the gunners, peering out over field and wood, eager to get sight of the enemy. At any attempt to plant a rebel battery, any demonstration of rebel infantry, any symptom of advance, some of them took sight, and sent a shot or shell shrieking among the trees. One of these batteries of our division is well worth visiting; it has lost this day thirty-eight officers and men killed and wounded, and twenty-eight horses; but here it is now posted, every gun brought safely out of the fight, the ranks of its heroic gunners now recruited by infantry volunteers. If one half be true which the staff tell me as we stand around this battery, hundreds of rebels must have fallen this day before the hurricane of grape and canister poured in a critical moment right into the face of the enemy from these wide-mouthed Napoleon guns.

Seated on this little summit, I listened to the deeply interesting recital of the events which occurred before I reached the field. How two of our staff appeased their hunger by a hoe-cake taken from the haversack of a dead rebel soldier; how one general of our division, at a doubtful moment, leaped toward a battery, ordered in double charges of grape and canister, and personally sighted the pieces into the enemy's teeth; how another general, not of our division, left his brigade to advance without him; how the horses of three of our orderlies were killed by a bursting shell as they rode behind the general, and yet no one was hurt seriously; how up to the last moment all was going well, when, just as our boys were pushing into some woods, leaving the cornfield behind them full of rebel dead and wounded, they found themselves confronted with fresh troops, fully fortified, who swept them with volleys so terrible that a retreat was unavoidable—these and the thousand and one little personal incidents, only uttered into friendly ears, greatly interested me, though of course there was in my own mind a natural feeling of regret that I had lost all these new experiences.

But little did any of us imagine that for us the battle of Antietam was nearly over; this seemed to be only the first act of the tragedy, and every moment might lift the curtain for a new scene. On our left, toward the centre of our main line, the din of battle had long been heard, and ever and anon one or more of our own cannon in front spoke out its thunder. As an attack on our position was momentarily expected, one or the other of the staff was constantly engaged in sweeping with a glass the presumed locality of the enemy. Meantime our infantry rested on the ground in long lines—thin, broken ranks at best, giving one a pang at the heart to see how small were some of the regiments now gathered about the torn and bullet-riddled colors. On our right were the Pennsylvania Reserves, and other troops were gradually posted behind us to aid in resisting the expected attack, each brigade in turn stacking arms and then lying down.

Thus every moment was a moment of expectation; of anxiety as to the result of the battle in the centre, and later in the day on our extreme left; of the suppressed excitement of men liable at any moment to be called into battle, and yet of practical rest and idleness. I passed much of the time out among the batteries, whence we had a good view of the woods in which the enemy might lie concealed until the moment of attack, and of the cornfield, which afforded admirable covert for infantry. At times we saw little squads of men at the edge of the woods—rebel pickets, or persons curious like ourselves. A horseman on a white horse showed himself several times on a slight elevation beyond the cornfield, and we christened him Stonewall Jackson. I found that a powerful imagination helps out a picture wonderfully, for several times I was assured by others that large bodies of rebels could be seen *en masse* at the edge of the woods, while the glass gave me a view of nothing but trees.

During the day we were able to get up a wagon or two with provisions, which the regimental quartermasters distributed among the men. I was walking down the lines, when a regimental captain thus accosted me, holding up a great piece of pork on his sword: "Look here, captain, this is the allowance of pork for my company, and I shall have to eat it all, for I am the only one left." I paused to inquire about it, and found it was even so; no commissioned or non-commissioned officer, no private, not even a drummer-boy remained to him. We talk with sadness about the decimated ranks of a regiment or company; here was a company simply annihilated by sickness, wounds, and death.

During the day some of our boys brought in from the adjacent fields the dead bodies of some of their comrades, and buried them in the rear of our little elevation, placing at their heads strips of cracker-box-covers, with the name and regiment of the deceased in pencil. Horses were lying all about us just where they were killed, for over this spot the battle had at one time fiercely raged. Hour after hour of inaction slipped away, while the battle-field on our left was fought over fiercely, terribly, with a stubborn desperation on both sides rarely exhibited since the world began. For the truth of this statement I may safely appeal to the statistician when the records of this day's work are made up, and the lists of dead and wounded are completed, or to any one who may visit with me two days hence the field of battle and witness the fearful result.

Sometimes it seemed as if the fighting had drawn so near to us that it must be in the next wood, and that our turn must soon come, and then the din of battle would move off to the left, leaving us quiet as before. Of course rumor had full swing on such a day as this; victory, defeat, large Union re-enforcements, the repulse of our left wing, the death of several of our prominent generals, the taking of several thousand prisoners, all were in turn buzzed through the ranks, and relieved somewhat the tedious waiting of this long day. About 4 P.M., General M'Clellan, with his staff, rode along our lines, and was greeted with much enthusiasm by the troops. We had now learned that our centre and left had been partially successful, the enemy having been driven back with much loss, though still holding firmly their new position.

One of our orderlies brought us about this time from a neighboring farm-house a loaf of bread, with a modicum of butter ingeniously stored in a hole cut in the loaf, and we sat down to enjoy it, with a cup of coffee, for the men had been permitted to light fires and cook their rations. We began to think that the fighting for the day was over. But about 5 P.M., sudden as lightning out of a clear sky swept over us another tornado of rebel wrath, and the shot and shell began to strike and burst over and about us in all directions. In an instant we were in the saddle; but, before we were fairly mounted, our thirty guns, which had been impatiently awaiting this opportunity for hours, swept woods and cornfield with a deluge of shot and shell. Never before had I known how tremendous may be the roar of mingled artillery. Thirty guns, each discharged as fast as the men could load! they actually shook the hill; nay, the concussion seemed enough to shake the planet.

As the rebel projectiles were supposed to be introductory to an infantry attack, the troops in front were notified to be ready, while those in rear fell in, took arms, advanced closer to the crest of the hill, and also lay down, prepared for action at a moment's notice. The Reserves still remained as before, except that each commander was getting his men into thorough preparation; every wagon went off at full gallop; the right wing was all ready; and now we sat on our horses, looking earnestly down to see what was to be the next move. General Meade, who succeeded to the command of our corps after General Hooker was wounded, rode up to the crest where we were stationed, and reconnoitred the position of the enemy's batteries as coolly as if at a review. Already decorated with a bullet-hole in his cap as a trophy of to-day's battle, his almost nonchalant manner, and the quiet way in which, amid the tornado of rebel wrath, he gave his orders to make ready for the storm, greatly impressed me. I saw the shot strike so close to our men as to fling the dust apparently over them; for perhaps ten minutes the enemy kept up a lively cannonade, but not a man was, to my knowledge, killed or wounded. This artillery firing at long range is terrible to hear, but is rarely fatal.

From some prisoners afterward captured we learned that it had been the intention of the enemy to attack with infantry, General Jackson's favorite time for flinging himself upon us seeming to be just before sunset. If this was his intention, the awful fire of our batteries must have admonished him of our thorough state of preparation, for in a brief period his batteries ceased to play, and our own thirty guns were silent also.

During a visit to one of our hospitals, I heard from the lips of a German, who was severely wounded in to-day's battle, a thrilling account of his personal experiences during this ten minutes' cannonading. He was lying under a tree, desperately wounded and unable to stir, with several other Union soldiers and a number of rebels, all in the same condition, in the woods, where some of the hardest fighting had been, and through which now crashed our shot and shell. The ground had been taken from the enemy and occupied by our troops early in the day, but was retaken by the rebels, so that wounded men in blue and gray lay indiscriminately together. He suffered little pain, but was tortured with thirst, relieved from time to time by some generous Southerner, who, in passing, shared with him the contents of his canteen. When, however, the shot and shell from our own batteries, in this five o'clock duel, began to shriek among the trees, killing some of our own wounded men, he described his sensations as truly horrible. Unable to move, planted by his wound just there, with these death-messengers crashing, bursting, striking sometimes within ten feet of him, what language could paint a scene so terrible! All that night, all the next day, and the next night also, he remained untended, only to be taken up at last when the enemy had retired and our own troops occupied the field. When I talked with him he was lying under a shelter-tent, outside a garden, every part of which was filled with the shelter-tent bedrooms of wounded rebels, waiting until his wound was sufficiently healed to enable him to be moved into the house. He told me that the surgeon had promised to save his leg, and added, in his broken way, a fervent hope that he might have one shot more at the enemy.

With this cannonading ended the fighting of the right wing for the day. The men were now permitted to bring in bundles of straw from the neighboring farms, with which they made themselves beds, and lay down in line of battle; the tired gunners made themselves similarly comfortable alongside their guns; pickets stood, with eye and ear open, close to the rebel lines, ready to give instant warning should a night-attack be attempted; and hardly had the darkness descended on hill and wood before we had also lain down on beds of cornshooks and straw, pulled our blankets over us, and all was still. No one removed even his sword; our horses stood saddled and ready for instant use at the fence near by; all felt the importance of getting as much rest as possible while rest was permitted us.

There was no tree over our heads to shut out the stars, and as I lay looking up at these orbs moving so calmly on their appointed way, I felt, as never so strongly before, how utterly absurd in the face of high Heaven is this whole game of war, relieved only from contempt and ridicule by its tragic accompaniments, and by the sublime illustrations of man's nobler qualities incidentally called forth in its service. Sent to occupy this little planet, one among ten thousand worlds revolving through infinite space, how worse than foolish these mighty efforts to make our tenancy unhappy or to drive each other out of it. Within a space of four square miles lay two hundred thousand men, some stiff and stark, looking with visionless eyes up into the pitying heavens; some tossing on the beds of the hospital, or lying maimed and bleeding under the trees; some hugging in their sleep the deadly weapon with which, to-morrow, they may renew the work of death.

Bound up with the lives and safety of these two hundred thousand is the life-destiny of millions; and even now, as through North and South the awful roar of this day's battle, borne by the electric wires, already echoes and re-echoes through city, and village, and hamlet, the streets pale with excitement, and all night long the fearful anxiety which kills shall keep watch and ward over many a sleepless dwelling. My God! why could not some pitying angel-messenger from Thee stand to-night upon one of these cannon-planted hills, and, with a voice which should almost awake the dead, send back home these insane children of the South lifting parricidal hands against their country? Through what other scenes of agony—through what other lanes of death, must this poor, childish human nature pass, before it learns by experience the utter brutal folly of war?

A man may see the grotesque absurdity of war, and yet be unable to devise a remedy which shall practically apply, taking things just as they are. As long as principle is weak and personal ambition strong; as long as man, instead of consulting and following heavenly oracles, forces into the low arena of the battle-field questions which were decided for him before his creation at the very throne of God, so long, I suppose, must his ambition and folly be met on their own ground, so long must he be resisted in his own arena. Of course no moral question can be decided in this brutal fashion. The right is by no means sure to triumph; the wrong is very often successful; the history of the world is one long record of the battle-triumps of injustice over justice, of vice over virtue, of wrong over right. "God is always on the side of the strongest battalions," said Napoleon, thus approximating the truth in a proposition which required to be complemented by Oliver Cromwell's order, "Trust in God, and keep your powder dry." For religious enthusiasm as well as gunpowder helped the Roundheads, and a little more religious enthusiasm would help us now.

Animal strength, animal courage, and skill in applying and using them, must thus be the main elements which enter into and decide a wager of battle. When we have conquered in the present struggle we shall not have decided that slavery is wrong in its claim to rule or to ruin, to destroy the republic because it can not bind the free North neck and heels at its chariot wheels, for this claim was decided against the South in the very constitution of humanity; all we can hope to do in this regard is simply to open Southern eyes so that they may see. The war will mainly decide as to the animal qualities of the two sections, and in this respect we must admit that the South had at first some elements of superiority, for it is the animal which their system has nourished, at the expense of the moral and intellectual. John Locke, who advocated slavery in the Carolinas, confesses that "the perfect condition of slavery is the state of war continued between a lawful conqueror and a captive;" and it must be acknowledged that this evil genius of the South, while it has defrauded the people of the highest arts and enjoyments of peace, has educated them wondrously well in the unnatural arts of violence needed in war. The land of the school-house, the printing-press, and the manufactory must pass through a necessary season of initiation before it can equal in these acts of violence the land of the bowie-knife, the duel, and the slave plantation.

But, look at it as I would, I could see no way in which the North could have avoided this war, and no doubts disturbed me as to her duty to fight it out to the end. For her it was indeed no ordinary warfare, but a crusade for freedom; the religious and patriotic element, the elements of self-denial, sacrifice, philanthropy, had come in to elevate and sanctify what is in itself low and mean. I was satisfied, therefore, that, despite my contempt for war, I was in the right place on this Antietam battle-field; and while other thoughts and visions ran riot through my brain, sleep at length came, and another long day was over.

CHAPTER XX.

THE ANTIETAM BATTLE-FIELD.

THURSDAY, *September* 18*th*. Long before daybreak, the little elevation whereon we had slept was alive with men making their coffee and eating their simple breakfasts, so that they might be ready for the day's fighting. The feeling seemed to possess every heart that this day was to be crowned with victory; the whole tone of conversation as we drank our coffee on the grass was hopeful, nay, almost exultant; the hour for crushing the rebellion seemed to have struck; the opportunity had come to drive the rebels into the Potomac, or capture their entire army. The natural dread of battle seemed to be lost in the hopeful feeling that the result of this day's dangers might be the ending of the war, and our return to our homes and families. The prize to be gained, for the country and for ourselves, was worthy of any venture, and I saw no one who did not seem anxious to make the trial. As well here as elsewhere, as well now as at the end of another campaign, might we enter the lists wherein alone the South was willing to try the momentous issue; and it certainly seemed that after yesterday's partial success we held the enemy at disadvantage.

But sunrise came, hour after hour slipped by, with no orders to advance, no attack by the rebels, and gradually a bitter feeling of disappointment began to trouble us, while the conviction forced itself upon our minds that the enemy was to be permitted to escape. I remember very little of this day save its sadness; our batteries still remained in position, looking down toward the enemy; our infantry rested on their arms as on yesterday, but silence brooded all day over the locality held by the foe. Toward evening a paulin was stretched over an upright for a bedchamber; our servants had brought up sufficient provisions, and about dusk the orders came to be ready for action at sunrise to-morrow. On the whole, matters began to look a little more cheerful; there was still hope that the rebels had not escaped; the growlers ceased their growling; the victory was only postponed for one day, not indefinitely. A messenger was sent off to Hagerstown with letters, and with the sun we also went to rest.

Friday, Sept. 19th. Up again at 3 A.M., we drank our coffee, saw that the division had a good breakfast, and made all ready for battle. Only to be again disappointed, for the expected order did not come. Finally, at 8 A.M., we learned that the rebels had slipped through our fingers and retreated across the Potomac. The river, lately in their rear, and forming one side of the angle into which we had driven them, was now their best defense against us. The battles of South Mountain and Antietam were robbed of any decisive significance. The campaign must now be transferred to Virginia; the long, weary days of marching and nights of shelterless discomfort were all to be again endured; and there seemed little hope that, after again overtaking the enemy, there would be any more decisive result. It is not for me to attempt any criticism of military measures or military men, but only to delineate truly the bitter feelings of disappointment shared by so many in our army that day. My heart almost sunk within me at the dreary prospect before us; this was to me blue Friday indeed.

An orderly was now sent to head-quarters with letters for home, written in pencil. I always carried in my saddle-bags several envelopes properly directed and stamped, and was thus able to send off by every opportunity pencil dispatches written in the saddle or on my knee. A sutler bound for the nearest railway station, an officer going to the rear, a newspaper correspondent or messenger, will always wait for you to scrawl a couple of lines, and this couple of lines may save mother, wife, or lover many an hour of anxious unrest.

Shortly after sending off our letters orders came to advance across the battle-field toward the river, and after the division was drawn out into the road I rode back a couple of miles to order up the wagon-train. Through torn-up cornfields, robbed of their tasseled grain by hungry horses and hungry men, past farmhouses, barns, and outhouses crowded with the wounded, I came at length to a quiet little grove near the roadside, and here I found the train. How charmingly to my somewhat jaded senses appeared the scene which now presented itself! At a camp-fire sat the teamsters, cooking their noontide meal of mutton, potatoes, and coffee; the horses stood, half asleep, tethered to the wagons. It was a sudden and quick transition from the battle-field, with its constant strain of excitement, to a picnic scene in peaceful woods. Who would not be an army teamster?

My faithful sergeant soon had my mare feasting upon unaccustomed oats, and brought up to the tree beneath which I was reclining a supply of meat and vegetables, which he spread out on the grass before me without even saying "By your leave." My reply was equally silent, but equally satisfactory. The *al fresco* meal seemed positively luxurious; it medicined mind as well as body. I sat down sad and moody, but what mind so dark as wholly to resist the influence of mutton, potatoes, and raw tomatoes, after having feasted so long on fried pork and hard bread? When I arose I saw a little more hope ahead, but not this day nor the next could I wholly lift off the shadow.

Meanwhile the wagon-train was made ready, and, having seen it fairly started, I rode forward to the front. My route carried me over the late battle-field, and I spent much of the afternoon, part of the time in company with a friend, in visiting some of the most severely-contested points, to be awe-struck, sickened, almost benumbed by its sights of horror. Within this space of more than a mile square, this spot, once beautiful with handsome residences and well cultivated farms, isolated, hedged in with verdure, sacred to quiet, calm, content, the hottest fury of man's hottest wrath had expended itself, burning residences and well-filled barns, plowing fields of ripened grain with artillery, scattering every where through cornfield, wood, and valley the most awful illustrations of war. Not a building about us which was not deserted by its occupants, and rent and torn by shot and shell; not a field which had not witnessed the fierce and bloody encounter of armed and desperate men.

Let us first turn off to the left of the Hagerstown turnpike; but we must ride very slowly and carefully, for lying all through this cornfield are the victims of the hardest contest of our division. Can it be that these are the bodies of our late antagonists? Their faces are so absolutely black that I said to myself at first, this must have been a negro regiment. Their eyes are protruding from the sockets; their heads, hands, and limbs are swollen to twice their natural size. Ah! there is little left to awaken our sympathy, for all those vestiges of our common humanity which touch the sympathetic chord are now quite blotted out. These defaced and broken caskets, emptied of all that made them manlike, human, are repulsive merely. Naught remains but to lay them away quietly, where what is now repulsive shall be resolved into its original elements, shall be for a time

> "Brother to the insensate clod
> Which the rude swain turns with his share,
> And treads upon,"

and shall reappear in new forms of life hereafter.

Passing through this cornfield, with the dead lying all through its aisles, out into an uncultivated field beyond, I saw bodies, attired mainly in rebel gray, lying in ranks so regular, that Death the Reaper must have mowed them down in swaths. Our burying-parties were already busily engaged, and had put away to rest many of our own men; still, here as every where, I saw them scattered over the fields. The ground was strewn with muskets, knapsacks, cartridge-boxes, and articles of clothing, with the carcasses of horses, and with thousands of shot and shell. And so it was on the other side of the turnpike, nay, in the turnpike itself; ride where we may, through cornfield, wood, or ravine, and our ride will be among the dead until the heart grows sick and faint with horror. Here, close to the road, were the haystacks near which our general and staff paused for a while when the division was farthest advanced, and here, at the corner of the barn, lay one of our men, killed by a shell, which had well-nigh proved fatal to them also.

Just in front of these haystacks was the only pleasing picture on this battle-field—a fine horse struck with death at the instant when, cut down by his wound, he was attempting to rise from the ground. His head was half lifted, his neck proudly arched, every muscle seemed replete with animal life. The wound which killed him was wholly concealed from view, so that I had to ride closely up before I could believe him dead. Hundreds of his kind lay upon the field, but all were repulsive save himself, and he was the admired of every passer-by. Two weeks afterward I found myself pausing to gaze upon him, and always with the wish that some sculptor would immortalize in stone this magnificent animal in the exact pose of his death-hour. One would like to see something from a battle-field not wholly terrible.

Over this grave-yard of the unburied dead we reached a wood, every tree pierced with shot or cut with bullets, and came to the little brick church on the turnpike. This must have been a focal point in the battle, for a hundred round shot have pierced its walls, while bullets by thousands have scarred and battered it. A little crowd of soldiers were standing about it, and within, a few severely wounded rebels were stretched on the benches, one of whom was raving in his agony. Surgical aid and proper attendance had already been furnished, and we did not join the throng of curious visitors within. Out in the grove behind the little church the dead had already been collected in groups ready for burial, some of them wearing our own uniform, but the large majority dressed in gray. No matter in what direction we turned, it was all the same shocking picture, awakening awe rather than pity, benumbing the senses rather than touching the heart, glazing the eye with horror rather than filling it with tears.

I had, however, seen many a poor fellow during my ride, something in whose position or appearance had caused me to pause, and here, lying side by side with three others, I saw a young rebel officer, his face less discolored than the rest, whose features and expression called forth my earnest sympathy, not so much for him as for those who in his Southern home shall see him no more forever. No one knew his name among the burying-party, and before night he was laid in a trench with the rest, with no head-stone to mark his resting-place, one of the three thousand rebel dead who fill nameless graves upon this battle-field. So ends the brief madness which sent him hither to fight against a government he knew only by its blessings—against his Northern brothers, who never desired to encroach upon a single right or institution of his—who were willing that he should hug to his breast forever the Nessus shirt of slavery, asking only that he did not insist upon forcing its poison-folds over their shoulders also. So disappears the beloved of some sad hearts, another victim of that implacable Nemesis˙ who thus avenges upon the white man the wrongs of

K

the black, and smiles with horrid satisfaction as this fearful game of war goes on.

Very slowly, as men move through the burial-places of the dead, we rode through these woods back of the church, and reached the rocky citadel, behind which crouched the enemy to receive our charging battalions, sweeping their ranks with destruction, and compelling their retreat. I was astonished to see how cunningly Nature had laid up this long series of rocky ledges breast-high for the protection of the rebel lines. In front of this breastwork we found a majority of the dead dressed in blue. At this point commenced also the long barricade of fence-rails, piled so closely to protect the rebel lines, and stretching off toward the north. Here is one more evidence of the use to which the rebel generals put every spare moment of time, and of their admirable choice of position.

One more scene in this battle-picture must be seen, and with a visit to this our ride may end. It is a narrow country lane, hollowed out somewhat between the fields, partially shaded, and now literally crowded with rebel corpses. Here they stood in line of battle, and here, in the length of five hundred feet, I counted more than two hundred of their dead. In every attitude conceivable—some piled in groups of five or six; some grasping their muskets as if in the act of discharging them; some, evidently officers, killed while encouraging their men; some lying in the position of calm repose, all black and swollen, and ghastly with wounds, this battalion of the dead filled the lane with horror. As we rode beside it—we could not ride in it—I saw the field all about me black with corpses, and they told me that the cornfield beyond was equally crowded. It was a place to see once, to glance at, and then to ride hurriedly away, for, strong-hearted as was my then mood, I had gazed upon as much horror as I was able to bear.

As we rode back, I noticed close by the lane several trenches already covered in, one with a strip of wood at its head marked with this inscription: "Colonel Garland and eighty dead rebels." Details of our soldiers from the various regiments were collecting their comrades, bringing in the bodies on fence-rails, identifying them, and laying each in his own separate grave, with a head-piece inscribed with his name and regiment. Of course I can not personally speak with positiveness as to the comparative numbers of the dead on each side, but from my own observation, and the opinions of old experienced officers, our late foes seemed to outnumber our own dead in the proportion of four to one. Two days of laborious sepulture will be necessary before they are hidden away in the bosom of our cherishing mother; during two days more of sunlight and darkness, of hot noontide and chilly midnight, must some of these poor mangled forms lie here untouched, untended, to be hurried by stranger hands at last into a common and nameless grave. Thank God that to the former occupants of these defaced bodies, now dwellers in far other mansions, the fate of these their former habitations is no longer of interest.

Not for these poor shipwrecked forms, then, need we reserve our pity, but for the broken circles of which every man among these unburied thousands formed a part—for the homes throughout the South and the North made wretched this day with the first hints of their new sorrow—for the widow, the orphan, the lover! Oh war! war! war!

Out of this sad presence silently we rode toward the setting sun, to find our head-quarter tents pitched on the edge of the battle-field, and to be soon seeking in sleep forgetfulness of war and all its horrors.

Our next day was a quiet one. At our mess-table in the morning it was generally thought that we might move before night, and every moment was therefore occupied in bringing up arrears of staff business. Late in the afternoon, however, I rode out to visit a portion of the battle-field I had not yet seen, once more to have a partial return of yesterday's impressions. The van of that immense army of visitors, which for several weeks came pouring in to visit Antietam, had already arrived, and many citizens were now picking up relics of the battle, and exploring every part of the field. Hither came the father or the brother from New England searching for his dead; here, also, the distracted wife sought out the grave of her heroic husband. The Hagerstown turnpike for weeks saw every afternoon almost one continuous funeral procession, bearing away to the North the bruised bodies of the North's bravest sons. More than a thousand, perhaps, were thus carried home to sleep among their kindred, to repose beneath commemorative stones, to which all of their name and family shall point hereafter with natural and patriotic pride.

At first it had seemed to me better to permit our brave boys to rest undisturbed under the bullet-scarred trees, in the little glens, or out in the fields, where they died for the good cause, and where they had been laid to rest by their comrades; but when I saw the gratification with which their graves were discovered by relatives who had come hundreds of miles to claim their own, and the affectionate tenderness, not unmixed with pride, with which they lifted the beloved forms, shrouded only in uniforms of blue, into their coffins, and the evident relief with which they commenced their journey home, I had reason to change my mind.

Stretching in front of the fields adjoining our camping-ground was one of the long fence-rail barricades of the enemy, and behind it a continuous pile of straw indicated their sleeping-spot at night. They had left behind them some fifteen thousand muskets, and details of men were engaged in collecting them. The burial-parties were still busily engaged; it seemed, indeed, that their sad work was hardly half accomplished. As we rode on, we met a friend guiding a couple of ambulances; as he was not a surgeon, we inquired his destination, when he told us that during his afternoon ride he had discovered, in a barn on the edge of the battle-field, some twenty rebels so desperately wounded that they had been unable to help themselves, and had therefore remained untended and without food ever since the battle. He was now going with the ambulances to bring the poor fellows into one of our hospitals.

Our visit this evening was to the ruins of a once handsome residence, burned by the rebels, its owner being suspected of too strong an attachment to the old flag. Near this spot was some of the hardest fighting of the battle, and around the ruins clustered thick the newly-made graves.

CHAPTER XXI.

CAMP NEAR SHARPSBURG.

SUNDAY, *September* 21*st.* We were now enjoying the finest marching weather of the year, and that we were to advance immediately was taken for granted. Whither? when? how? ruled the hour. The sound of distant cannonading this morning also gave rise to some conjecture, but this music had become too common to awaken much curiosity. It proved to be an artillery duel across the Potomac. I remained in my tent all day, busily engaged in writing, and went very early to bed. At 11 P.M. I was awakened by the adjutant general, who put his head in to say that we were ordered to move to Harper's Ferry on the morrow. As I was all ready in my department, I thanked him for his good news, and so off again to sleep.

But we didn't move the next day, nor the next week; indeed, the next month found us encamped on the battle-field, or in its immediate vicinity, helping to guard the Potomac, lest the enemy should get across again and try another battle. Did I not rightly say in the beginning that "waiting" is one of the elements of war? But it was not for subordinates, unacquainted with all the reasons for this delay, to trouble themselves on this point, and so we made the best of it, gradually settling down to bear with cheerful philosophy the monotony of tent-life. The accessions to our staff consequent upon the enlarged command of our general as chief of a division consisted of an inspector general, whose duty it was to inspect the regiments and brigades; a chief of artillery, who had supervisory charge of our four batteries of flying artillery; a chief of ordnance, and an additional aid, with an increased number of mounted orderlies. Our head-quarters had thus become in itself quite a village, located nearly at the extreme southwestern corner of the battle-field. A few hundred feet in front was the head-quarter camp of General Meade, now in command of the corps, and our division was encamped by brigades through the woods directly west of us. All day long the music of their axes indicated that they were putting up their huts and making themselves comfortable. The weather was delightful; an abundance of food was supplied to them; the sutler was always ready to eke out the government ration with supplementary trash, and ere long the country farmers in the vicinity brought in fruit, home-made cakes, pies, and other edibles, all of which found a ready market.

Of reading matter there was, for the most part, great lack, the men paying eagerly ten cents for the New York Herald, almost the only New York journal which, for some reason, reached us. Now, if there be any thing which the soldier needs in camp or bivouac, it is something to read. A season of terrible excitement, great fatigue and privation, and constant strain upon his nerves and feelings, is followed by a season of almost entire calm and monotony. Once a week, perhaps, he is on guard taking his turn as sentinel with the rest; more or less of drill consumes a portion of the day; a dress parade occupies a short half hour at sunset; for the rest, his time is chiefly his own. A game of cards is well enough in its way as an occasional pastime; but, if this be the only resort, it is apt to degenerate into gambling, out of which grow quarrels and the acquisition of bad habits not easily overcome. I have very seldom seen our troops playing base ball or indulging in any athletic sports; hidden away in the woods, with no companions of that sex without whose influence man becomes rough and brutal, they are exposed to the enervating influence of many idle hours.

If you wish to demoralize a man, to dilute his manliness, corrode his patriotism, steal away his cheerfulness, destroy his enthusiasm, and impair his health, pen him up in an isolated camp with little to do, no books to read, no resource against idleness; if you wish to demoralize an army, march it off from a severely-contested battle-field into the woods, and condemn it to a month or two of listless do-nothingism. At such a time the men need, as never so much before, books of a cheerful and moderately-exciting character, strong, bracing stories like those of Charles Kingsley, quiet pictures of home life like that fascinating sketch of "John Halifax, Gentleman," military tales like those of Lever, the wonderful character-pieces of Charles Dickens, and the choice productions of our American authors. In these later days the novel has arisen to its true position; it has become, in our own country and in England, almost the rival of the pulpit as the medium of patriotic impulse, elevated sentiment, moral and religious culture; and thus the good novelist becomes to the soldier not only his physician to animate and invigorate him, but his preacher to elevate and inspire him.

I sincerely wish that some good citizen would send to our army through the Sanitary Commission a supply of mental food for the men in the shape of a thousand or two copies of each of our leading monthlies—the Atlantic, Continental, and Harper's. Every copy would be physic and nourishment to body and mind; the men would feel better in camp, would fight better on the battle-field. I speak from my personal experience; for, with all my privileges as a staff officer, I found it difficult to keep a book on hand for an occasional leisure hour. Now and then a book-peddler came along; but even a famished brain can not find food in "The Torn Pocket-handkerchief—a Tale of Love and Murder," which, with other books of the yellow-covered family, composed his stock. The soldier will get neither mental nourishment, incitement to duty, nor patriotic impulse out of such shallow and frothy cisterns. Were it in the power of the Sanitary Commission to distribute after every battle some good wholesome books to the uninjured and the healthy, as they supply medicines, clothing, and nourishment to the wounded and the sick, they would do much toward sustaining in our army a good *morale*.

Every day now witnessed about our head-quarters a levee of officers from the different brigades, and there was always straying in, to take a seat at our mess-table or sit around the evening camp-fire, some good fellow with a fresh atmosphere of thought and experience, to keep the social currents ever in motion, and prevent any mental stagnation. This evening camp-fire, built every night in front of the general's tent, had become our usual place of assemblage after supper, and here any man who could talk was especially welcome; then were our old stories brought out once more, refurbished and newly decorated, as fair barter for his novelties; the old battle-scenes were re-enacted; fresh bits of humor sparkled around the circle, struck out, like fire from flint, by the concussion of wit and fancy. Our general, from his extensive *répertoire* of Mexican and Florida experiences, his personal acquaintance at West Point and elsewhere with most of the leaders in the rebel army, and his budget of entertaining anecdote, led the camp-fire congress, delighting us constantly with something fresh and new. There came in also upon us about this time a new division quarter-master, truly a fellow of infinite wit and humor, as well as an energetic and able officer. Our mess had now been necessarily divided, the lieutenants setting up housekeeping for themselves; and when our new friend and the general entered the lists of humor, either at the mess-table or about the camp-fire, great was our enjoyment.

One of his stories illustrates so well the manners and customs of a large class who follow up the army, that it will bear repeating, though there's a great difference between a written tale and the same tale told by a man who can twist his face into a knot, talk Dutch or English alternately, and fairly personify its several characters.

"While I was post quarter-master at Aquia Creek, the armies of Generals M'Clellan and Burnside were both debarked, and you can readily imagine that all sorts of queer customers occasionally found their way on shore. One very hot day I was busy in my office, when a not very prepossessing head was thrust into the open window, and its owner, in breathless haste, inquired,

"'Ish dis de quarter-mashter's offish?' Upon being answered in the affirmative, he continued,

"'Well, Mr. Quarter-mashter, I've just got mine schooner in de river, mit sutler's goods on board, and I wants one place vot I can sell dese tings to de soldiers. You give me one place, hey?'

"'It is against my orders, sir, to give permits to any body to put up tents or houses for the sale of goods of any kind.'

"'Well, Mr. Captain, I would not take much room for dese little tings, and den I can make up some monish vot I lose on de Chickahominy.'

"Finding the fellow bound to worry the matter through, and being up to my eyes in work, I told him to call again in the afternoon, when I should be more at leisure.

"'Oh yes, captain, I vill come den. Now, captain (with a polite leer), you trinks wine, hey?'

"'Yes, sir, I drink wine.'

"'Very goot; den I sends you one case of the finest wine vot comes into dis creek. You will smack your lips, captain, ven you trinks dis wine, hey?—oh, dis is good. Vell, I sees you dis afternoon.'

"Away went Mr. Sutler; but hardly had time enough elapsed for a journey to his schooner before I was again reminded of him by the appearance of one of his men, bearing on his shoulders a basket of Champagne, and lustily inquiring for 'de quarter-mashter.' On a card attached to the basket was the following address:

"'To Captain Vesh, Qr. Maister.
    Fon Henri Weisenheimer & Co., Sutlers.'

"The wine was duly stowed away in the locker,

and almost forgotten in the press of business, when, late in the afternoon, that same head, undergoing now the process of drying and polishing with a red bandana, was again thrust in at my door. Our friend was now the quintessence of politeness.

"'Vell, captain, I come down to look at dat little place vot ve speak about dis morning.'

"'What place, sir?' (sternly.)

"'Vy, dem place vat you would give me to put up one little tent ven I sell my goods.'

"'You must be mistaken, sir. I told you distinctly that we granted no such privileges, and being busy, and finding you would not take no for an answer, I told you to call again.'

"'Vell, now, captain, look at dis! Dis morning I send you von basket Champagne, cost me sixteen dollar mit de wholesale. Now I lose all dem too. I don't like dese tings, captain.'

"'Yes, I understand you perfectly. You thought to buy me with Champagne. I'll keep the *bribery* to remember you by; the *corruption* you anticipated don't follow. Now, sir, I give you two hours to get your vessel under weigh and out of this creek. If you are caught again on shore, you will be placed under arrest.'

"And away went Mr. Weisenheimer, probably cured for life of any desire to bribe a quarter-master."

Another pleasant fellow, the correspondent of a New York journal, with a lively budget of news and a good assortment of stories, frequently joined our circle around the blazing logs of hickory. By-the-way, the army correspondent is decidedly an institution. When we belonged to a brigade, these gentlemen did not favor us with many visits; but, now that our general commanded a division, we saw much more of them, and were glad of the opportunity. Thoroughly posted as to the latest news at home and at army head-quarters, in familiar relations with general and staff officers of the higher grades, the experienced correspondent can scent out an intended move with almost unerring instinct. In brief, he knows all that has happened or is to happen, and sometimes a good deal more.

A dozen or more of the journals of the large cities have their regular army correspondents, and three of them maintain a considerable staff, the chief usually being at head-quarters of the army, while his subordinates accompany the several corps. Such is the rivalry in this department, that they are instructed to spare no expense and to make any exertion, however desperate, to collect and forward the news in advance of each other. Thus the admirable report of the battle of Antietam, which appeared in the New York Tribune, and was copied into every New York paper and some fourteen hundred other journals, was written, I understand, mainly in the cars. The Tribune had in various parts of that field several correspondents. At nightfall they rode in with their various reports to their chief, who had been disporting himself in the front of the fight, acting for a while, indeed, as aid to General Hooker. With these reports and his own notes he was off at once on a fresh horse for a night-ride of some thirty miles to the nearest railway station. The cars once reached, he rode and wrote steadily on, and finished his letter in the Tribune office while the first portion of it was being set up by the compositors. I understand that this same enterprise has since been exhibited by one or more of the other New York Journals.

The newspaper correspondent, usually quick in noting the signs of the times, intelligent, and personally agreeable, is thus a welcome visitor at head-quarters. Occasionally, however, a black sheep creeps into the whitest flock, and even an army correspondent is not always immaculate. A young man, announcing himself as connected in this capacity with a certain journal, received so characteristic a dismissal from the staff mess of a brigade camped near us that I may be excused for narrating it. He was evidently of the genus sponge; thrust himself upon the mess without invitation, contributed nothing pecuniarily or socially to the common stock. It was a most hospitable mess, at whose table I have enjoyed several of the best dinners I ever ate in camp; and yet so insufferable became the intrusion that the caterer was requested to dismiss him. He commenced blandly, but with voice rising from piano to forte by rapid transition.

"My dear sir, it gives us all a great deal of pain that we have been compelled to set before you such poor fare, that we can offer you so few delicacies; indeed, it harrows up the feelings of the mess so much that they don't enjoy their meals. It would be very gratifying if we could entertain you as we should like to, but we can not, and—*confound it, sir, you must leave, and there's an end of it!*"

This transition from the bland to the blunt, from the lively to severe, must have slightly astonished the listener, who probably felt a little as if he had been struck by lightning, and incontinently disappeared. But this exception only proves the rule.

The weather during these days of waiting was so delightful that I passed no day without an hour or two in the saddle, wandering through the pleasant forest paths in the vicinity, among the finely-cultivated farms filling all this fertile region, usually calling in at one or more of our hospitals on the way. Sometimes I gave my horse a drink in the Potomac near the ruins of the bridge leading to Shephardstown. The rebel pickets could be seen lying or sitting on the opposite bank, and sometimes the thought occurred to me that the staff-trappings of my horse might tempt a bullet; but, by tacit consent, the pickets on both sides had ceased firing, and I never heard that this tacit consent was violated. Quiet and still slept the fields, a "solitary horseman" occasionally moving slowly along, engaged like myself in a peaceful reconnoissance.

One morning, however, I found the little village of Shephardstown opposite, and the river bank below it, quite in a state of excitement. A general and his staff had taken position near a church, decorated, as were many other buildings, with the red hospital flag, and full of rebel wounded, while parties of cavalry were sitting motionless as their horses at various points along the river bank, and the road in their rear was quite alive with mounted men. On the bluff on which I was standing an artillery battery watched, open-mouthed, these suspicious proceedings, while our infantry pickets lining the river bank below kept their eyes in the same direction. On inquiry, I learned that yesterday one or two of our cavalry regiments had crossed the river, stung the rebels a little, and brought over a few of them as trophies; and the rebel hive was evidently anticipating a similar incursion to-day.

A walk over the battle-field always developed new features of interest. All that was horrible or repulsive had now disappeared, but other reminders of the battle were not wanting. Less than a quarter of a mile from my tent stood a thick grove of oak, maple, and hickory, every tree pierced with bullets and perforated with shot, or mangled and torn by shell. Here were great trees decapitated and reft of their head-dress of foliage, others with their limbs amputated close to the parent trunk, or with splinters torn from their sides. Through one hickory-tree two solid shot had passed, one about six feet above the other.

As I wandered sometimes through these groves of hickory and chestnut, the old days were vividly recalled when I was a schoolboy in this same State of Virginia, and went out nutting with my schoolmates, one now a rebel major general, another killed one day in the Sunday streets of Washington, most of the rest probably in the rebel army. I remembered as if but yesterday with what intense interest we watched for the time when the bursting bur announced that the nut was ready for gathering, and with what eager industry we devoted every leisure hour to collecting and storing our treasures in the dormitories.

I had not been among the hickory-trees since those schoolboy days, and determined to have, as soon as practicable, a nutting all to myself, *in memoriam*. Finally, I pushed off alone, one lovely afternoon, into a hickory grove, determined to be a boy again. The trees hung thick with fruit, the hour was propitious, but the excursion was a failure. Every thing was provided; but the schoolboy, exulting in his escape from weary tasks, his veins full of fire, his pulse at fever heat, to whom nuts were worth more than are dollars now, was not there. The wild, exuberant joy of the schoolboy time, which filled the woods with laughter and shouts of excitement—the enthusiastic rivalry with which we climbed the trees and risked our necks on the bending limbs, had long since departed; I would hardly have struggled up this tree to-day were its fruit golden. A few nuts flung down by the wind were gathered, still fewer were cracked, and so ended my nutting. Ah! this was not the first time that I had endeavored in vain to bring back the delirium of my boyhood by revisiting old scenes or renewing old associations; and yet our schoolboy days, for real happiness, bear no comparison with those of our later years. The former may have more sparkle; it is certain that the latter have more true joy. A schoolboy's life is like the little brook which goes laughing and singing on its way, but is easily fretted into foam, and bubbles up with impatience over every pebble; a man's life resembles the river, to whose surface such obstructions hardly send even a ripple.

Our evening sessions at the camp-fire still continued, and at one of these our quarter-master, who had before illustrated the fact that bribery and corruption do not always go together, gave us a pleasant story at his own expense, illustrating how, when post quarter-master, he was distanced by a Yankee sutler, a story which seems to come in naturally enough as a part of this mosaic of campaign experience.

"It was our busiest period at Aquia; troops and stores were coming almost hourly, and I had been at work day and night for at least three weeks, with scarcely time enough for an occasional nap. You may imagine how, under such circumstances, a man would feel bored by useless questions, and how he *might* lose his temper.

"One busy day a clean, dipper-dapper, keen-eyed down-Easter presented himself, and at once proceeded to inform me that he had brought down on the steamer Keyport a large lot of "perishable goods," which he desired to sell to the soldiers, and wished me to assign a spot whereon he might put up a tent for a couple of days.

"He was at once informed that no such permit could be granted; but, unwilling to give it up so easily, he commenced a series of undertone mutterings, such as, 'Well, this *is* hard!' 'Out two hundred dollars!' 'Don't allow *any body* to sell!' 'Pies will spoil,' etc.

"Finding that there would be no such thing as getting the fellow off without ordering him out peremptorily, I at once told him that time was precious, and that he must leave. This order seemed to have little effect on the muttering. Finally, in piteous tones, he 'wanted to know' if I couldn't make an exception in his case.

"'Now, sir,' said I, 'leave this office! I told you NO, and that is law. If you want to sell your old pies, go over on the hill and peddle them to teamsters and contrabands; you can't sell 'em any where about here!'

"The 'hill' was about half a mile from my office, on the edge of the swamp, and, as I thought, entirely outside the limits of our sale-ground; but he bowed and departed in a hurry.

"Some ten days afterward, when this little incident was forgotten, as I was going down the pier to the boat just arrived, a man accosted me very politely,

"'Captain! there's a box on board the Keyport for you.'

"Supposing the stranger to be a new clerk, I asked him what it looked like, when he commenced a series of killing bows, and faltered out at last,

"'Three dozen of Scotch ale, sir!'

"Being still somewhat puzzled, I asked from whom it came.

"'Why, captain, I—I—bought it for you!'

"'But, my dear sir, you are an entire stranger to me, and why—* *'

"'Captain, don't you remember me? I was here about ten days ago with a little stock of pies and other perishable goods. You very kindly permitted me to go over to the hill yonder to sell them, and I made about three hundred dollars. I want you to drink my health.'

"So we parted. When I reflected more seriously on the matter, I remembered that on the same day I had sent him off so roughly, General Burnside told me he intended to *march* his troops to Falmouth instead of sending them on the cars, 'for,' said the general, *men* can walk, *stores* can not.'

"It appeared that my Yankee friend, all dressed in gray, had heard of this order, and located himself on the hill past which marched at least five thousand men during the next twenty-four hours. Thus he sold his pies and a quarter-master at the same time."

CHAPTER XXII.

THE HOSPITALS AND THE SANITARY COMMISSION.

DURING all these weeks I never wandered over the battle-field without meeting parties of visitors, men, women, and children, come to seek out its most famous spots, to glean every little relic, to cut the buried bullets out of the trees, to picnic somewhere under the pleasant shade, and then to drive home with their curiosity fully gratified. One thing quite impressed me, and that was the rapidity with which the more marked traces of the battle disappeared. The roar of the last cannon had not ceased to reverberate among her leafy aisles before Nature, silent but ever active, had commenced to purify herself from the soil and stain of battle, and cover up the bloody footprints of War. In two weeks' time, only the broken-down fences, the shattered and ruined buildings, the torn-up cornfields, and the frequent clusters of graves reminded the traveler of the late struggle.

A year or two, and even these evidences will disappear. These bullet-marks in the trees will be overgrown with fresh bark, fences, and fields, and farm-houses will resume their wonted appearance, and over the graves and trenches, where lie the buried thousands, will once more wave a thick green mantle of bearded grain. Would that thus might disappear from every Northern and Southern home the sad memories of this battle; that Time the Comforter might thus heal the wounded hearts and dry up the bitter tears in every Northern and Southern family! Would that thus speedily every reminder of this rebellion might disappear from the national memory, every rankle from the national consciousness; that our present national wound might be healed to the central point of difficulty, never to break forth afresh, and leaving no ineffaceable scar!

The little village of Sharpsburg still bore striking evidences of the fearful nature of the late cannonading. At one period in the battle it must have been a target for both armies, and there was hardly a single house in the whole town, no matter how humble, whose roof, walls, or doors were not pierced and torn with shot and shell. And yet quite a number of its residents remained in their cellars during the whole raging of this iron storm. I can imagine few situations more trying to the nerves than to be thus pent up in gloom while that tempest howled and shrieked through the air, or came hurtling in the rooms overhead. A good Union lady, who visited our head-quarters, gave us a description of this season of horror which greatly interested us. How they made their little preparations of food and clothing, and went down, children and all, as soon as the first shell burst over the village; how they listened, expecting every moment to hear some of the shrieking fiends burst through their own walls, perhaps to penetrate into their retreat; how her husband was forced to rush up and put out the fire caught from a shell which exploded in the second story; how hours lengthened out into seeming days of suspense and fear; how they all mutually sustained each other, she narrated as only a woman can. After hearing her story, I felt that a far pleasanter position would have been the very front of the battle.

It was pleasant to converse with these true Union women, of whom I met several in this vicinity. Some of them were slaveholders, but declared that they preferred the Constitution of our fathers even to slavery. Well and faithfully did they do their duty also in the hospitals, with which this whole region was now filled. The army of the wounded, numbering at least ten thousand, occupied more than seventy of these impromptu hospitals, stretching from the Potomac out over the battle-field, through Sharpsburg, Keadysville, and Boonesborough, even to Frederick and Hagerstown, while miles of ambulances bore daily northward their precious freights of patriotic pain. Over the river, also, we could see the red flag waving from many a dwelling, the hospital of the wounded rebels, whom the enemy had carried with them in their late escape. In barns, and sheds, and farm-houses; in churches, halls, and residences; in colonies of hospital *marquées;* in yards and gardens crowded with shelter-tents; wherever, in a word, there was space for the narrow hospital-bed, there lay a soldier chained to his couch by a wound more or less severe. No matter what flag he followed into battle, an equal surgical aid surrounded him, an equal kindness soothed his agony. Once within the hospital, the distinction between the patriot and the rebel was forgotten; and I was touched in noticing that, in some of the little grave-yards which sprang up, ah! so rapidly, near the different hospitals, the men of the North and the men of the South slept side by side together.

Most of the rebel wounded lay in the barns and

other buildings near the river and inside their former lines, these localities having been selected by their brigade surgeons during the battle. Miserably deficient at first, they gradually put on an air of comparative comfort; every one had in a day or two his own bed and a plentiful supply of food; but the rebel surgeons, who had been left behind in charge, did not, in general, impress me either with their ability or their tenderness. Nor was I particularly impressed with the average appearance of the rebel wounded, the rank and file lacking, to some extent, that look of intelligence and self-reliance which their general want of education and the social despotism of the slaveocracy of the South had not tended to awaken. Occasionally, however, an interesting face attracted me, while the fact that they were sufferers invested all of them with a certain dignity. Lying among rough, commonplace-looking men, I saw here and there a boy, too young for war, doubtless the darling of some Southern home, lying pale and weak after the loss of a leg or an arm, yet still full of pluck and courage. Some were only lingering for a moment on the shore of the Great Ocean, with hardly a breath of life fluttering through their rent canvas; some moaned despairingly in their agony; some lay still and motionless in the borderland between sleeping and waking; but most of them were not severely wounded, and responded in pleasant terms to every kindly utterance. Had there been any personal repulsion in the atmosphere of those rebel hospitals I should have discovered it; but after these visits I always felt like asking myself what devil it was that had made these men my enemies.

Sometimes I listened to their little histories, not

eventful usually, but interesting as part of the same old story of the affections, ever old and ever new, which, when truly told, comes home to all of us. One thing surprised me, and that was the strange pleasure which some evidently experienced in exhibiting their half-healed stumps. Imagine a man proudly uncovering the stump of his leg or arm, and holding it up with the exultant remark, "Doesn't it look splendidly, sir?" The sight somewhat appals you, but it will never do to betray a hint of this feeling to the pale-faced youth looking up so eagerly into your eyes. "Yes, it does look finely," you respond, with the mental addition, "very finely for a stump;" and then you talk with him about the new improvements in the manufacture of limbs, and each helps the other, until you both reach almost to the point of declaring that a leg or two more or less is a matter of very little consequence; and then you look again into the still pallid face glowing with temporary excitement, and think of this mere youth launching out upon the great sea of life in such a shattered bark as this, and you turn away lest your feelings should betray you.

One young rebel, handsome and generous-looking, became one day quite enthusiastic as he spoke of his future career, but the initial fact upon which that future turned was the going to Philadelphia to get a false leg—going to the land of those who had just hurt him for the means of cure. Is there not something a little suggestive in this? In the same hospital I saw the poor maimed hulk of a man propped against the wall, both legs having been shot off in the battle, while another with seven distinct bullet wounds was likely to recover. The majority seemed hopeful, but there were very many whose fate was written out upon their emaciated countenances; there was no need for the surgeon to whisper it to you as you moved by.

I learned from several of our surgeons that wounds of a precisely similar character were far oftener fatal with the rebels than with our own men, the stamina of the former being impaired by scant food and great privations. Poor fellows! one needed only an occasional interview with them to be convinced that they —to whom freedom would be a savior, while slavery has been a destroyer—were led into this rebellion by the same motive power which impels the Hindoo mother, who, at the bidding of her priests, her ignorance, and her prejudices, flings her first-born into the Sacred River.

I found the rebel officers frank, courteous, and willing to converse, admitting, with little qualification, their failure in Maryland. We discussed the different positions of the late battle, how this or that division was located, and so branched off into other subjects, but the very word slavery was tabooed as too exciting for a hospital. I felt instinctively that the bare utterance of that word might cause the maimed man with whom I talked to leap from his bed in defense of his idol.

Of course the main feeling, as we passed through the rebel hospitals, was that of pity rather than of sympathy. Sincere and brave as they unquestionably were, they were to me the victims of a wicked cause. Poor consolation must it be for a young man condemned to limp through life, that he lost his limb in the service of a confederacy whose foundation-principles are so contrary to our ideas of natural justice.

L

Pity, and pity only, was about all one could feel for such a victim.

But when I entered the hospitals of our own brave boys far other feelings thrilled me. Never did I get over the half-reverent feeling with which I moved among them. This was no place for pity, but rather for a sympathetic encouragement which usually flowed forth in words of proud congratulation. A very large majority of our wounded suffered little pain, and though their confinement was tedious, yet their permanent cure was only a question of time. For the life of me I could not feel much commiseration for such as these. A man who goes home from this war decorated with a deep-laid scar or even deprived of a limb, will bear henceforth to his grave the honorable insignia of American chivalry; his wounds, like the battle-crosses of the great Napoleon, have admitted him into the republican Legion of Honor. His town and neighborhood shall be proud of him; his family shall have rich possessions in the memory of his patriotic bravery; when he dies, his maimed body shall be laid to rest as that of a public benefactor, and his children and grandchildren shall speak of him with honest pride as one who, in the crisis of his country's destiny, in an hour when right and wrong were struggling for the possession of a continent, bared his breast on the right side. But there were some already passing through the pearly gates into the Great Hereafter, and others, still encouraged by hope, who were forming plans for a future they would not live to enjoy. In such a presence a man feels the poverty of his own commonplaces; nor dares he, unless in his highest mood, interfere between the departing spirit and its

God. But if he have any thing of his mother left in him uncongealed by the frosty touch of the world's collisions and cares, be sure it will leap up into his eyes, perhaps even moisten them a little. We will stammer out our little word of sympathy and pass on, thankful at least that, though his earthly life ends here, yet is every one of these men, now dying for us and for his country, really going home.

The saddest thought which I brought with me from these hospitals was that so much suffering and death seemed all in vain; that still fiercer battles must be fought; still other fields crimsoned with patriotic blood; still other thousands of our brave countrymen must suffer and die. And yet not wholly in vain, for all this death is part of the great sacrifice which always has preceded any advance of humanity toward the right, the just, and the true; all this suffering is part of the great agony out of which a truly free nation shall yet be born.

Not one complaining word did I hear in the Union hospitals. Courageous, hopeful, and patriotic, they bore without a murmur their painful wounds, their tedious confinement. Would that between these miles of beds could pass the procession of Northern traitors; these peace-men who would stab these brave boys behind their backs; these men who by their treason encourage the South to persist in its rebellion; who rejoice in our defeats, and turn pale at every Union victory; who are sold to the South body and soul, but have not courage enough to join the rebel ranks. It is possible that even these might be shamed by the sight of so much patience and constancy into something resembling patriotism.

It is probable that never, in the whole history of warfare, were the wounded in any battle so expeditiously and comfortably cared for. The surgical department of the army is, in general, admirably organized and conducted; the Sanitary Commission greatly aided in the good work, while volunteer nurses and private donations lent valuable assistance. As speedily as they could bear transportation, our own wounded were carried to Frederick in ambulances, and so on to Washington or elsewhere, while the rebels were paroled and allowed to pass on their own way. Many of these came North, and were lost to the rebel cause forever.

I have referred to the Sanitary Commission, and no one could visit these hospitals without becoming a firm believer in the importance and value of this institution, as supplementary to the regular surgical department. Think for a moment of the terrible exigency of the occasion! As the result of one day's fighting, more than ten thousand Union and rebel soldiers were thrown upon our hands at Antietam, needing beds instead of the blankets of their usual bivouac, food more delicate than the ordinary army ration, bed-clothes and under-clothes of every description, and the many other articles which a sick man requires. Take into consideration the deficiency of army transportation, except for the absolute necessaries of the battle-field and the hospital, and the fact that for days after such a battle the surgical staff is busied incessantly in the primary operations and in the first dressing of wounds, and you will see how this commission, with its thorough organization, and lavish expenditure of its means for these extra supplies and their transportation, becomes to our poor wounded boys the source of incalculable comfort and solace. It follows hard upon the footsteps of our advancing armies, so that within three days its forty agents had distributed food and clothing among eight thousand wounded men; and during this battle month of September it divided more than $400,000 worth of supplies among the various Eastern and Western armies. I regret to add that some of our hospitals at Antietam were indebted to this commission for their first supply of chloroform; the surgeon found without it should have been instantly sent home in disgrace.

So extensive are the ramifications of this commission, and so thoroughly have its agents been drilled in the good work, and so completely has it the confidence and aid of government officials, that one dollar expended through its channels is equal to about three expended by private benevolence or state societies. It is natural that our kind-hearted women should desire that their offerings should go to their special friends, though, if they reflect, they could hardly wish that one man should enjoy these delicacies, while his brothers in patriotic devotion, the men who stood shoulder to shoulder with him in the hour of trial, are left without them. Surely, if there be a place in the world for impartiality in the distribution of articles of comfort and solace, it is the hospital of those who have been wounded in a common cause. An orange, a jelly, a glass of wine, would choke a patriot if he saw his pale-faced companion on the next cot going without one.

Besides, this private bounty is simply impossible. At Antietam, for example, though we were in a friendly state, with railroads connecting the North with

Frederick, Hagerstown, and Harper's Ferry, it was well-nigh impracticable, so entirely was every means of transportation required for the purposes of government, to get even a small package from home during all these days of waiting. What the fate of such a package must be under less favorable circumstances may be easily estimated. A wounded man would probably die or return to his regiment before any such private gift could reach him. What we need is to have these supplies ready at once, even before the battle is over, and this is the office well performed of the Sanitary Commission.

For one, I believe that this commission is one of the first-fruits of our most advanced Christian civilization, the first inroad into the domain of war of a practical Christianity which shall yet throttle and destroy this demon forever. When I seek to estimate its value and significance in its various supervisory, reformatory, and scientific, as well as benevolent operations, to say nothing of those exceedingly valuable statistical collections which are to be the corner-stones of future history, I confess that I know of no calculus by which correctly to compute them. Could the tens of thousands of the blue-uniformed sufferers it has relieved utter their testimony, we might reach some adequate expression.

As to the Western Department, says General Rosecrans, February 2d, 1863, "While the general commanding highly appreciates and does not underrate the charities which have been lavished on this army, experience has demonstrated the importance of system and impartiality, as well as judgment and economy, in the forwarding and distribution of these supplies. In all these respects the United States Sanitary Commission stands unrivaled. Its organization, experience, and large facilities for the work are such that the general does not hesitate to recommend, in the most urgent manner, all those who desire to send sanitary supplies to confide them to the care of this commission."

As the result of these combined efforts of the surgical department and the Sanitary Commission at Antietam, the men were soon made thoroughly comfortable, and the feeling was sown broadcast throughout the army that the soldier who perils his life in battle is sure of kind and humane treatment should he receive a wound. How much our foes appreciated this kindness was well illustrated by the remark of a rebel officer, who said to me, as he looked up laughingly from his bed on the floor of a barn, "I declare I am almost sorry to quit; I haven't been so comfortable since I entered the army."

CHAPTER XXIII.

ANTIETAM AND HARPER'S FERRY.

THE interior life at our head-quarters during these days of waiting was, on the whole, lazy, tedious, uneventful. A certain amount of routine work in the morning, a gallop on official duty, or to one or more of the hospitals, or for exercise, in the afternoon, pleasant evenings around the camp-fire, early to bed and late to rise, so moved on the leaden-footed hours.

Under some circumstances this might have been very agreeable. With little to do, surrounded with pleasant friends, why not be perfectly easy and happy? Why, amid the jokes at the mess-table, the ever-recurring question, "Why don't we move?" The fact is, that all this would be very delightful as a picnic, but it was not to picnic in Maryland we had left our families and deserted our Northern homes. The weather was too fine to permit the thought of winter-quarters, so that it was impossible to divest ourselves of the belief that to-morrow, or to-morrow, we should certainly move on.

I found it well-nigh impossible to read with much profit even the few books I was able to procure. Outwardly, indeed, all was calm, broken only by the review by the President, or the cannonading of an occasional reconnoissance; but still there was a good deal of electricity in the air; exaggerated reports lent their incitement; there was always a feeling that the next hour might see our canvas houses disappear, and the camp-stool exchanged for the saddle. It is difficult to study profitably on board a ship at sea; in a tent, during a campaign, it is well-nigh impossible. A quid nunc can not be a student, and no coterie of quid nuncs has a more restless expectancy of the something which is to turn up than has a staff mess when within striking distance of the enemy.

All this while, lazily stretched at ease along the banks of the river for a distance of several miles, rested and slept the Army of the Potomac, every man of them with plenty to eat, plenty of sleep, and little to do. A regiment or two, usually of cavalry, was occasionally sent across the river to find the bear, but to return when the "tracks got too fresh;" and as week after week of the lovely weather slipped by, we began to accustom ourselves to the idea of winter-quarters. About the pleasantest hour of the twenty-four was that of our evening gathering around the camp-fire, lighted at dusk by Berryman the faithful in front of the general's tent. Among the many military experiences thrown into the general fund, the following, related by one of our mess, will bear recording here.

"When I was out West, a military commission was appointed to examine regimental officers as to their qualifications, and some of the colonels and majors used to be forever in my quarters, questioning me as to the probable style of examination, and looking very uneasy and miserable. One day, after the examining board had adjourned, I went up to their examination room and sketched out on the blackboard some fearfully complicated plans of impossible fortifications, together with a few little interesting propositions, such as $\frac{a^m + b\sqrt{xy}}{p^n - q^m} = \sqrt[c]{\frac{x^m - y^n}{a^n}}$, followed by a long series of hieroglyphics, which purported to prove the truth of this highly important equation.

"Shortly after my return to my own quarters, one of the candidates for examination presented himself, looking nervous and wo-begone, to talk over his anticipated martyrdom. 'Captain, I wish this confounded examination was over!'

"'Why, colonel, it seems to me that you are making more out of it than it deserves; I don't believe it is going to puzzle you much. They will, of course, begin with some very simple question, as, for example, 'What are the constituents of gunpowder?'

"'But I don't know what gunpowder is made of, though I know well enough how to shoot it.'

"'Well, colonel, then they'll probably ask you what is the velocity of a cannon ball the third second of its flight, and how many grains of gunpowder it takes to start it.'

"To this a long-drawn-out whistle of wonder was the only response. 'By-the-by, colonel, the board has adjourned; let's go up, and perhaps we can see on the blackboard what kind of questions they have asked to-day.'

"On entering the examination-room, and catching one glimpse of its mysteries in chalk, the colonel started back, exclaiming, 'Christopher Columbus! Well, if it takes all that to make a colonel, then I'm floored, that's certain!'

"The next day, however, the colonel's agony was over; as he was a good practical officer, he readily passed, and many a laugh we had afterward over my little *ruse de guerre*."

October 10*th*, 1862. Having some business at Harper's Ferry, fourteen miles distant from our camp, I rode thither to-day, followed by my sergeant, and accompanied by one of our aids, a smooth-faced son of New York, cool and brave in battle. The ride was one of the pleasantest I ever enjoyed. Through all this portion of its devious course the Potomac has elbowed the Maryland hills out of its way, leaving only space enough at their base for the Chesapeake and Ohio Canal, and a narrow roadway partially scooped out of the side of the mountain. The Virginia bank is more level, less bold and striking, relieving the view with glimpses of green fields and fertile farms. The yet youthful Potomac is not yet far enough from its birthplace among the Alleghanies to be very sedate and quiet—is indeed quite turbulent and frisky at times, only to be cured of these fevers of youth when at Harper's Ferry it weds the pleasant Shenandoah, after that growing calmer and more dignified every day, as they glide on to the ocean together.

A canal is in general about as commonplace an object as can well be devised, but this section of the Ohio and Chesapeake looked any thing but commonplace to-day. On one side overhung by mountains, cut out, in fact, at some points from their rocky base, on the other fringed with a narrow belt of tall, o'erspreading trees, its waters undisturbed by the nondescript half-vessel, half-box canal-boat, its locks all closed and silent, it was actually picturesque in its many windings. The road was so crowded with army-wagons, and withal so dusty, that we were glad to quit it for the shaded canal pathway. The little belt of trees between us and the river was picketed by our troops, snugly ensconced in the shade, and ready to give the alarm should the enemy attempt to cross.

We had this pathway almost exclusively to ourselves; stopped to pick a few wild grapes, or to enjoy some new vista of autumn loveliness, as a curve in the canal path treated us to a fresh view of the river or opening through the hills; and so we found ourselves about noon riding under Maryland Heights, opposite the town of Harper's Ferry. The shallow, foaming river boiled and bubbled between us and this little elevated angle thrust out at the point of junction of the Potomac and Shenandoah, and frowned upon, buttressed by, absolutely pent in by mountains. On its left Maryland Heights overlook the town, on its right and front are Loudon Heights, with Bolivar Heights in its rear, every one of these now crowned by our batteries and whitened with our camps. It adds to the aggravation caused by the late capture of this spot, with its garrison of ten thousand men, to see how carefully the stable has been locked now that the horse is stolen. It will not do to think of this, however, or we shall lose all pleasure in our visit.

The river is here some five hundred feet wide, and we crossed it at the ford, to enter by a gateway into the government inclosure, with its work-shops, arsenals, and store-houses all in ruins and black with fire. Near the main entrance, the engine-house wherein John Brown and his little party defended themselves still stood uninjured, as also the gate which afforded him a temporary barrier. We also paused to take a look at the now ruined bridge, the scene of other impressive incidents in this exciting tragedy.

I have never been able to unite in the wholesale

praise or the wholesale denunciation which has surrounded the name of John Brown. He was a compound of the old Puritan of Cromwell's time and Don Quixote de la Mancha, walking ever in the felt presence of his God, and fighting with his Bible in one hand and his musket in the other, as did the one, and yet imbued with that native chivalry of soul, that self-forgetting spirit of knighthood, exaggerated, half-frenzied, regardless of practical consequences, or unable to foresee them, which make the old Spanish knight one of the sweetest and best-beloved of all real or imaginary characters. The old man stood before me in actual bodily presence as I paused at this spot—this spot which is to be hereafter classic ground, as time throws into shadow the more rash and Quixotic features of his undertaking, to bring into the foreground his deeply religious spirit, his wonderful devotion to what he deemed his God-given duty, his real greatness of soul.

When I think of this Harper's Ferry tragedy, I am reminded of an incident in the late English war in India. A battery planted by the natives on the heights beneath which the English army was passing had been very troublesome, and a small detachment of a dozen men was sent out to reconnoitre its position. Clambering through the woods, they at length reached a spot where they discovered that the battery was formidably posted and held by a large force of the enemy. Just then the notes of an English bugle reached their ears, sounding their recall, but unfortunately they mistook it for the signal to advance. Without a moment's hesitation, they charged the battery, and were killed to the last man. The English sent out afterward a large force in quest of them, which charged and took the battery, to find them all laid out side by side behind the guns, every man with a red cord about his wrist, the proudest decoration of Indian valor, placed there by their admiring enemies.

Like these brave Englishmen, John Brown, who felt himself called of God and enlisted for life in the great cause of freedom, evidently in this case misunderstood his orders. Like them, also, he extorted even from his foes the tribute of their hearty admiration, and went to his grave decorated with the red cord of valor which makes his name immortal. His rude prison-house became for them a temple where men who came to scoff remained to reverence. Times have indeed changed since then. John Brown's detachment was only very little in advance of the main body, and I could not help wishing that, in this stand-up fight between Freedom and Slavery, we had a few more men of religious enthusiasm like his—men possessed, inspired with the great idea—God's hammers for crushing out wrong.

Harper's Ferry is a little, narrow-streeted, dusty, dirty hamlet. There is only room on the little plateau at the apex of the angle for one main street; it was now crowded with sutlers' shops and with military visitors, and I was glad to mount the heights in rear to be rewarded with a fine view of the Shenandoah and a glance down the Potomac. About 3 P.M. we started on our return, reached camp in the midst of a driving rain, and were soon occupied in discussing a good beefsteak, with baked potatoes and other accompaniments, at our pleasant mess-table.

The butter was unusually nice this evening, and

had its little history, which was related with great gusto by our quarter-master. It seems that a brigade quarter-master, in need of forage, had sent out a team of wagons, and taken some hay from a well-to-do farmer in the vicinity. A day or two after, the farmer, fat, healthy, and weighing over two hundred, brought into our quarter-master's tent a greasy-looking document like the following:

"Reseaved of —— —— fife tuns and a haff of Timithy hay, at fifteen dolers a tun—Seventy 5 and 7 dolers and haff. Altogether 82 dolers and haff.
"THOMAS RITCHIN, Wagen-master."

Of course the farmer wanted his money, and had somehow discovered that vouchers like the above were not current at Washington. The matter did not belong to our quarter-master in any way, but he very kindly made out proper vouchers for the man, and instructed him how to get them signed, and so get his money. He was, of course, profuse in his thanks.

A few days after he again presented himself with a similar paper belonging to a friend, and, as his friendly protestations had won the heart of our quarter-master, he was again furnished with the proper set of vouchers.

Upon entering the tent this last time, he handed the captain a small roll of butter, saying that he had brought it for him, knowing that good butter was scarce. After many thanks for the present, the butter was turned over to our mess.

His business over, our portly friend still sat in the tent, until, as the captain was about to leave, he stammered out,

"Oh! that butter, captain, is a matter belonging to the women-folks, and they'll expect their pay."

Greatly surprised, the quarter-master inquired how much he should pay him.

"Well," said he, "I git a quarter at home, but as I came through Sharpsburg this morning they told me that butter was selling for thirty-five cents a pound."

"Then you confess," said the captain, "that while you are satisfied with a quarter at home, you are willing, on account of the friendship you feel for me, to charge ten cents a pound extra. However, we want butter, so here is your money."

"Captain, won't you get me the butter-rag? The women-folks always expect it back now cotton is so high."

We had several similar experiences in our Southern tour. But the butter was good, and was worth more than the sum it cost our quarter-master in the mirth it elicited.

Sunday, October 12th. Last night, about midnight, orders came to send out one of our brigades on picket; quite a warlike demonstration, which disturbed somewhat the quiet on the Potomac. To-day we moved our head-quarters to a spot nearer Sharpsburg, where the general hired rooms in a house, and the staff encamped in a field close by. This quarter-of-a-mile move was highly encouraging; it was at least evident that we were not permanently located for life on the Antietam battle-field.

Our tents were this time pitched in two parallel lines, a more sociable arrangement; and about midnight I was awakened by what I at first thought a cavalry charge, but which proved to be the rush of a herd of army bullocks on a stampede. In a twinkling down fell the tent of our inspector general, leaving him struggling in its folds and calling lustily for "Amos," his black shadow. Other tents rocked and swayed hither and thither; our fat friends fell over and over among the tent-ropes, picked themselves up again, and rushed on still more madly into the rain and the darkness. The colonel was soon extricated from his canvas winding-sheet, and took refuge with the adjutant general; the list of killed and wounded was made out in blank, and all was again quiet on the Potomac.

Wednesday, October 15*th.* Some excitement at our mess-table to-day over a complete set of white stoneware and other table finery. This eating and drinking from "silver washed with tin," however fashionable in the army, is not, after all, the *ne plus ultra* of luxury, and the thanks of the mess were incontinently tendered to our quarter-master, who had made the purchase for us. But this gentleman was not himself just now, being grievously troubled with what he called "neuralgia" when seriously inclined, and "spiflications" when humorously moved, but which was, in the vernacular, "old-fashioned rheumatism." We joked him after the usual fashion, accusing him of "preparing the public mind" for an application for sick-leave, but it was evidently no joke to him.

Friday, October 17*th.* This afternoon I walked with a friend down toward the river. On our way we passed through the encampment of the 118th Pennsylvania, and noticed that the men were all falling in in their company streets, and that the tents of the field and staff were surrounded by quite a crowd of general, staff, and other officers. On inquiry, we learned that a new flag was to be presented to the regiment by a committee of Philadelphians, and paused to look on a while. The regimental line looked finely, every man in new uniform, and gave us a good specimen drill.

While this was going on, the field officers and their guests enjoyed a collation spread upon an open-air table. Not being expected at the feast, we concluded to take our look at the river, and return in time for the presentation. It was convenient to pass the regimental guard, some forty men drawn up on the left, and now standing at ease. What was my horror when, as I drew near, the sergeant called out "Attention, battalion! shoulder arms! present arms!" thus thrusting upon me a salute not due to my rank, no doubt to the amusement of the officers standing near, and to his own mortification when his mistake should be discovered. There was no dodging it, so I received and acknowledged it as if I were Field Marshal the Duke of Wellington, or one of our new-fledged brigadiers. On our return, however, from our glimpse at the sunset, I took care to pass in another direction. The collation was still in full blast, and it was getting late, so that we did not, after all, assist at the flag presentation.

Sunday, October 19*th.* To-day I resolved to go to church, if such a thing were possible. All the little meeting-houses in the adjacent villages were occupied as hospitals, but I had heard of an Episcopal chapel some seven miles away, and thither I now proceeded. It was a lovely autumn day, soothing but not melancholy, and a pleasant hour's ride up the Hagerstown turnpike brought me to the pretty stone chapel just in the mood for a quiet hour within. I was at once courteously welcomed to a seat; the congregation, composed mainly of young ladies, came in; the choir gave us some music; but the minister was not, so that after waiting half an hour I retired.

Determined not to be foiled, I now rode off to a Dunker meeting-house, whose locality had been described to me. And a romantic ride that was, through narrow country lanes, beneath the arches of forest-aisles, and among some of the finest orchards and thriftiest farms I ever saw. This Dunker settlement would be considered remarkably inviting every where; but to a man tired of camps and sick of war, it was positively enchanting. Houses chiefly of stone, large and well-appointed barns and outhouses, fields of the finest corn I ever saw, orchards heavy with fruit—what else could a quiet man desire?

Through this paradise I reached at last the plain brick meeting-house, now surrounded with comfortable family carriages, tied my horse with the rest, and entered the large square room full of worshipers. At a long table extending across the head of the room sat the elders of the community, the males dressed in a semi-Quaker garb, the females wearing plain dresses and pretty white caps by no means injurious to their personal appearance. The body of the house was filled with benches, whereon sat the men on one side and the women on the other.

The services consisted of extemporaneous addresses by such of the brethren as were moved to speak, of short prayers, and hymns plaintive and peculiar sung by the whole congregation. To me it was an impressive service, full of earnest religious spirit. At its close the fraternal kiss was exchanged among the brethren, and it was announced that a sort of love-feast would be soon in order.

This religious fraternity, which is found in various parts of Pennsylvania especially, is bound together as a sort of community, though each member owns his own farm and enjoys the fruits of his own labor. It is of German parentage, and seems to combine the characteristics of the Methodist and the Quaker. The members own no slaves, and are very strong for the Union, though opposed to war; they greeted me with great cordiality after the service, and I rode back to camp quite satisfied with my morning's experience.

CHAPTER XXIV.

FAREWELL TO MARYLAND.

MONDAY, *October* 24*th*. Our division was this day ordered to Bakersville, half a dozen miles up the Potomac, and after breakfast I rode thither with the general and our topographical lieutenant, in order to select proper locations for the different brigades. Even so small a change was pleasant; the morning ride very agreeable; wood and water were found in abundance, and long before the brigades arrived their camping-grounds were ready for them. By nightfall they were comfortable; pickets were sent out to line the banks of the river; every body but the division staff was at home.

The general, who now had his wife with him, had taken rooms in the chief residence of Bakersville, and we had selected a pretty spot close at hand for the head-quarter tents. But day glided slowly into night, and our head-quarter wagons had not arrived. As it turned out, they had mistaken the road, and gone off upon a reconnoissance in another direction. The night was rainy, and it was after 8 o'clock before they came slowly rumbling along. All ready stood the division guard to unpack and pitch our tents; all ready were our servants to set up our simple housekeeping gear; our cook seized at once his mess-chest, and in half an hour I was sitting comfortably in my tent, every thing in its place, hearing the rain patter down upon the roof, and indulging with a friend or two in a late dinner of coffee, bread and butter, and pickled oysters. I declare that it is worth while to stand on a wet and dismal hill-side for half an hour, so as really to enjoy the satisfaction of being once more pleasantly housed.

Bakersville rejoices in one store, with a motley stock of groceries, medicines, and dry goods, consecrate to barter and country gossip, and in some half a dozen residences, so that our staff and attendants doubled its population. Our tents were perched upon an elevation overlooking the little hamlet; our division guard and orderlies encamped in a field on the opposite side of the road, while in the rear our cooks and servants reigned supreme. As the evenings were now cold, a big fire was built at nightfall in front of each tent, the tent-flaps flung back, and a portion of the heat thus penetrated within. Two of our lieutenants had confiscated somewhere a sheet-iron stove with a long piece of pipe, which, when thrust horizontally out of their tent-flaps, looked like a gun protruding from an embrasure.

The general now occupied himself in thoroughly exploring the vicinity, while our topographical officer was busied in mapping it out. During our stay here I rode twice to Hagerstown, some twelve miles distant, a pretty town; and as one or two rebel raids around our quiescent army had just stirred up the apprehensions of its citizens, it was overflowing with uniforms.

Our stay here was to be very brief; the usual order to have three days' cooked rations was issued to the men shortly after our arrival, and at length, on Sunday, October 26th, the order to march actually came. Once more we were to cross the Potomac into Virginia; probably a long and weary march was before us. The wet season was also at hand, and on this day of moving the rain came down in a deluge. But every one was glad of the expected change. By noon the whole column was in motion; our head-quarter tents were all struck save my own and the quartermaster's, and the wagons moved off, sinking to their hubs in the mud as they rolled slowly along.

I have noticed that the rougher the day and the more horrible the marching, the more jovial and exhilarated are the troops. As they came plunging along through the deep mud, almost staggering under the torrents of rain, past my tent on the roadside, I have rarely seen them in better spirits. I had appropriated the stove of the lieutenants, and its long pipe now projected from my tent-flaps and pointed straight over the road. Not a company passed by without some fling at my canvas fortress. "Don't shoot!" would cry, in imploring tones, some wag in uniform, as he plowed through the mud, his heavy knapsack dripping with rain, his shelter-tent wound round his shoulders, his bayonet ornamented with a tin cup, and a frying-pan strapped to his side; and "D—o—n—'t shoot!" came in all sorts of laughing tones from the waddling chorus. "Lie down, boys, lie down!" the usual order given to infantry when under artillery fire and not themselves engaged. "Boys, we've got to charge that battery!" interspersed with variations, gave the bedrenched column a good deal of fun. There was one good feature about this day's march. It was not one of those doubtful days when, by picking your way, now here, now there, you can partially protect yourself, for the mud was deep and universal.

There was no anxiety about it; your first plunge settled the matter, and you had wet feet and the entire freedom of the road for the rest of the day.

> "John Brown's body lies mouldering in his grave,
> His soul is marching on,"

was ever and anon wafted to my ears by a chorus of marching singers. What a dearth we have in America of good common songs! I have heard fire companies returning from a fire actually compelled to sandwich a good old hymn between two bacchanalian refrains, having quite exhausted their favorite melodies. "We are bound for the land of Canaan" does not flow naturally from a great two-fisted, red-shirted fellow, nor could I ever enjoy hearing a crowd of roughs yelling out at the top of their lungs, "I want to be an angel," especially if they qualified each verse with an intermediate dash of oaths. In all seriousness, that man would be a public benefactor who would give our soldiers some simple patriotic songs, each with a good chorus, to lighten their weary marches and cheer their evening camp-fires.

So very slow was the movement of the division that it was after nightfall before the rear brigade marched by, and still poured down the driving rain. Fortunately, the night's march was not a long one; yet I felt almost a compunction of conscience as I laid down in my camp-bed and thought of the poor fellows bivouacking in the wet fields.

Monday, October 27th. This morning the rain had become more reasonable, did not come down so uncompromisingly, and at noon the heavens had gotten over their weeping-fit, and once more smiled on us. Great was the loading of wagons with quarter-master and commissary stores, and the last two tents disappeared from beside the school-house, my own masked battery being one of them.

At breakfast I had achieved a horse-trade. My mess having departed yesterday, I breakfasted at a farm-house, and there sat at meat with us a stranger, uncouth, unkempt, unclean. Happening to mention that I should require another horse, my mare being overworked, he of course had just the animal, and after breakfast brought to my tent a beast, large, black, clumsy, and strong, with big feet for wading through the mud. It was my duty to inspect and try him. Now if there was any one quality for which I was noted among the staff, it was my entire ignorance of the good points of a horse; but I mounted the black Bucephalus, rode him a couple of hundred yards, and returned looking very wise and saying nothing. Thus I left it to the horse-dealer to make the first move, and the trade began. As it is the common belief that in a horse-trade the most honest man will try to cheat his own brother, I armed myself at all points with objections, but finally made an offer, which was, after much demur, accepted, and the beast was mine. I never repented of the bargain. Though evidently intended for a truck-horse, he was invaluable for the slow, heavy work of a muddy campaign.

On my new black, then, my mare being ridden by my servant, I was soon plunging through the mud out of Bakersville, passing mile after mile of wagons, and reached, about 4 P.M., the head of the column. The division was just going into bivouac in the fields lying under South Mountain, in the highly picturesque region at the western entrance of Crampton's Pass. On the road I had passed our quarter-master riding in an ambulance. The "spiflications" had proved too much for him; but, though suffering much pain, he was jocose to the last, informing me that "the surgeons had set on him," and given him the necessary document of disability, and so we lost him.

It was late before the head-quarter tents arrived, and as my own was still in the rear, I accepted the invitation of our colonel, a man with very correct ideas as to comfort, to pass the night at the pleasant residence of Mr. Crampton. Colonel Phelps, commanding the 1st brigade, and his staff soon joined us, and with these gentlemen, of whose bravery in battle and open-hearted hospitality I had enjoyed abundant evidences, we supped and lodged. Among my many pleasant campaigning memories, that merry evening round Mr. Crampton's blazing logs, with its mixture of solid conversation and sweet cider, has pleasant prominence.

Tuesday, October 28th. A good sleep and a capital breakfast prepared us for our morning march. As we rode up and through Crampton's Pass we enjoyed a fine sweep of landscape, and saw the town of Birketsville sitting up on its own little knoll, keeping watch and ward over the broad checker-board of farms and orchards. The general was riding at some distance in front of the troops, and, having joined him, I was ordered to ride on to Berlin, the little town on the Potomac which had been selected as the crossing-place of the army. My ride was, as usual, through a region crowded with troops; the turnpikes were now helped out by roads extemporized through the fields on both sides; mile upon mile stretched the great caravan, pressing slowly forward. It was evident that the Army of the Potomac was at last in motion.

Berlin was a very interesting place to staff officers about this time, being situated on the railroad which brought up all the army supplies, but ordinarily it has few attractive features. For the next two or three days the village and the region about it became one vast military camp. General M'Clellan had already established his head-quarters in a grove back of the town, and long wagon-trains were at once sent across the river over the pontoon bridge with subsistence stores, which they left in great stacks along the roadside, and then returned for more. Berlin was to be our only dépôt until we reached Warrenton, and every effort was necessary to provide against contingencies.

Having finished my business, I rode back, to find the division bivouacked about a mile out of town. The evening air was lit up with ten thousand camp-fires; and when tattoo was sounded by the bugles in every direction, we went to our beds, rejoicing in the belief that the Army of the Potomac was so soon to bid farewell to Maryland.

Thursday, October 30th. Yesterday was a very busy day for me, passed chiefly at Berlin; and to-day, at 1 P.M., we struck tents for the last time in Maryland, and the division moved at once into the town. But so many thousands were now pressing forward over the pontoon bridge that our march was delayed for an hour or two, and we sat with the general on our horses, amused by the evident exhilaration of the troops as they hurried by. The day was beautiful, and every one had quite a touch of the old enthusiasm. At last it was our turn to cross; the men who had been standing at ease along the streets and road fell in, the bands gave us their most exhilarating music, and at the head of his division of eight thousand men the general, with his staff, moved toward the pontoon bridge. All our tedious waiting at Antietam was forgotten; only the pleasant reminiscences of our Maryland campaign were left in our memory, and never have I felt more sanguine of success than on this lovely afternoon.

Just as we reached the bridge my hand was seized by a strong, two-handed grip, and, turning, I saw the pleasant face of one of our Fredericksburg friends, a good Union farmer of intelligence and thorough loyalty, who had been compelled to fly when our army relinquished that city. His "God bless you!" and fervent hope that we might free his state in this second trial, so that he might once more return home, greatly impressed me. I accepted it as a good omen to be thus cordially welcomed at the threshold of his state by a patriotic and warm-hearted Virginian.

CHAPTER XXV.

ONCE MORE INTO VIRGINIA.

"ALL hail, Virginia! may we be better friends before we again leave you!" exclaimed one of the staff as we rode off the pontoon bridge, and the birds responded with their merriest music; the trees, tinted with the rich hues of autumn, bowed before the gentle breeze, and whispered a God-speed; the Old Dominion was giving us pleasant welcome to her sacred soil. After such a greeting, who could remember the inhospitable treatment received from the people during our last campaign in Virginia, or feel that we were now among our enemies? Nor was there, during the first few days of our march, any thing to disenchant us, for we were moving through a lovely country, as yet undefaced by war, and received many a kindly greeting, especially in that portion wherein peaceful Quakers feasted on the fat of the land. For good living, commend me to a community of Friends!

It is true that we had no public demonstration of welcome, but found many who still loved the old flag, and whose greeting was affectionate and sincere. The whole region impressed me with its loveliness; it was seen under the auspices of delightful days and moonlit nights; the roads were in excellent condition, and the men marched so well that before nightfall on our first day we had reached our camp-ground at Bollington, nine miles from the river. As I sat that evening in my tent I heard once more the old Virginia music—a distant cannonading—and thought that perhaps to-morrow might bring us face to face with the enemy—*Quien sabé?*

But the division remained quietly in camp at Bollington during the next day, and I rode back to Berlin, returning in time for supper. Our epicurean staff-colonel had discovered a social oasis in the home of a pleasant Union family, and here some of us messed during our brief delay at this point. During this day there was great excitement among our contrabands. The idea of going back to their former homes greatly disturbed them; nor could we blame them for desiring to keep out of the old net. Our cook had no wish to fry any more buckwheats for General Lee, his former master, and my own body-servant came to me with a look so piteous that I had not the heart to say him nay; so we paid them, and sent them back to Berlin rejoicing.

Only two were now left of the old set who linked their fortunes with ours at Fredericksburg—Berryman, the old gray-headed darkey, whom I have seen so often sitting in the shadow of the general's tent, teaching himself to read, the ugliest and apparently least serviceable of the whole party, whom the general took out of mere charity, but who gradually became useful, faithful, and wholly reliable, attending the general with the same solicitude felt by a good nurse for her little charge, and never known to be away from the head-quarter wagons on a march; and Charles, a handsome, six-foot, finely-formed native of Maryland, who came nearer to Mrs. Stowe's Uncle Tom in the simplicity, truthfulness, and deep religiousness of his nature than any I ever met with. The latter, now that my former servant had departed, became attached to the adjutant general and myself jointly, and the whole care of overseeing the pitching of my tent and furnishing it was safely intrusted to his hands.

Saturday, November 1st. A hurried breakfast, especially for the lazy ones, for the order to march had come, and our general, as usual, was ready on the instant. It was a fine day for marching; our route was a little to the west of south, skirting the eastern slope of the Blue Ridge, and gladdening us with many a bit of romantic scenery. The men marched rapidly, so that about 3 P.M. we reached Purcellville, where a halt was ordered. We were now within a mile or two of Snicker's Gap; General Pleasanton, with his cavalry brigade and some flying artillery, was in advance beating up the enemy, who were on the other side of the Blue Ridge, and made demonstrations at each of its gaps of an intention to push through and attack us. The cannonading in front had been kept up all day, and our general, in putting his division into camp, was unusually careful in the formation and supports of his infantry line, and in the posting of his batteries.

About sunset our general ordered our old brigade, now under the leadership of Lieutenant Colonel Hoffman, of the 56th Pennsylvania Volunteers, a very gallant officer, to the aid of General Pleasanton. They were absent from the division three days, during which period they stirred up the hiding rebels in a manner which won the encomiums of all. Of course it would not do for our army to march past these gaps, leaving them in possession of an enemy who might pour through one of them upon our flank at any moment, or cut off our rear whenever so disposed. These gates must be ours, and our own men must keep the key, before we could venture farther. Each was guarded by rebel skirmishers with strong reserves, and each in turn was taken and held by General Pleasanton. At Ashby's Gap our old brigade did the work nobly. Deployed as skirmishers, they advanced slowly up the well-wooded sides of the narrow opening, drove in the enemy's pickets, rallied on our own reserves, and advanced in line of battle, had a brisk fight with the rebel reserves, and finally drove them altogether out of this important passage. The contrabands of the vicinity, here as elsewhere, acted as guides, and did excellent service.

As our former brigade moved up the road, with the hearty God-speed of those of us whose first military experiences were intermingled with its history, I was standing in front of a house selected by the general as head-quarters—a Secesh house, I regret to add, but its owner did not seem at all conscientious on the subject of greenbacks. Here we messed during our brief stay, and here the general and one or two of us lodged. We had lately received an addition to our mess in the person of an army correspondent, a man who, despite his name, was any thing but a *cipher* around an evening camp-fire.

The next day, Sunday, I was again compelled to ride back to Berlin through almost a solid mass of men in uniforms, of artillery, and of wagon-trains. It was useless to attempt to move my train against such a crowded tide, for miles upon miles of wagons were drawn out in the fields waiting for a clear road. All day long the hurrying mass moved forward toward the front, but at night, when the troops were bivouacked, the wagon-trains would have the turnpike to themselves. So I left my own train to come on at nightfall and park in Berlin, and rode on ahead, to pass the night at the house of a pleasant lady, whose rebel proclivities neither spoiled my supper nor disturbed the comfort of my bedchamber.

I had been compelled to leave a subordinate and a guard of a dozen men at Bakersville in charge of government property, and right glad was I next morning to see the little squad marching toward the railway station. Footsore from their hurried march, they were equally glad to be relieved of their knapsacks, which I directed to be carried in the wagons, and in a couple of hours the wagon-master reported all ready for a start. But to get within a hundred feet of the bridge was simply impossible, Berlin being crowded with advancing troops and artillery. Six long hours we waited for the road to be clear, and it was three o'clock in the afternoon before the train started. Once fairly in motion, I rode on ahead as usual, reaching Purcellville about sunset, and here learned that our division had moved on. As I had ordered my train to park here for the night, I went to a farm-house and secured supper and lodging. Many thousand troops were bivouacked all about us, and some of the field officers of a New Jersey regiment shared with me the evening meal.

As I sat in the parlor that evening, I discovered among the books usually found in such places the biography of Rufus Choate. A gleam of the Orient, verily a chapter out of the Arabian Nights, was thus flung in upon me at a moment when, tired and dusty with travel, I needed just such a stimulant. In five minutes I was in Boston, listening to the soft, sweet, fascinating tones of that most sympathetic voice, catching a beam or two of the light which sparkled in those deep-set eyes, magnetized and enthralled by the very presence of the orator, as he stood flinging ever fresh enchantment from his elfin locks. Our plain, practical America has thus far produced few men of genius, though many men of great talents; but this man was a genius. How such an imagination—Oriental, torrid, mystic—was ever ingrafted upon his logical, comprehensive New England understanding has always seemed to me a mystery. His political creed had in these later years seemed to me all wrong, but this never affected my feelings toward the man. Never could I forget how in my student-days he carried me captive, compelling my affection in the few brief words I ever exchanged with him, and forcing me to sympathize with his argument, even though I knew it was on the wrong side.

The good farmer came in about bedtime with his hints and suggestions as to sleep, but I asked only for another candle, agreed to look out for the house, trimmed the fire, and sat enjoying this book, not critically, but lovingly. A little after midnight the curtain dropped upon the fascinating life-drama, and I went up stairs, having passed the pleasantest night of the campaign in the society of Rufus Choate.

Tuesday, November 4th. My train did not come up until this morning, having been detained in the crush of wagons, and compelled to go into park some miles in the rear. Leaving it to push on as rapidly as possible, I rode forward some ten miles to Bloomfield, getting a good view of the roads winding up through Snicker's and Ashby's Gaps in the Blue Ridge, and enjoying greatly the delicious autumn air and the many-hued foliage of the forests. At about 8 P.M. I found our head-quarter tents pitched in a pretty spot near a farm-house, and I was soon at the mess-table.

That night the major of the 76th New York, whose adventures on the first night of our battle at Bull Run I have before referred to, came in to visit us, having just been exchanged and rejoined his regiment. Among other incidents, he told us that one of the 76th, also a prisoner, looked a little as if he had negro blood in his veins, and at once the cry went up from the rebels, "Hang him! hang him!" The rope was actually procured, and nothing but the most strenuous remonstrances prevented the catastrophe. At length the officer in charge consented to wait until morning, and during the night the man got mixed up with the crowd of other prisoners, was paroled, and sent off during the excitement and confusion caused by next day's battle.

That night also I enjoyed for the first time the greatest of all campaign comforts, which I see memorialized in my little diary thus, "SIBLEY STOVES." The nights had now become so cool that the usual fire in front of our tents, though pretty to look at, was rather a delusion in the way of warmth. In our future encampments, five minutes after our tents were pitched these simple sheet-iron rolls filled them with a pleasant glow. For these comforts we were indebted to the thoughtfulness of the general, aided by the energy of our new quarter-master, a dry humorist, one of your men who will almost knock you over with a joke, looking as solemn the while as a judge when passing sentence.

My own tent not being pitched when I arrived, I accepted the invitation of our surgeon, also a late addition to our staff, and a fine specimen of the American gentleman. We had indeed been very fortunate in the changes incident to a division staff, and I still felt, when returning after an absence, like one who is coming home, sure of a hearty welcome.

Wednesday, November 4th. A march not long, but tedious, brought us to-day into camp near Rectortown. Early next morning we again moved forward in a southerly direction, marching about 9 A. M. through Salem, a village sitting, like its ancient namesake, on a hill. A mile or two beyond this spot our march was incontinently stopped. The scouts had brought in tidings of the movement of a force of the enemy in a direction threatening our right, and our division was ordered to leave the road and push up toward the threatened point of attack; so we moved over the fields and up through an opening in the hills, where we formed in line of battle. The day was raw, and the wind had a fair sweep at us as it came rushing through the hills; but this was the only enemy we met with. It was soon discovered that the tidings were incorrect, and the march toward Warrenton was again resumed.

Warrenton was occupied by our troops without opposition; a rebel force had just left it, and we found four hundred of the rebel wounded still here. Our reception this evening was not enthusiastic. Every store was closed; hardly a light glimmered in a private residence; the whole town was evidently indulging in a fit of sackcloth and ashes. The hotel was of course open, or, rather, its basement-office; but even that looked black and sullen, and anxious to turn upon us a very cold shoulder. This marked coolness, combined with the chilliness of the night air, and a plentiful lack of food, was not exhilarating. Our division bivouacked at the southern edge of the town, and, as our wagons were in the rear, we went into a wayside school-house, doubtless a good enough temple of learning in its day, but now *sans* windows, *sans* doors, *sans* every thing like comfort. Even its walls were ornamented with legends any thing but suggestive of its former uses. One prudent staff officer brought out a candle or two from his saddle-bags; another produced a paper of crackers and cheese; a roaring fire was built in the ample fireplace; and thus provided with a supper which could not induce dyspeptic dreams, we waited patiently until midnight brought up our wagons, and sleeping became possible. A blanket was now hung up as a substitute for the door, another did duty as window-shutter, and so we managed, after all, to pick up a few crumbs of needed sleep.

CHAPTER XXVI.

WARRENTON TO FALMOUTH.

WE remained in Warrenton four days, during which period General M'Clellan was relieved by General Burnside. Our staff tents were pitched around the school-house, which was still used as a mess-room; the weather was cold, and quite a heavy snow-storm gave notice of approaching winter. The first two days were to me full of anxiety, as there was no subsistence dépôt at Warrenton; the railway connection was not completed, and no one seemed to know positively where or when supplies could be obtained. I have before expressed my opinion as to the admirable organization and management of the commissary department; but when the railways are broken up, and other transportation is limited, it is a Herculean task to feed a large army. Some military authority has said, with laconic point, "An army moves on its belly;" and it was clear that unless food was procured our division would have to pause. And most of the other divisions were similarly situated.

In the midst of a driving storm, I sent off a subordinate with a wagon-train a mile long, and with a sort of roving commission among the stations where supplies might be reasonably expected. Great was my relief when, late at night, after being two days out, he reported the train coming in with rations for our eight thousand men for nearly a week. Early next morning the different brigade commissaries were notified, and in two hours the square acre of stores was distributed, and we were now ready to move.

During our stay I hibernated in my tent, for the air was cold, and I had much to do. Hearing that an old Californian acquaintance of mine, a rebel officer of some distinction, who was wounded at Antietam, was at home on parole, I called to see him. But he had left Warrenton when our army reached it, and I was most courteously received by his wife and family. That gentleman has lost one son, and been himself twice desperately wounded in this rebellion, and yet no allusion was permitted to mar the kindly courtesy of our interview. I mention this incident because it sent me home pondering the old question, always suggested to me by the interchange of kindly courtesies with the Southern people, Why have they forced this whole nation into war?

I wish I could describe one scene which greatly charmed me during this stay at Warrenton, the view of a large camp at night. I was not in the habit of leaving head-quarters after dark, but on this occasion desired to visit my good friend "Don Carlos," a captain on the staff of my old brigade. As I walked along the ridge occupied by our division, I found myself passing through long avenues of fire, for before each shelter-tent blazed a pile of hickory logs, each vying with its neighbor in architectural order and grandeur of illumination. Around each pyramid of flame sat the men, engaged in various avocations; some, of course, cooking, for no camp-fire was ever without a soldier making coffee, no matter what the hour; some reading or playing cards; the majority simply keeping warm and conversing together. As I proceeded, I saw the tents of the field and staff hiding away beneath the foliage, each fronted by a camp-fire, around which sat a group of officers, while the fire-light went leaping up among the trees, lending a weird appearance to the forms hovering about its glow. The brigade head-quarter tents were pitched around a hollow square, lofty trees standing like sentinels at its corners, while within was a blazing pile in front of each opened flap, making the quadrangle light as day, and tropical with warmth. Within the tents the various staff officers were amusing or employing themselves; all of the commonplace was transfigured. This was tent-life under its most romantic aspect, and I paused for some time to enjoy this, to me, novel night-scene.

Very picturesque all this, but when I returned to my tent and saw my little conical-shaped roll of sheet-iron glowing with a welcome, I once more repeated mentally my old benediction, "Blessings on the man who invented the Sibley stove."

Very little occurred worthy of record during this my second visit to Warrenton. Here, as in other places, young men were not, all its male residents, save old men and little children, being off to the wars, and the pretty town looked far more wo-begone and gloomy than on my former visit. Of goods of any kind, drugs and medicines, and the like, there was absolute dearth, as no communication with Alexandria had been for some months permitted. To me it was no longer pleasant to ride through the disconsolate streets, and I therefore kept very much at home. The last review by General M'Clellan took place while here, on which occasion our late commander was heartily cheered by the troops as he rode down the lines, and seemed considerably affected at leaving them.

Tuesday, November 11th. At 11 A.M. our corps marched in a direction nearly due south to the town of Fayetteville, distant seven miles. I did not, however, accompany the march, as we were expecting every hour the arrival of railway trains of subsistence stores, and it was desirable to secure as many supplies as possible before moving. Several other officers remained with me, and, about 4 P.M., having passed the day at the railway station in rain, we went up to the pleasant residence of a lady, and sat down to an excellent dinner bespoken by one of our number. Despite the poverty of the land, the mahogany was well covered, and a merrier party has rarely surrounded it. The lady of the house was decidedly Secesh, and the conversation flowed naturally into dangerous channels. She was confident of the ultimate success of the rebellion, but remarked not long after that they were trying to sell their place and move North.

"Oh yes," said one of our party; "you think the plank is going to break in the middle, and don't mean to be on that half which falls overboard." A quiet laugh around the board was followed by an impetuous protest that she could not see it in that light. She was not the first respectable Virginian whom I have met who feels bound to talk strongly for the South, and is yet plotting and planning desperately to get out of it.

Our excellent dinner had only sufficient earnestness of converse to flavor it withal, and we were so much pleased with our hostess that, later in the day, finding we must remain in Warrenton all night, we engaged lodgings under her roof. I think no one of that party but looks back at this evening around a home fireside as one of the pleasantest experiences in Virginia.

The next day the railway trains arrived, and we rode out to Fayetteville, all of which town I saw except the houses. I remember this as the prettiest camp of the campaign, and here we passed four days, during which I made another business visit to Warrenton. Cannonading was occasionally heard in the direction of the Rappahannock; every hour we expected orders to move; but the hoof-disease had broken out among the horses, and it was necessary to replace many of them with fresh stock. The men had delightfully-situated bivouacs, and from my tent I could look out at evening upon continuous lines of camp-fires covering the ground for acres. Some of the oldsters of the staff had now fallen into the pleasant custom of playing a few games of whist before retiring for the night. There seemed to be a general understanding, as the weather grew more wintry, that there would not be much more marching or fighting at present, and that the true philosophy was to make ourselves comfortable. It takes a man about six months really to learn how to accept with entire equanimity the frequent changes and disappointments in campaign life, and to enjoy it properly as he moves along.

Monday, November 17*th.* A pleasant morning after yesterday's storm! Bright and early came down our tents, breakfast was dispatched, and the general and staff mounted and led off the division. Having sent a train to Warrenton Junction the day before with orders to meet us at Bealeton, I rode ahead with two knights of the quill, Argus-eyed, and ever on the watch for items, and much I enjoyed their company and the lovely bits of scenery, and the fresh morning air. We had not ridden far before we caught up with the other divisions of our corps drawing out into the road, and at Bealeton I found my train, which had just arrived. Relieved on that head, I dismounted, seated myself on a cracker-box at a camp-fire deserted by the second division, and waited a couple of hours for our division to come up. Our march was slow and uneventful, and we were glad at 5 P.M. to fling ourselves from the saddle at the house of a gentleman which had been taken for head-quarters. It was quite dark before the tired troops reached their camping-ground, where our adjutant general, never weary in the performance of duty, remained to see each brigade comfortably located. Our wagons then came slowly on through the mud, our tents were pitched by the light of lanterns, our horses quartered in the capacious barn, and supper, which we had engaged in the house, was ready.

It almost repays a man for going without his dinner, and passing the day on a tedious and chilly march, the sense of comfort which steals over him when, seated at a well-filled table near a cheerful fire, he feels that he has earned the right to a few hours rest. Our host was a man of far more than average intelligence and shrewdness, and during the evening and next morning I enjoyed some free conversation with him. He commenced, of course, with the stereotyped Virginian formula, "I was strong for the Union, but when my state went out I had to go with her;" but he was well read, had a good deal of reasoning power, and had evidently pondered upon this subject, and as he was also frank and anxious to reason fairly, we soon brushed all extraneous questions away, and came down to the question of slavery.

I may add that to this question of slavery every intelligent and candid Southerner always reverts in speaking of the rebellion, all other pleas being considered merely side-issues. Doubtless many in Virginia, as I have before remarked, persuade themselves that it is for the doctrine of state rights they are contending, and for the honor of their native state "invaded" by Northern myrmidons; but when an earnest and candid man seeks to go to the root of the matter, he always brings you down to the question of slavery.

Of course I do not propose to transcribe this conversation. In the course of it, however, I quoted some of the well-known results of our census statistics as indicating the difference, in all the elements of progress, between the free states and Virginia; but he knew more about these figures than I did, and at once admitted frankly, as I have heard many other Southerners admit before him, that slavery was a curse to the white man and a curse to his state.

"Why, then," said I, "are you so anxious to sustain it?"

"Because emancipation would be ruin and destruction to our slaves. Poor creatures, they are left on our hands, and never could take care of themselves; it would be cruel to turn them off."

"Well, it must be admitted that you Virginians are the most Quixotically benevolent people I ever met with; to the negro you are willing to sacrifice your state and yourselves. Certainly, if I were so philanthropic and such a negro-worshiper as you are, I also would be a slaveholder."

My host couldn't help laughing at this *reductio ad absurdum*, and at once changed his position. His plea, though so weak, is very common among slaveholders, who, unable to wink out of sight the facts of the census tables, try to ease their consciences by the belief that they are unadulterated philanthropists, suffering all these evils of slavery for the good of the slave. Accustomed to fling the title of "nigger worshiper" into the teeth of the Northman, it somewhat puzzles them to find it fixed so clearly on themselves. It struck me, through the whole conversation, that my host probably felt more doubts as to his position than he cared to admit to a man wearing the federal uniform.

Tuesday, November 18th. Still on the march, the day being rainy and the roads becoming more difficult of passage, to reach about dusk a camping-spot on the Stafford Court-house road, having moved some eight miles. The general selected a farm-house for his head-quarters, much to the joy of the occupant, who knew that this secured him at least partial protection for his cattle, sheep, and other movables. He had a piteous tale to tell of his losses, and was one of those whining, inefficient do-littles who keep a few negroes to do their work, bring up a family of drones like themselves, and pass most of their time in smoking a pipe or shaking with the fever and ague. The slaves looked sleek and comfortable, and really more respectable than their master, and we were told that one by one they were setting off on the Northern tour.

The next morning it again rained hard, and the roads became well-nigh impassable. I was now quite unwell, and remained as long as possible with our last night's host after the division had marched. As I sat by the fire, feeling weak and miserable, constantly occupied in futile efforts to convince the members of this family that one use of outside doors was to shut them, I became practically aware to what perils a wayside farmer is exposed during the march of troops. Behind the main body, wherein discipline exercises at least partial restraint, linger the squads of stragglers, and, aided by the army teamsters, they scour the country far and near. The proprietor of the house became quite frantic this morning as these locusts in uniform settled down upon his possessions, and made such strong appeals to me that I remained with him for several hours. Once I put a stop to a horse-trade, much to the chagrin of some cavalry-men; at another moment I halted a fellow as he was riding off on the farmer's only saddle; while of provost duty in the matter of chickens, sheep, and oats I had my hands full.

I had no objection to protecting the poor man all in my power, but this paddling to and from his barn in the midst of the driving rain was hardly the thing for my illness. My wagon-train had not moved, so slow was the advance of the troops; but I at length tore myself away, having secured for him a temporary guard. After wading through the deep mud for five miles, I found our corps encamped at the sides of a marsh a few miles from Falmouth. The general and staff stood upon a hill-side waiting for our wagons. About two hours after they were discovered plowing through the marsh; forty stout fellows, with long ropes, aided the tired horses; our servants and the division guard soon had our canvas houses erected, and one tired and miserable campaigner went immediately to bed.

Over the two days spent in this slough of despond, during which the rain overflowed the shelter-tents of the men, driving them into the woods, and ran over the trenches of our staff tents, saturating their floors with moisture, and defying even the Sibley stove; days in which, being fairly under the care of my friend the surgeon, I kept my tent, to enjoy without interruption his medicines—verily the two gloomiest days of the campaign—I should prefer to draw a veil. To be moderately sick at home I consider rather a luxury; to be sick in a mud-puddle, covered by canvas, is simply horrible.

On Saturday, the 22d, we moved five miles, and encamped at the side of the railroad between Aquia and Falmouth, a pleasant situation, and prettily located camp. Every one was of course full of disappointment at the failure of the pontoons, over which it had been intended that we should cross the Rappahannock. Who was to blame we knew not. It was only another stanza of the old refrain, "Some one had blundered." A few days ago, and a single division might have occupied Fredericksburg and its heights. Now it was understood that the whole rebel army, which had been dogging our footsteps ever since we left Maryland, was occupying and fortifying the fords and the surrounding heights. With all our confidence in General Burnside, it was evident that his position in a strategic point of view was an unfortunate one.

Very pleasant are my remembrances of our sixteen days passed in camp near the railroad. Concluding that the Fates were against us, and that the failure of the pontoons had put a stop to any more Richmond-ward for the present, it was, by mutual consent, agreed to accept the fact of winter-quarters, and to make the best of it. A room in a neighboring house was engaged for a mess-room, and our caterer was spurred up to his best efforts, our tents were fitted up with additional comforts, and every effort made to bear with cheerful philosophy what seemed an inevitable delay. Frequent rides to Aquia Creek, or over to Falmouth to have a look at the rebel pickets lining the river, and at the fortifications daily going up behind the city; a review by General Hooker of his corps, which impressed me more than any review I ever witnessed, from the number of bullet-pierced flags, and the well-known fighting fame of the reviewing general and many of the regiments; a visit to all the old spots so familiar when we occupied the "Camp opposite Fredericksburg"—these, with other excursions, varied the routine of staff duty and the monotony of camp life, and brought us to the mess-table with good appetites and cheerful minds.

During the last day or two of this period the movements of the pontoon trains began to look a little suspicious. A pontoon train is usually composed of some forty-eight narrow, flat-bottomed boats, thirty feet in length, set upon wheels and drawn by eight horses. With each boat are the necessary girders and planks for the construction of a bridge, and the different trains are under the immediate charge of two regiments of engineers.

The usual orders as to three days' rations, additional ammunition, etc., also came in, and at length, on the evening of Monday, December 8th, orders to move on the morrow toward the river reached us. At 10 A M. on Tuesday our division was in motion, crossed Potomac Creek, and bivouacked in the woods south of it, our own tents being pitched among the trees in a spot cleared for them by the pioneers. Our own general was absent in Washington, and the division was under the command of the senior brigadier.

Wednesday, December 10*th*. At 9 A.M. we struck tents, but moved only a couple of miles, bivouacking near White Oak Church. Our orders were to march at two o'clock to-morrow morning, and it was understood that we were then to attempt the passage of the river. We got up two or three staff tents, however, and the men made themselves as comfortable as if permanently located. We were right in the midst of the woods; one of the brigades was bivouacked within twenty feet of my tent door, and I watched with very deep interest the movements of these brave fellows— the veterans of half a dozen fiercely-contested battles —to see if any shadow of the impending conflict obtruded itself; but I remarked no change in their usual manner. It was evident, however, that they were well aware of the serious business before them, as their cheerful remarks ran usually in one channel. Systematically they put up their shelter-tents, built their fires, and cooked their suppers, and very early in the evening all was still through this immense camp save the sentinels pacing their usual rounds.

Every one was busy during the afternoon at headquarters in writing letters and making the necessary preparations, and after an early supper all retired to bed. About midnight I was awakened by our general, who had just arrived from Washington, and was groping his way among the tent-ropes, and greatly did his well-known voice rejoice us, as we had feared he would arrive too late to lead the division in the coming struggle. We were all speedily assembled in the office-tent, where a hearty breakfast or supper was soon served up; the different brigades were already falling in, and by 4 A.M. the whole column was in motion. The division, however, did not attempt the passage to-day, but was halted within a mile or two of the river, where the men stacked arms and awaited orders. Meantime the attempt to lay the pontoon bridges across the Rappahannock in face of the enemy had begun, and some account of this desperate undertaking will fitly occupy the next chapter.

CHAPTER XXVII.

THE PASSAGE OF THE RAPPAHANNOCK.

THURSDAY, *December* 11*th*. Our entire army was now filling the woods and fields skirting the Rappahannock, and stood grimly face to face with the enemy. But the river must be crossed before the desperate storming of the Fredericksburg Heights was possible, and the laying the pontoon bridges was the first thing in order.

Our own, the 1st corps, under command of General Reynolds, and the 6th, under General Smith, constituted the left grand division, commanded by General Franklin, and the spot selected for its crossing was some three miles below the city, where, beyond the rather steep bank, spread out a broad plain toward the rebel heights. Here early in the day the pontoons were brought down to the river's brink, and while our leading brigades looked on with almost breathless suspense, and the long line of our gunners on the heights overlooking the river stood ready to open fire at the least hostile demonstration, the laying of the two bridges was at once commenced—the one by the 15th New York Engineers, and the other by the United States Engineers. The work is simple enough, but I can conceive of no duty demanding more true courage. In the charge even of a forlorn hope, every man, as he grasps his musket, is fired by the common enthusiasm, lifted on the wave of a common excitement, feels to the tips of his finger-ends the martial inspiration; but this duty had in itself no warlike incitement—none of the fervid intoxication of a desperate charge; these men were for the nonce not warriors, but bridge-builders, grasping not the musket, but the hammer; not borne forward in a rush of excited valor, but penned up in narrow boats, from which neither advance nor retreat was possible. Every plank they laid brought them, living targets, closer and closer to the rebel sharpshooters, now coolly sighting each his man from the rifle-pits on the other side.

But there was no hesitation. The boats were floated out into the stream; each in turn was brought into place; coolly and systematically the engineers united it to the rest with girders, upon which, one by one, they laid down the plank. Nearer and nearer to the opposite bank grow the floating causeways; already they are more than half way across; the anxious thousands watching so eagerly the operation are already beginning to breathe more freely; the silence and suspense are awful, when suddenly a line of fire fringes the rebel rifle-pits, and volley after volley from the rebel sharpshooters is poured upon the courageous workmen. Some are wounded; all fall at once into the bottom of their pontoons, where they are partially protected; and now our artillery posted on the heights sweeps the opposite plain with grape and canister. These terrific discharges soon make every rifle-pit too hot for its occupants, and finally drive every rebel out of his hiding-place. Once more the heroic workmen resume their task of peril, the last boat is floated to its place, the last girder spans from boat to shore; and as the foremost engineer leaps upon the bank, one long, loud, enthusiastic cheer relieves the pent-up excitement of ten thousand spectators, and renders to these brave men the homage of their applauding comrades.

Farther up the river, and just opposite the city—the point at which General Sumner's right grand division was to cross—our engineers were not so fortunate. Very early in the morning the leading divisions were marched down as near the crossing-place as possible, where they rested on their arms, the pontoons were floated out, and the engineers sprang to their work. The same silence and suspense brooded over the river; boat after boat was brought into place; the engineers were within twenty feet of the opposite bank, when suddenly, at the report of a single rebel cannon—the death-signal to some of our heroic volunteers—the rebel sharpshooters, posted in the rifle-pits and houses at the river's brink, swept the unfinished bridge with their rifles, and three officers and twenty men fell killed and wounded before their murderous fire. To continue the work in the face of this continuous storm of bullets became simply impossible.

Then from more than a hundred guns of various calibre poured for hours a deluge of shot and shell upon the doomed city, especially upon the houses near the bank which protected the enemy's sharpshooters. Some have estimated that five hundred shells in a single minute were hurled from these miles of batteries. I had ridden over to our old Phillips's House headquarters, now occupied by General Sumner, and selected as his own post of observation by General Burnside, and stood watching with a hundred other officers this terrific bombardment. In rear of the house were troops, massed in solid acres, awaiting the orders to cross; the steps and slopes in front swarmed with generals and staff officers; every face had a waiting look of anxiety, while every eye sought to pierce the foggy cloud now resting upon Fredericksburg. All the while the rebel batteries, save that solitary death-signal just referred to, had not given tongue. The air was full of the smoke-wreaths of shell bursting over the town, and two or three perpendicular columns of smoke rising above the fog indicated the site of some of the burning houses.

As I stood here, an artillery caisson passed by with a poor fellow crimsoned with gore and held up in the arms of two others. What was my surprise when I saw the white face turn wistfully toward mine, while a low voice groaned out my name. In an instant I was at his side, recognizing him with difficulty as one of our orderlies. He had preceded the division with a companion on a private reconnoissance toward the river bank, and both had been severely wounded by the premature explosion of one of our own shells. A surgeon was soon found, and the stretcher-bearers bore the wounded man down into the glen to the right of the Phillips House, where some hospital-tents were already pitched, and where, safely out of range of the rebel batteries, long streets of these temporary houses of refuge were quickly going up. I found the surgeons in charge ready and willing to do all in their power; chloroform was administered, and in twenty minutes John, minus an arm, was lying in a clean bed and feeling quite comfortable, and I left him to go down to the bank of the river in search of his comrade. As I rode back through the glen, already the sad procession of ambulances had begun, and I paused a moment to gaze at the poor fellows as they were lifted out and carried into the canvas hospitals—heroes every one of them, for they had been wounded in the desperate efforts, as yet unsuccessful, to lay the upper pontoon bridge.

It was now about noon; the fog had lifted, and the city was distinctly visible, showing at this distance but few battle-scars, though I saw rising from several houses columns of smoke and flame. There had been for some time a lull in the bombardment; the rebel batteries during the while had remained obstinately silent, but the rebel sharpshooters were not yet dislodged, and every attempt to finish the bridge had been defeated by their murderous fire.

John had described the locality of his accident as well as he could collect his thoughts to describe any thing, but my search up and down the river bank proved unavailing, and it afterward appeared that the other wounded attaché of our staff had been taken to a hospital, where he lost his leg. Both, however, recovered from their severe wounds.

Rumors of every conceivable description filled the air, and I finally had to ride down about 3 P.M. and take a look at the pontoon bridge for myself. It was then more than two thirds completed, but no effort was apparently being made to continue it; the batteries were silent; for a moment all was quiet on the Rappahannock. I saw a person at the open window of one of the houses waving a white handkerchief, probably intended as a notice to our gunners that he desired to be considered as claiming exemption from their rather pressing attentions by virtue of this flag of truce. The man certainly deserved consideration for the novelty of his idea, and the bravery with which he carried it out.

Hardly had I returned to my former post of observation when with renewed violence burst forth the storm of war, and it was under cover of this last bombardment that the movement began, by the aid of which the pontoon bridge was at length completed. It had become evident that the rebel riflemen could not be dislodged from their hiding-places by artillery, and men were now needed who would cross in the pontoons and drive them out at the point of the bayonet. The call is for volunteers. Hundreds at once step to the front, men of Michigan and Massachusetts, for to regiments of these states has been given the perilous honor of leading the way into Fredericksburg, and for hours they have been waiting near the bank for the completion of the bridge; one hundred only can be selected, lest the boats be overcrowded; hurriedly they leap in; one youngster, Robert Hendershot, drummer-boy of the 8th Michigan, made of heroic stuff, forcing his way in among the rest, and so making his name and fame historical.

And now, boys! brothers! heroes! give way! Ten thousand faces pale with intense excitement look down upon you; ten thousand anxious hearts hang upon every stroke of your oars. It may be that the future destiny of that country you love so well depends upon the issue of this hour's business. With desperate strength the boats are speeding on their dangerous errand. In vain the rebel sharpshooters seek to check their progress; the shore is gained; with loud cheers our heroes rush up the bank, charge with the cold steel upon houses and rifle-pits, capture fifty prisoners, and put the whole rebel gang *hors de combat*, with wounds more or less severe, or send them flying toward the rear. Five minutes of this bloody work does the business, and they are soon recrossing with their captives, having met with small loss, to be received by wild and tumultuous cheers and congratulations. Hardly have these cheers died away before the bridge is finished, and at double-quick our impatient volunteers are crossing to secure and hold it.

Nearly at the same period, by a sudden and gallant dash, the 87th Pennsylvania threw another pontoon bridge across a little below this, and now four floating ways span the Rappahannock, and afford free passage to the rebel lair.

Why has not every man who distinguished himself in this passage of the Rappahannock received ere this some decoration of honor, to be worn proudly on his heart while living, to be handed down as a precious heir-loom when he has departed? Why, at least, is not his name published in some roll of honor, as a reward to him and an encouragement to others? Can we afford to neglect those appeals to an honest pride and an honorable ambition which Napoleon and every other great captain have found so valuable? I consider that every man who steadfastly aided in laying those pontoon bridges, or who crossed in those boats in face of the concealed enemy, was a hero, and is fairly entitled to a hero's reward.

General Howard's division at once commenced to cross, and his third brigade, under command of Colonel Hall, and consisting of the 7th Michigan, 19th and 20th Massachusetts, and 59th New York, led the way across the bridge and through the streets of the city.

In this street-fighting the brigade lost about one hundred in killed and wounded, among them the heroic Chaplain Fuller, who seized a musket and led on into the fight the men for whose welfare he had so zealously labored and prayed. One hears some bitter things said in the army about chaplains, but were they all true, the life and death of such men as Fuller and Conant, and others of similar stamp, would more than counterbalance them.

Having obtained full possession of the lower streets, General Howard's division bivouacked in the city for the night. About the same time General Newton's division, led by General Devens's brigade, rushed across the pontoon bridges assigned to the left grand division, moved at double-quick up the steep bank, and at once deployed as skirmishers, and began to force back the rebel sharpshooters. The latter fell back briskly as the remainder of Newton's division crossed, and our men were soon drawn up in line of battle on the plain. Here they remained for some time, but, for some reason, it was deemed best to leave no troops on the right bank for the night; the division was withdrawn, and bivouacked near the river, in readiness to cross on the morrow.

Our own head-quarters were in the woods by the roadside, perhaps a mile and a half from the lower bridges, and here we cleared away space enough for some tents. A cheerful camp-fire was built, and as we sat around it many and various were the speculations as to our own movements and the intentions of the enemy. All were in excellent spirits, but I felt ill at ease, for the general had just directed me to remain on this side and attend to my own department, and, though never less anxious to go into battle, I could not help feeling a little regret that my comrades were to go in without me. They brought me their money, with letters and messages for home, and the whole affair was to me very dismal. As they were to be in the saddle with the early dawn, we separated early for bed.

Friday, December 12th. Shortly after sunrise the general and staff rode off at the head of the division, leaving our quarter-master and myself in possession of head-quarters. In a couple of hours the fields about us were deserted by all but the wagon-trains and the tents of the quarter-masters and commissaries of our different brigades.

After an hour or two of necessary duty, I mounted my horse and rode over toward General Sumner's head-quarters. Every road leading to the river was crowded with troops of the right and left grand divisions, while the centre, under General Hooker, which was to be held in reserve, remained under arms, ready to move at a moment's notice wherever their services were most needed, but did not cross until the morrow. Our batteries still lined the bank, but rested a while from yesterday's labors, while the city and all the rebel fortifications were hidden from view by a thick veil of fog.

I could not resist the desire to ride once more through the familiar streets of Fredericksburg, and was especially curious to see the result of yesterday's bombardment. A brother officer joined me, and we were soon in the current sweeping down to the river. As we crossed the pontoon bridge which had cost such an expenditure of blood and patriotism, every pontoon, with its frequent bullet-marks and splintered sides, eloquently attested the perils of bridge-building under fire.

The lower streets, through nearly their entire length, were crowded with troops, now standing at ease, and leaving only a narrow passage-way in the centre for horsemen. Most of the men maintained a proper military decorum, and did not leave their colors; but I saw numbers enjoying a thorough ransack of a few of the houses, bringing therefrom measures of flour and meal, eatables of every description, with some other articles of a heterogeneous description. Soldiers have sometimes queer ideas in these respects. I have heard of one who, having found somewhere a volume of Congressional documents, bore the weighty, bulky book around with him in his knapsack for several days, until they seemed heavier to him than they even do to the man who attempts to read them. I saw one fellow to-day rejoicing in a huge stuffed monkey, an absurdity so great that I halted him to learn its history. Of course "another soldier gave it to him;" while to my question as to how he intended to transport his monkeyship, he replied practically by slinging it over his shoulder as a counterbalance to his shelter-tent. Whether he stormed the heights with the creature on his back I have never learned.

One man walked demurely along decorated with a woman's bonnet, while another wore a beaver hat, which seemed almost as incongruous. The humorous element, not the rage for plunder, was evidently predominant; and of all that army I did not see one hundred engaged in pillage, and nearly all these were content to remove eatables alone. Numbers had boxes, half boxes, and smaller parcels of tobacco, but, as this had been fished from the river, it was legitimate prize of war. And it is my belief, judging from personal observation, that the accounts in the papers of the wholesale pillaging of our troops were an exaggeration. I am no apologist for this military misdemeanor, and have the strongest aversion to private pillage; still, it is not fair that our whole army should suffer for the errors of a few. If any one has imagined that our troops, immediately on crossing, broke ranks and commenced to pillage and destroy, he greatly mistakes the general deportment of our volunteers. As the long lines of men picture themselves in my memory to-day, I see them mainly serious and determined, leaning on their guns, evidently thinking of the work before them, and not of a little private pillage. And I desire also to say, after my campaign experiences, that our American army, if we may believe history, is less liable to the charge of pillage than any large army ever before organized.

One would naturally expect, after the battle of yesterday, to see a city of ruins, hardly a brick wall standing, hardly one stone remaining on another; but, to my great surprise, that iron storm had made comparatively little outward impression. The row of inferior houses immediately on the river's brink, which had been the rebel hiding-places, were, of course, riddled and torn with shot and shell; perhaps twenty buildings in all were destroyed by fire. Many of the churches and residences were decorated with one or more shot-holes, while a few were considerably torn by bursting shell; but a large majority of the buildings had not suffered at all. The gaping ruins and dismantled dwellings I had expected to see were not visible, and as I rode through the upper streets where the soldiers were not drawn up, the old sleepy town looked very much as before. We saw quite a number of the citizens, of different colors, who had remained in their cellars during the bombardment, and it was a touching sight to see some of the women, still half frenzied with their late excitement, as they dragged themselves and their little ones down to the bridges, anxious only to escape the scene of so much terror.

I always felt an interest in the mansion wherein we passed our first night in Fredericksburg, and was glad to find that it bore no evidence of damage. A row of superannuated contrabands stood leaning over the fence, the last remnant of their tribe, and from them I learned the history of two or three persons in whom I felt some interest. Nearly all the residents had fled to the mountains or to Richmond.

We were now two or three streets above our troops, but saw here and there an occasional soldier, and were riding leisurely up street, thinking all was safe, when one of our pickets remarked to me, "Captain, if you don't want to be shot, you'd better not go any farther. The rebel sharpshooters are just above us." As we were now nearly at the edge of the town, we thanked him, and concluded to pursue our investigations in another direction.

After visiting other parts of the town, to be every where struck with the little damage done by our bombardment, we rode once more through our troops, still standing at ease in the lower streets, recrossed the bridge, and again ascended to the elevation near the Phillips House as, on the whole, the best post of observation. Many officers were here, seeking, like myself, to pierce the fog resting upon the rebel intrenchments, but in vain. All was still; the passage of the river seemed to be the only work for to-day, and it was time for me to be back to camp.

An hour or two later, hearing the booming of cannon, I left my tent and rode down to the river bank. The fog had at last lifted, and the rebels were amusing themselves by throwing a few shells into the city, and exchanging compliments with two or three of our batteries; but the day passed with nothing more exciting than these occasional artillery duels, the infantry on each side being passive, and so in anxious suspense we awaited the coming morrow.

CHAPTER XXVIII.

THE BATTLE OF FREDERICKSBURG.

SATURDAY, *December* 13*th*. I awoke this morning with the same feeling of intense and anxious expectation which had sent me early to bed last night; and, with my friend the quarter-master, hurried through breakfast, attended to my necessary duties, and then visited the commissariats of the different brigades. It was perhaps ten o'clock before I was ready to ride over to a point on the bluff bordering the river, where our batteries were posted, which, without being too far from camp, commanded a fine view of the rebel fortifications, and of the plain back of the city. Here, with the exception of occasional visits to camp to learn if any orders had been sent over, I remained for the greater part of this most exciting day, in company with a large party of staff officers, whose duties detained them on this side the river.

Shortly after we reached this look-out, the fog had lifted sufficiently to afford a complete view of the arena whereon Sumner's right, now quietly occupying the city, were to enter the lists against a concealed and fortified enemy. It is a gradually ascending plain, lying back of Fredericksburg, with many inequalities of surface, and bounded by a line of heights, more elevated as they recede, which not only overlook the plain, but by a sweep toward the river on the rebel left, flank it also. As I looked toward this extreme left through a field-glass, I saw the rebels still busily engaged in putting up fresh earthworks, and it was evident that they intended to use the spade until it was absolutely necessary to take up the rifle. Near the turnpike I saw also, glistening in the sun, the pieces of a brass battery, planted so as to enfilade this plain, and cut down any advancing column.

With our field-glasses we could not discern the numerous batteries which crowned the heights for several miles, but some of the rebel forts and embrasures were distinctly visible. One fort, especially, on a low elevation just back of the city, seemed to command the plain perfectly, and here, protected by earthworks, were the guns of the Washington Artillery, a famous rebel battalion. Just at its base, and connecting with the turnpike, ran a narrow country road, skirted by a low stone wall, looking quite insignificant. We shall know more about this stone wall anon.

Over this plain, thus fronted and flanked by hostile batteries, and line upon line of infantry, must move to the storming of those fortifications the forlorn hope of Sumner's right grand division. The morning was one of the loveliest of the year; the city, the plain, and the rebel heights slept silently in the pleasant sunshine; only an occasional smoke-puff above the trees, followed by the deep boom of a heavy gun, would remind the casual observer of the dread reality of war. But none of this present group of spectators needed any such a reminder; an awful sense of deep and anxious expectancy weighed upon every heart, and we talked together as men might talk upon the brink of some great peril. I can truly say that never among my limited experiences, whether during the entrance into battle or in the shock of the contest, have I suffered any such feelings as oppressed me during these fearful days of suspense, especially during the brief hour of calm of this very morning.

About noon, as I kept my eyes riveted upon the plain, I saw a long black line coming into view from behind the houses in the rear of the city, and advancing steadily toward the enemy's works. This is General French's division, which has moved in solid column up the streets, deployed in line of battle, and now, preceded by skirmishers, marches bravely up to the assault. Not far behind them shortly appears another thin black line, Hancock's division I have since learned, while Howard's division, being held for the present in reserve, is not yet visible. One must look earnestly, or he will almost fail to distinguish these two lines; at this distance it seems impossible that this is the force which is to attempt to throttle the foe in his own den. And yet yonder they move, on, on, unmolested, as if the rebels, awe-struck and fascinated like ourselves, have forgotten the very use of their artillery. Already they are half way across the plain; we are actually beginning to breathe more freely, when, as if at a given signal, from the fortified plateau, from the enfilading batteries on the left, from invisible artillery on the right and front, pours down a continuous hurtling tempest of shot and shell. With strained eyes we see our brave boys pause, the gaps in their lines are distinctly visible, their ranks quiver, many a poor fellow lies down wounded or dying, while some hurry back to the rear. And now the spot whereon we stand, and all along the bank above and below us, trembles with the thunder of artillery, for our eager

THE BATTLE OF FREDERICKSBURG. 307

gunners have sighted their guns, and now fling back at the rebel batteries a responsive tempest, which may perhaps silence or divert their fire. But these rebels know too much to waste ammunition upon our distant batteries; a few shot go shrieking over our heads into the field beyond, some indeed striking so near as to cause a little excitement among those under fire for the first time; but nearly the whole rebel fire, every shot of it, is concentrated as upon one focus, on that forlorn hope, now so exposed to the pitiless storm upon that unprotected plain.

And these Northern heroes are worthy of the occasion. Of course there are some cowards who fly to the rear, but the ranks of the brave close up their gaps, and once more they advance to the front. Every thunderbolt of rebel wrath is launched with merciless skill on their devoted heads. Forward, however, is the word; but how thin grows their line; how clear is it that, if they persist in advancing, they will reach the foot of the hills with only a handful of men. Shot down by tens and by fifties, what can they do but bend beneath the storm, and finally melt away before it, and so, with broken ranks, to the rear.

A few minutes pause, and now for the second act of the drama, as a second long black line moves out upon the plain, again to advance midway, again to be mowed down by that whirlwind of fire. Is it not awful to sit here and see our heroes thus done to death by those invisible guns, to sit here unable to help them, unable also to take our eyes from the terrible picture! This time, thank God! they seem to hold their own; this time the gaps torn through their ranks are rapidly closed up; they are two thirds of the way across the plain; the awful storm which howls about them may destroy, but it can not stop them. Once under that hill, with its plateau covered with earthworks, which now vomits smoke and fire, and they will be somewhat out of range, somewhat sheltered from the rebel batteries. Ah! how earnestly I have been watching the effect of the shot after shot hurled by the battery just in front of me seemingly into the very embrasures of that Washington Artillery. Several times I have seen the dust fly up apparently among their guns; but they hardly notice us, continuing to rain down grape and canister upon the heads of the advancing infantry.

Expressions of joy, and thanksgiving, and congratulation are thrilling through our circle of spectators, for now our attacking line, thinned but firmly advancing, is within a few hundred feet of the foot of the hill, and here these death-dealing batteries will be shorn of half their power. Five minutes more, and the worst will be over; then for the desperate bayonet charge up the heights, and the attack on the fortifications. But under that hill is the stone wall already referred to, and just as the heartfelt prayer of gratitude to the good God is thrilling through the soul, that stone wall seems actually fringed with fire. Every foot of it conceals a rebel sharpshooter safely protected, and able to select his living target and take deliberate aim. God help our poor boys now. Their only safety is to rush desperately on, with no pause to answer the enemy's volleys, on to the stone wall, trusting to cold steel alone, or every man of them is lost. Out on that plain, just in the vortex of that hell of flame, enfiladed by batteries, within point-blank range of that mile of rebel rifles, nothing but a desperate charge can save them, nothing but the bayonet do the needed work!

But see! are they not pausing—halting—actually halting to deliver a volley—a volley against earthworks and stone walls, not a bullet of which will harm the hair on a traitor's head? Alas! it is even so, and, of course, a retreat becomes inevitable. The opportunity for a dash is lost, and five minutes of exposure like this will not leave a man to tell the story. Already many a heroic soul has gone back to God, lifted on the red wing of battle; already many a wounded patriot baptizes Virginia with his blood; the broken remnant must fall back or perish. But even this falling back is in good order. Not in disorderly rout, but with hot faces still ever and anon turning defiantly at the earthworks and stone wall which have been their worst enemies to-day, they retire perhaps half way across the plain, where, in a ravine affording partial protection from the artillery, they halt, close up, and remain firmly all day.

A little to the left of this main attack I noticed another body of men, who had advanced through a ravine which partially concealed their movements, and who held a somewhat isolated hillock more than half way across the plain, on which was a house and some farm-buildings. Only after careful scrutiny with the glass did we finally decide that the flags flaunting over these troops were really our own stars and stripes. I afterward learned that this was the division of General Sturgis. They had one battery with them, and remained at this point all day, flinging at least disdain into the teeth of the rebels.

And this, as I understand it, is about the whole of the sad story of the attack on the rebel centre. We had won a position half way across the plain, but thousands of our bravest soldiers had been killed or wounded; not a rebel battery was silenced, not a single earthwork carried. Behold an epitome of this day's disaster. The artillery on our side the river still kept up the semblance of war; a few rebel missiles howled insultingly over our heads; but toward evening all this ceased; fresh divisions of General Hooker's reserve were sent out to relieve the troops in front, and the battle was over. We had absolutely gained almost nothing, and had made fearful sacrifice.

Yes, one thing we had gained, and that was the proud assurance, which must have thrilled the bosom of every man who looked on at this day's assault, that, with a fair chance for success, our volunteers would be invincible. The men who boldly plunged into that sea of death will save our country yet against the Southern rebel, and the still more unworthy traitor of the North. If any one doubts this, I would that he could have stood with me this day, and every such doubt would certainly disappear. Never have I been so proud of my countrymen; and, despite the sickening conviction that those heights could not be carried by our troops, I felt as never so strongly before that, with heroes like these, the defeat of treason was only a question of time.

How had it fared meanwhile with the left grand division? All day long we had heard the din of their contest with the enemy, and two or three squads of prisoners in gray had already passed us, indicating that the fight had been at close quarters. Riding over toward their bridges at the close of the battle on the right, I met an officer who reported that we had early in the day driven the rebels from some of their outworks at the point of the bayonet, and captured several hundred prisoners; but that an attack by a superior force had compelled our men to relinquish the advanced position won by their valor and fall back, and that thus the enemy still held intact their line of works. It was but too evident that here, as on our right, the work was all to be recommenced on the morrow. Meanwhile the hospitals were full of agony, and out under the cool evening sky lay hundreds of our unburied heroes.

Sunday, December 14*th.* Early this morning, having gotten through with some necessary business, I started to the front. As I drew near the river, I halted a moment on the bluff just above the pontoon bridges of the left grand division to survey the striking picture. Far as the eye could reach on either hand, up and down the river, stretched our batteries, with the artillery bivouacs sheltered in their rear. The men were now standing lazily around their pieces or gazing out toward the wooded heights two miles away over the river, where crouched the rebel cannon, and where the rebel infantry lay in wait for an approaching foe.

The battle had not yet recommenced; occasionally a puff of smoke might be seen among the distant trees, followed by a muffled roar and the shriek of a projectile, to be met by instant reply from one of our own batteries; but, for the most part, our guns were at rest. Just below the bluff, a plain of an eighth of a mile extended to the river, upon which ammunition wagons were parked, while over it wound to and from the bridges a continuous procession of staff officers and orderlies, and of ambulances now engaged in bringing over the wounded to the hospitals on this side. The inequalities of surface concealed from my view most of our troops on the other side, and only the skirmishers disturbed the prevailing quiet.

Descending to the plain, I was soon crossing one of the bridges, here guarded by detachments of infantry and cavalry to prevent the egress of stragglers. I then ascended the sloping bank on the other side and reached the plain. Here, a short distance in front, were troops drawn up in line of battle and standing at ease, composing the reserves, held back in readiness to dash in to give the finishing blow for victory, or perhaps to cover the retreat of our discomfited battalions.

My own division held the extreme left of our lines two miles or more down the river. As I rode along most of the troops were lying on their arms, and I was struck with the rather small show the thirty or forty thousand troops of the left grand division made in so extended a plain. A wide, well-shaded road, running parallel to and about half a mile distant from the Rappahannock, marked our main line of battle. Here our batteries were posted, with this tracery of blue uniforms behind them. Once in a while a reminder would come from our friends on the heights in the shape of a shrieking shell, followed by a sudden and sulphurous response from one of our own watch-dogs, while the sharp crack, crack of musketry, perhaps an eighth of a mile in front, indicated the whereabouts of our pickets, now briskly skirmishing. Occasionally a quartette of stretcher-bearers came slowly along with a wounded soldier, his face covered, and his wound crimsoning the earth with drops of blood as he was carried to the hospital.

Two large and handsome residences very near the river had been appropriated by the surgeons, and in the rear of one of them were the head-quarter tents of General Franklin. It was while sitting under one of these trees, near the stone house, that the gallant Bayard was mortally wounded by a chance shell.

The attitude of the troops was that of expectancy, but, for the present, the gunners rested alongside their pieces, and the infantry were standing at ease. As I drew near the extreme left the rattle of musketry increased, for our skirmishers were just then having a hot time of it. The general and staff were sitting under a tree by the roadside, and I was soon listening to yesterday's experiences. To our division had been assigned the duty of extending our left down the river and driving the rebels over Massaponix Creek, while to the divisions of Meade and Gibbon were given the storming of the heights in front of this position. From all accounts, both duties had been splendidly performed. The 1st division advanced for more than a mile and still held the extreme point gained, while the 2d and 3d had charged into and through the woods upon the enemy's fortifications, captured several hundred prisoners, and needed, as it would seem, only sudden and quick re-enforcement to pierce the rebel line, gain his flank, and probably defeat him. How well General Smith's corps and General Hooker's reserves did their duty; how the rebel batteries swept the plain with a murderous fire of shot and shell; how our own men behaved—this, with the various personal incidents of the fight, greatly interested me.

Two sons of New York on our staff had been especially fortunate. One had been sent out to the skirmishers with orders for them to push into a certain piece of woods, and the other obtained permission to accompany him. Instead of delivering their orders and returning, the young scamps led the skirmishers in person, made a brilliant cavalry charge of two into the woods, captured and brought off several rebel cavalry-men, and, what they seemed to value still more, three fine horses as prize of war. One of them had his horse so badly wounded at Bull Run as to be unserviceable ever since, and was now willing to call his account with the rebels, in this regard, square.

After hearing the news I again mounted and visited the several brigades. Our loss thus far had been small, and the men were in good condition and fine spirits. It was especially fortunate that during the whole of this Fredericksburg tragedy the weather was mild and delightful—a great blessing to the wounded and to the men, who were not permitted to light fires. While thus engaged among the brigades, a solitary Whitworth gun, the only one I have ever become acquainted with, which had been planted by the enemy on the other side of Massaponix Creek, and close to the river, and which thus enfiladed our entire line, began to throw solid shot among us very uncourteously. Though more than a mile distant, its aim was quite as good as was desirable, for sometimes the projectile struck a hundred feet or so in front, and rebounded over our heads, while the next perhaps struck in our rear. It was agreed by all that the yell of this projectile was the most ear-piercing we had ever listened to. It is oblong and grooved, so as to give it a rapid spin or rotation in the air, which adds to the music of its flight. I saw one strike apparently in the very midst of a group of our old brigade, and ricochet; there was a cloud of dust, a sudden jump of the men, but no one was injured. Another cut through a soldier's knapsack in a very artistic manner, not wounding the man, but flinging into the air, among other things, his pack of cards—an expeditious deal, though not according to Hoyle.

"I declare," said to me one of our staff, about as cool and brave a fellow as I ever saw, "that confounded Whitworth half scares me." The unpleasant feature about this particular gun was that we could see the smoke-puff so long before the shot struck or went howling over our heads. It was supposed to be introductory to an attack by the enemy, and every preparation was made to resist it, General Reynolds riding at once to the front, accompanied by our own general and staff, who at once got the brigades well in hand. But only this solitary Whitworth kept up the ball, accompanied, it is true, by the music of one of our own batteries, which sought to return the compliment. I did not hear of a single one of our men being killed or wounded, so that this was rather an expensive luxury to the enemy, every discharge costing them about ten dollars, and they soon ceased firing.

And this quiescent position of affairs was maintained along the entire line of both armies, the skirmishers having all the fighting to themselves. On my way back I called in at the hospitals, where I found every thing comfortably arranged, the wounded having for the most part been already sent across the river. During the afternoon I took a look at the position on the right, but only an artillery duel or two at long range, and occasional skirmishing, made up the record of the day.

Our tents being close to the roadside, we kept open house, having sometimes three sets of hungry officers at our mess-table at a single meal; but these were days of such anxiety that the duties of hospitality were only mechanically observed.

Monday, December 15th. Another foggy morning, and I once more crossed the river and rode out to the division to find every body quiet, but still in a state of constant expectancy. During this morning the pickets by common consent ceased firing, and, pending a flag of truce, they not only met half way and exchanged coffee for tobacco, but sat down on the grass and had a friendly game of cards in a quiet way. Perhaps an hour before these card-players had been straining every nerve to get a good shot at each other; for the present, however, all this fighting was to be considered in a Pickwickian sense, and so merrily went on the game.

On my return from the front, having some business to transact at the office of the provost marshal general, I rode up to head-quarters, a canvas city with one wide street leading up through double lines of tents to the marquée of the commanding general. General Burnside was just riding out of camp with half a dozen aids, and as I saw the patriot hero, my whole soul responded to the wish that he might yet succeed in his desperate undertaking.

The next day, Tuesday, was another quiet day,

though a very busy one in my department, as it was necessary to send supplies to the front. Every day we had expected the renewal of the battle; every hour was one of anxious expectancy; every night we had said at parting, "To-morrow will surely be the decisive day!" These were the longest days of the campaign for those who, having none of the excitement of personal participation, experienced the doubt and uncertainty, the mingled turmoil of hope and fear, which one might see painted upon the countenances of even the most careless among us. For one, since the result of the first day's fighting, I had felt but little hope of our ultimate success; and it has always been a mystery to me why our forces were permitted to remain so long unattacked, especially on our left, where our defeat must have resulted in the capture of the left grand division.

I had retired early to my tent on Tuesday evening, glad to be alone with my own thoughts, and was soon a candidate for sleep. About midnight our little camp was aroused by the sound of voices; I turned over, rubbed my eyes, listened, could not believe my own senses, for the voices sounded strangely like those of the general and staff. What could it mean? Not an intimation of a retreat had reached us; at sundown I had been ordered to send over certain supplies; but this must be a retreat! The night was stormy; the wind howled drearily through the tents, and General Burnside had taken advantage of this propitious circumstance to withdraw his army.

To Lieutenant Rogers, of Wisconsin, who had lately joined our staff as acting aid, had been assigned the duty of bringing off the pickets of the left grand division, a most responsible office, only to be entered upon after the main body had crossed the bridges. His description of his midnight experiences greatly interested us. Sitting on his horse beneath the pelting storm, he waited patiently at the bridges until the last brigade was moving down to the river. Two miles away, out in yonder darkness, a few hundred of our men stood leaning on their muskets, peering anxiously out into the night toward the picket-line of the enemy. Not a man of this line of scattered sentinels, three miles long, suspected that he and his comrades were the only Union soldiers on that side the river; not a man, as shivering beneath the midnight blast he thought perchance of his Northern home, even dreamed that the long lines of artillery and infantry he saw behind him at sunset had all disappeared; that the whole host of his brothers had departed, leaving him close to the enemy and almost alone.

The time has come to ride back and bring off these outlying sentinels, so that every man of them shall be rescued without arousing the suspicions of the enemy. One sudden exclamation by a surprised soldier may bring down upon the little handful the ever-vigilant foe. Two long miles must be traversed by the pickets on the left before they can reach the bridges, and their course is to be immediately in front of the enemy's lines. How easily they may be cut off! how much faster than men these rebel bullets travel! It is certainly fully time for our staff comrade to be off on his perilous journey.

Splendidly mounted, he takes ditches and fences at a flying leap, and rushes down to the extreme left with no regard to the roads, but straight as the bee flies. The left once gained, he moderates his pace, and coolly whispers into the ear of each astonished officer his orders. "Order every man in your command to fall back steadily, and very silently; gradually close up your ranks, and move swiftly to the bridges. Whisper these directions into their ears man by man." So quietly but rapidly he speeds down the picket-line; the propitious storm howls with unabated fury; not a rebel sentinel gives the alarm; one by one our drenched boys are falling back and drawing in together. The last officer has notified the last man; silently as shadows the whole picket-line steals across the plain. And now, as the ranks close up, now for rapid marching. Double-double-quick is about the pace. The wild sweep of the storm sounds ever and anon terribly like the murmur of excited pursuit, but no rebel thunderbolt comes darting out of the darkness, no rebel bullet strikes down a single man. Half an hour after the order was whispered into the ear of the soldier standing guard on the extreme left, the whole picket-line is moving swiftly down the bank, and reaches the bridge. Only one bridge remains, for the others have been already removed, and at its head stand the engineers, all ready to take up the planks, cast off the pontoons, and float them across the river. Another minute, and the floating causeway, already partially cut loose from its moorings, trembles beneath the quiet tread of the rejoicing column; another minute, and our lieutenant, grimly smiling as the last files reach the bridge, moves over also.

And now, engineers, to your work! It may be that the foe has discovered the escape, and is hurrying forward in quick pursuit; it may be that even yet a volley of leaden hail may come hurtling down from yonder bank, or a desperate charge endeavor to capture the pontoons. It is astonishing how quickly the bridge comes up under such urgent reasons for haste. It falls to pieces as if by magic. The pontoons are floated over, and at once drawn up the bank. Not a single soldier is left on the other side of the Rappahannock; every gun, ambulance, and wagon is safely across; and thus is accomplished a retreat which almost negatives the sad reverses of the battle of Fredericksburg.

CHAPTER XXIX.

A CAMPAIGN IN THE MUD.

THURSDAY, *December* 17*th*. I fancy that the rebel pickets must have been slightly astonished this morning when the gray dawn revealed the fact that the plain, so lately bristling with hostile cannon and bayonets, was now deserted, and that our forces had taken French leave. Probably a little rage mingled with their astonishment, for, as we sat at breakfast, several shots from our old friend, the Whitworth gun, came shrieking over our mess-tent, too high, however, to do us any damage.

And now, for more than a month, with one or two changes of camp, we hid away in the woods south of Potomac Creek, forming part of the cordon of troops protecting the government dépôts at Belle Plaine. Our line of infantry pickets stretched from the Rappahannock to the Potomac, while the whole neck between the two rivers for twenty miles was patroled by our cavalry. It would have been quite worth the while for a citizen unacquainted with army matters to visit the quarter-master and commissary dépôts lining Aquia and Potomac Creeks, for thus he might get some idea of the immense equipments and supplies required by a large army. Several roads were cut to and from these dépôts, and the wagons were busily engaged in hauling the necessary supplies for subsisting the men and fitting them out for another trial with the enemy. As the troops had now abundant leisure, they exhibited a good deal of taste and skill in the building and decoration of their huts. A good wide fireplace at one end, bunks for beds, carpets of cedar twigs, cracker-box tables, and pork-barrel armed chairs, with neat racks for their muskets and other equipments, made these winter houses almost luxurious. The rebels had passed the last winter here, and left behind them two villages of substantial log houses, to which our boys now fell heirs, and valued them accordingly.

During these days, by one of those changes resulting from priority of rank, our division received a new commander, while our former general was transferred to the command of another division in the same corps. Of course the withdrawal of the latter created a profound sensation among officers and men. It was natural that the troops who had followed him through so many scenes of difficulty and danger, who had learned to love, and, what is far more important, to trust in him, and who had become proud of their leader, should experience deep regret at the parting, while those of us who had entered into military life as members of his staff felt like men who are parting with their best friend. As only his aids are attached to the person of a general, most of the staff still remained at division head-quarters.

With our new general, late military governor of Washington, whom we had long known by reputation, we were soon quite at home; and as such a man usually surrounds himself with gentlemen, we found his personal aids very pleasant companions in camp, and every thing soon fell into the usual comfortable routine at our head-quarters. Our tents ran along a little ridge among the trees, extra comforts were laid in, and we did our best not to think too much of home in these winter-woods of Virginia.

My servant Charles had now a confrère in the duty of waiting upon the general's mess in the person of "Cupid," about the ugliest personification of the God of Love it has ever been my lot to meet. Charles was now in trouble. The resources of the quarter-master's department had been taxed in vain to find shoes of sufficient capacity for him, while one or two attempts at Washington in the same direction had as yet proved unsuccessful. He could wear "twelves," but "thirteens" fitted him better, and his feet were now daily exposed to contact with a good deal of cold or snow-covered ground. One day I found him sitting on the floor of my tent with several pairs of dilapidated shoes lying about him, which he had brought in from a late visit to one of the camps. "I'se gwine to take two pair of sixes and make one pair of twelves out of 'em, shure!" said he, and for days he devoted his leisure time to this new experiment in pedal architecture. It was entirely successful, and I soon had another convincing proof that twice six makes twelve.

Charles was more busy than ever in learning to read and write. Berryman, of course, left us with his general; the literary efforts of this sixty-year-old pupil had been rewarded with success at last. I declare there was something really touching in the sight of this gray-headed negro painfully spelling out his letters. Charles still remains with the division, but Berryman accompanied a scouting party one day into his old country, and brought back with him Mrs. Berryman and half a dozen children. He now left the army, and is residing comfortably on free territory. One can not help becoming strongly attached to these children of slavery. They are, of course, very far as yet from reaching the standard of availability or energy attained by men whose natural powers have been trained and incited by the stimulus of free labor, but they are wonderfully faithful and trustworthy, and I felt safe in permitting to Charles free access to every thing in my possession. I firmly believe that we have the destiny of this race in our own hands; that they are capable of great development, and are to be hereafter a blessing or a curse to us, just as the ruling classes shall decide.

Road-making and corduroying were now the order of the day. Detachments from the different brigades were daily engaged in this business, and our general frequently superintended the work, and sometimes gave the men a little practical aid in order to show them how these things are done. Some of the boys, greatly pleased at this, christened him "Old Corduroy." I wonder what they called him afterward, when he swam his horse across the Rappahannock alongside the forlorn hope sent over in boats to dislodge the rebel sharpshooters? It was then evident that, however much he liked a good road, he was by no means particular when the object was to get at the enemy.

But this road-making, drilling, and head-quarter routine was for a while suspended by orders received on Friday, January 16th, to be ready to march on the following morning. This order was, however, countermanded, but on the following Monday it was renewed, and on Tuesday we struck tents, and by noon the division was on the march. If I may judge from my own observation and the opinions of brigade commanders, the men were never in better spirits, never more ready to do their whole duty. They marched forward well knowing that another attempt to cross the Rappahannock and to attack the enemy was before them, and every body was willing to lend his best help to secure, this time, an entire success.

But about 4 P.M. it began to rain; not a gentle shower which lays the dust, and is rather refreshing than disagreeable, but a cold, driving storm, which, aided by the gale, penetrated the clothing and cut the faces of the men as they staggered on. The deep-cut Virginia roads became in two hours quagmires, through which artillery and wagon-trains were with difficulty dragged at the rate of a mile an hour. It was after dark when we reached Stoneman's switch on the railroad, near which the brigades were bivouacked in the woods, made fires, and sought a watery repose.

By the light of lanterns we pitched a couple of tents on a bleak and exposed plateau for division head-quarters, where at every step we sank deeply into the mire. For at least half an hour our patient cook sought to work out a rather difficult problem, viz., how to make a fire of green wood in a mud-puddle out in a driving rain. Fire and water were here brought into fierce opposition, but fire finally got the best of it, and we were soon standing in the mud around a table in the general's tent, supping on coffee, canned meats, and hard bread.

The large office-tent had been put up as a common

bedchamber for the staff; our cots were brought in, and, when put up, looked like islands of refuge surrounded by water. My servant had located mine in one corner; beside it was a lake growing gradually larger; a gentle rivulet meandered through the middle of the tent. The scenery was peculiar, though not picturesque. How to get one's boots off, and where to leave them, except in a mud-puddle, was the first question. Some of the staff immediately went to work digging trenches and canals for drainage purposes; and having, in the mean time, gotten into my bed as into a bag, lest the wind, now eddying under and through our canvas walls, should tear away my blankets, I looked out from the top, considerably interested in these new experiments in hydraulics.

Our cots sank down, of course, into the mud; but, as long as they did not float off, we were safe. Only one trouble now disturbed us. The storm had evidently determined that our canvas roof should not stand; the ground was too wet to hold the tent-pins securely, and the whole affair was now swaying from side to side like a balloon impatient to be off on its aerial travels. As I was in the windward corner, my sleep was agreeably diversified by being roused several times to grasp the fluttering canvas, and scream for the guard to pin it once more down.

At last, about three in the morning, with one wild yell of triumph, the eddying storm tore up our tenement, sent its frail rafters clattering about our ears, and carried it off bodily in its arms, leaving us delightfully exposed, out on a naked hill-side, to the pitiless tempest. At first I resolved to remain in my bag. Unfortunately, it opened the wrong way, affording free entrance to the rain and wind, which rushed in so desperately as to compel me to leave. Rising, I groped my way to the general's tent, which had long since lost shape and symmetry, and was flapping about like a ship's topsails in a calm. He was sleeping so comfortably that I did not disturb him, but, after putting in a pin or two more to restrain his bedchamber from flying away, I went into the orderlies' tent, where we passed the rest of the night in trying to keep our feet as much as possible out of the mud. On the whole, this was a very proper introduction to our campaign in the mud.

Very early next morning, after a cold and hurried breakfast, the troops began to wade on to glory. The rain still deluged the earth, the usual mud-holes became miniature lakes; to get the pontoons, the artillery, and the ammunition wagons along was next to impossible. It was painfully evident that, to succeed in this movement, our men and our horses ought to have been made web-footed. After an aquatic excursion of about five miles, the division reached at 3 P.M. our stopping-place for the night; but the batteries were still plowing up the mud in the rear, and did not get up until the next day. The whole country about us was full of troops; but the main supply trains of the entire army had been left behind at their old parks, our own being in charge of the lieutenant who so handsomely brought off the pickets after the late battle.

The men had time to build for themselves rustic dens and huge camp-fires before night shut in, while the general and staff bivouacked on the lower floor of a comfortable roadside house. That night our bedchamber did not blow away.

Thursday, January 22*d*. The division remained to-day quietly in the mud, but I passed most of it in the saddle, having to retrace my steps on the old business. It was a most slow, uncomfortable, and splashy ride, out of which my horse and I came looking more like an equestrian statue done in clay than like living beings. Shipwrecked wagons, dead and dying mules and horses, pontoons stuck in the mud, guns dragged along by doubling up their usual teams, a few regiments on their dismal march, and mud-incased staff officers like myself filled the roads, and imparted a doleful look to the whole picture. It was on this day that some facetious rebels erected, on the opposite side of the river, for the delectation of our pickets, a signboard with the legend, "Burnside stuck in the mud."

I returned to our wayside house in time for a late dinner, and by 7 P.M. our room was once more floored with cots, for the general had ordered lights out early, and an equally early turning out on the morrow. Hardly were we snugly under the blankets before the music of a regimental band broke in upon the stillness of the hour, and rarely have I enjoyed any serenade so much as this one given to the general. We were now aware that our last effort was a failure, and that we were on the morrow to return to our old quarters, and were of course feeling a little blue, so that the music just fitted my mood.

Very early next morning we were on our return. The men were anxious to secure their old huts and articles of comfort, and marched through the mud as I never saw men march before. As we once more erected our canvas houses on the well-known ridge, the sun burst forth from the clouds, its first greeting since we commenced our ill-starred enterprise. And so ended the celebrated campaign in the mud.

CHAPTER XXX.

WINTER-QUARTERS.

THWARTED by the elements in its late movement, there was nothing for the Army of the Potomac to do but to go into winter-quarters, and await a more propitious season. Baffled but not discouraged, this was only one more of those disappointments through which that army has passed, with a courage and determination more ennobling than any success, on its way to future victories.

Its day of glory is sure to come. On many a battle-field it has illustrated a heroic valor which has won for it on the Peninsula, in Maryland, and in Eastern Virginia magnificent partial successes — the promise and prophecy of that substantial and decisive victory yet to come. Let me pay to it the homage of my admiration and gratitude for its past sacrifices, and attest my belief, founded upon the evidence of my own experiences, that it is yet to cover itself with patriotic glory. How splendidly this army can fight; how, when a forlorn hope was needed, the men have been always ready; how, after weeks of hard marching and fighting, they have moved with alacrity against the enemy, has been partially delineated in these pages. If the fault has been with its leaders, this is not the place to criticise them, nor do I feel in the mood. Let the dead Past bury its dead.

When this war began, there existed among officers

of the regular army a strong prejudice against the volunteers; but this has, among those who have seen much fighting, almost wholly disappeared. Still, one serious defect, the want of proper discipline, greatly vitiates and impairs the fighting value of our citizen troops—a defect having its origin mainly in the method of their enlistment. Under that method a captain found in his ranks his equals, his friends, his schoolmates and neighbors. To subject these to a strict military discipline was, from the nature of the case, well-nigh impossible. Moreover, a good many poor sticks, from one reason and another, managed to get into positions for which they were totally unfitted, and it took some time to get rid of them. I have known an entire regiment, made up of excellent fighting material, rendered comparatively worthless by having at its head a skulker or two with shoulder-straps. And if there be one lesson which I think I have well learned during my limited experiences, it is the absolute necessity of having for field officers men who respect themselves, men who stand firmly on their own feet—self-possessed, self-contained, elevated and strengthened by a sense of patriotic duty. Imagine a whining incapable leading a regiment upon a desperate bayonet charge!

The very first element of discipline is of course respect, and only a whole man can command the respect of his inferiors. No regimental field officer should hold in his hand the great responsibility of the leadership of a thousand men unless he has passed a thorough examination, which shall test not so much his knowledge of tactics as his self-respect, manliness, reserved force, character. Given a man, and all the rest becomes easy, whether you want him for a colonel or a general, or even commander-in-chief. It took a very short time to make out of Oliver Cromwell a leader who put to shame the former driveling timidity of Essex, and led his men through an almost uninterrupted path of victory.

Says Macaulay in his article on John Hampden, "It is a remarkable circumstance that the officers who had studied tactics in what were considered as the best schools, under Vere in the Netherlands and under Gustavus Adolphus in Germany, displayed far less skill than those commanders who had been bred to peaceful employments, and who never saw even a skirmish till the civil war broke out. An unlearned person might hence be inclined to suspect that the military art is no profound mystery; that its principles are the principles of plain common sense; and that a quick eye, and a cool head, and a stout heart will do more to make a general than all the diagrams of Jomini."

Even our West Point school, to whose thorough sifting processes we owe that annual platoon of accomplished officers, scholars, and gentlemen, whose military knowledge has drilled and organized our newly-formed armies, and whose valor and discipline has set so good an example to our volunteers—even West Point, with all its training, can not manufacture a first-rate officer unless that indispensable ingredient be furnished—a man.

Good regimental leaders being thus selected by a commission more anxious for manhood than for those matters of drill which come so easily to ordinary comprehension, we shall soon have that discipline we so much need—a discipline which to the inexperienced might appear almost cruel, but which is really merciful and humane. Absolute obedience at the risk of being cut down on the instant for neglect, the punishment of a coward on the spot—this in mercy to his comrades, and as a necessity to the country, should be the iron rule of our army in battle. War is the meanest and most brutal way of settling a difficulty; a battle is the lowest and most unnatural mode of trying and deciding a disputed issue; but when war does come, when a battle becomes necessary, it should be no child's play, but the desperate use of our fiercest fighting qualities, or we must necessarily be defeated. In a storm at sea, we know that if the master of the ship does not hold the wills of his seamen wholly lost and fused in his own, so that they will dare any danger at his bidding, the ship will probably perish; so in a battle, an even more terrible season of crisis, the commander must hold his troops in the very hollow of his hand, to be retained inflexibly, or hurled as one man in any needed direction. This straggling from the line of march should be stopped, even if it require the severest punishment, while the coward in battle should be made to fear the sword of his officer more than the bullets of the enemy.

The great majority of our volunteers, brave fellows as they are, are ready and willing to do their whole duty; it is in justice to them that I advocate a more careful selection of regimental officers, and a more rigid discipline. To stand up and face the dread realities of battle requires not only manly pride and the incitement of patriotic impulses, but also a severity of discipline which shall surround each command as with a ring of iron. What every soldier needs is to know that the quickest escape for him out of this bloody lane is to beat the enemy; that he stands here at the orders of those who will withdraw him when necessary, but will punish him on the spot for retreating without orders; and that his file-closer, his company, his regiment, his brigade, will not and can not desert him, will absolutely support him to the bitter end. One coward sneaking to the rear makes a bad gap, breaks the chain of sympathy, demoralizes all about him.

Closely connected with this subject of want of discipline is that of the enormous waste of ammunition in battle. Having gotten our soldier before the enemy, and compelled him by this iron rule to stay there and fight, the next point is that he fight to some purpose.

At first I concluded that the great disproportion in our battles between the number of ball cartridges discharged and the numbers of killed and wounded was due mainly to the want of presence of mind in our raw troops; but the very limited investigation I have been enabled to make has convinced me that our troops take much better aim, and consequently waste far less ammunition than is usual in European warfare.

During the wars of the French Revolution and of the Empire—Napoleon's wars—according to Gassendi, a French general of artillery, the infantry fired 3000 cartridges for every enemy killed or wounded. Piobert admits the same thing. Decker, a Prussian general, and one of the best military writers in Germany, estimated that not less than 10,000 cartridges are burned for every enemy killed or wounded.

At the battle of Vittoria the English are supposed to have killed or wounded one of the enemy for every 800 balls fired. An English officer states that at the battle of Cherubusco the Mexicans killed or wounded an American for every 800 balls fired, and that the Americans killed or wounded a Mexican for every 125 balls fired.*

The heroic Rosecrans, in his account of the bloodily-contested battle of Murfreesborough, declares, " Of 14,560 rebels struck by our missiles, it is estimated that 20,000 rounds of artillery hit 728 men, and 200,000 rounds of musketry hit 13,833 men, averaging 27 cannon shots to hit one man, and 145 musket shots to hit one man."

In the battle of Gainesville, spoken of in another chapter, there could not have been expended more than 100,000 cartridges, and the enemy admit a loss of more than 1000 men, thus averaging 100 musket shots to each of the rebel killed or wounded. Of course all such statements only approximate the actual ratio, but it is sufficiently clear that, great as is the waste of ammunition by our army, it is not only equaled, but excelled by those of Europe.

One trouble is that our men, in going into battle, are weighed down, overloaded with ammunition, having to stuff their pockets as well as their cartridge-boxes with the sixty or eighty rounds ordered. Of course very much of this is thrown away and wasted; but this is only a trifling evil compared with the encouragement thus given to the too prevalent idea among the men that he who fires the greatest number of rounds in battle is the best soldier. I have heard men

* See "Rifles and Rifle Practice," by Wilcox, p. 236, 237.

boasting of their achievements in this regard, and the result of such an idea is a hurried loading and discharge without any regard to aim; a wasting upon trees and foliage of ammunition which, if used at all, should be used so as to defeat the enemy. I was struck with a remark made by a rebel prisoner to his captors, "We never carry more than forty rounds into action, and usually expend about ten."

There is altogether too much of this wild, reckless firing, the men discharging their pieces before bringing them fairly down to a level, and utterly regardless of taking aim. Of course there are periods when heavy, rapid, and continuous volleys are necessary; still it would be well if every man could be drilled as a sharpshooter, taught to shoot slowly, and always take aim, either at the enemy or his supposed locality. This, and the more frequent trust in cold steel alone, the latter being especially necessary in operations against a fortified and sheltered foe, have seemed desirable for our volunteers. How gallantly they can charge, and how fatal have been their volleys, has been too often illustrated on many a bloody field to require any praise of mine; my only suggestion being that if they discharged fewer cartridges, and still more frequently depended on the bayonet alone, it might be better for our cause.

But I must pause, or I shall exceed even my privilege as a Yankee, as one of a race always ready to give their opinion on any subject "for what it is worth." I feel that in these military matters I have no right to give an opinion, but the terrible importance of this struggle to all of us must be my apology. I have seen troops in battle discharging their pieces at an angle of forty-five degrees, and the instances of their firing into each other are by no means rare. An appeal may safely be made to many of our officers whether the first duty to be taught an inexperienced soldier should not be this—to fire slowly and composedly, or not at all. I would rather have five hundred men who fired thus, once in two minutes, than a thousand who should be anxious only to discharge their muskets.

To the very interesting statements as to the ratio between the casualties in battle and the whole number engaged which have from time to time appeared, I can only allude. In the five battles of the late Italian campaign, for example, it was estimated that about 8 per cent. of the French and Sardinians, and $10\frac{1}{2}$ per cent. of their enemies the Austrians, were either killed or wounded. In the battles spoken of in these sketches our loss was not far from 10 per cent. of the whole numbers engaged, while certain divisions and brigades lost one third of their number; and in the fearfully bloody fight at Gainesville two of our regiments lost more than one third of their number engaged, as did also the 4th brigade.

The proportion between the killed and the wounded is about as 1 to 5, and of the wounded about 1 in 10 never recovers. If this be even approximative to the truth, it certainly robs war of some of its presumed fatality. As I have before remarked, the escape of so large a majority of the men, amid such storms of bullets sweeping and yelling around their ears, has always been the great mystery of war.

But to return to the Army of the Potomac. Much at different times has been said about its demoralization, but I believe that this has usually been a creature of the imagination in those who have had so much to say about it. These volunteers are not children requiring constantly to be petted withal, and feeling no personal stake in this momentous issue. Of course a man's fighting value may be reduced by fatigue, constant excitement, paucity of food and sleep, but a day or two of rest recruits him. No man likes to be beaten, but forty-eight hours afterward he has forgotten his disappointment, and is ready to "pick the flint and try it again."

Of course there will always be more or less grumbling among volunteers, especially when they have but little to do; though, as far as my observation goes, this Anglo-American privilege is not one tenth so common among our boys as it is among the semi-traitorous crew who sit at ease at home, and do nothing but grumble. In every army, the men who straggle, and who avoid arduous or dangerous duty, are always demoralized; but, as the fighting is done by the others, this may be considered only as the usual wastage. In this wastage may be included some, doubtless, who wear the straps of the officer, and their faces are always long, their tales always doleful and despairing.

I am inclined to think that a man thoroughly in earnest, and inclined to perform his own duty, seldom has much to say about demoralization. He does not see it; for he carries about with him an atmosphere of encouragement and hope, so that his men and his companions are never demoralized in his presence. The Army of the Potomac has several times practically refuted the slanders of these whining prophets,

P

and will do it again and again at the first opportunity.

In conclusion, then, let me once more record my heartfelt admiration of the Army of the Potomac as a worthy coadjutor of our glorious armies of the West, and my belief that it will yet crown its many reverses and sacrifices by decisive victories. And my last words can be only those of hope and encouragement; for, as I review the events of the past two years, I have greater love for our Constitution, which has proved itself a chart sufficiently comprehensive to guide us even over the untried and stormy seas of this rebellion; for our form of government, as challenging the world for the rapidity with which it has organized its power into immense armies and navies; for my country, hardly feeling this draft upon its resources, and growing richer every day; for my countrymen, now beginning to take hold in earnest of this war as a matter of settled and permanent business; for our great underlying principle of Liberty, every day attesting its applicability to men of every color and every rank.

It may be that we are to have more reverses mingled with our victories; but these delays are all right, are indeed necessary to insure for our national disease a permanent cure. One thing is certain, that the man who lends neither his wealth, his influence, nor his right arm to aid on the war, has no right whatever to complain of any delay in its prosecution. Rights and duties are correlative, and only he who performs his duty to the government has any right to criticise its action.

As yet, we have hardly begun to bring out our full

resources. England, in her twenty years' war with Napoleon, expended $5,000,000,000, and came out richer than when she went in. Adam Smith computes that one fifth of every population can fight, and this would give us four millions of fighting men. We must, if necessary, become a fighting nation. The vast importance of the issue justifies every sacrifice. We are fighting for Democracy every where. The European aristocracy recognizes this, and hence its opposition. Garibaldi knows it, and hence his enthusiastic sympathy. In such a contest, upon whose result Freedom herself depends, there must be no such word as fail. The omens are all propitious; patience, courage, constancy must be ours, and may God defend the right!

THE END.

www.ingramcontent.com/pod-product-compliance
Lightning Source LLC
Chambersburg PA
CBHW031857220426
43663CB00006B/656